A·CALENDAR·OF
SAINTS

A·CALENDAR·OF
SAINTS

The Lives of the Principal Saints of the Christian Year·

James Bentley

LITTLE, BROWN AND COMPANY

First published 1986 in Great Britain by Orbis Publishing
Limited

This edition published in 1993 by Little, Brown and
Company (UK)

Reprinted 1994

ISBN 0 316 90813 4
Printed in Spain by Graficromo S.A., Cordoba

Little, Brown and Company (UK)
Brettenham House
Lancaster Place
London
WC2E 7EN

Above: *Saints Crispin and Crispinian*, Franco-Flemish
(Musée Sandelin, Saint-Omer)

Title page: Raphael (1483–1520), *The Holy Family with Saint
Elisabeth and Saint John* (Alte Pinakothek, Munich)

Page 6: Barnaba de Modena (fl. 1361–c.1383), *Saints Anthony
Abbot and Eligius* (Victoria and Albert Museum, London)

Contents

January

'The difference between a good
person and a devout one is this:
the good person keeps God's
commandments, though without
any great speed or fervour; the
devout not only observes them
but does so willingly, speedily,
and with a good heart.'

Francis de Sales (January 24)

Concordius

Basil the Great and Gregory of Nazianzen

St Basil the Great

'Let it be assured that to do no wrong is really superhuman, and belongs to God alone.'

St Gregory of Nazianzen

St Gregory of Nazianzen

Saint Concordius spent most of his adult life alone in the desert, meditating and praying to God. About the year 178, when the Emperor Marcus Aurelius was presiding over a systematic persecution of Christians, Concordius was captured and brought to trial at Spoleto. The governor of Umbria, Torquatus, promised to release the saint if only he would renounce his faith and worship a statue of Jupiter. Concordius refused, so Torquatus ordered his soldiers to beat him with clubs.

Still Concordius seemed not to care about Torquatus's threats but treated the governor with scorn. When Torquatus demanded his name, Concordius merely answered, 'I have already told you, I am a Christian and confess Jesus Christ.'

The governor decided to torture the saint on a rack. While this was being done, Concordius sang a hymn of praise to Jesus. Torquatus flung Concordius into a prison and two days later soldiers came to behead him. They made one more attempt to persuade him to make a sacrifice to an idol. Instead the saint spat at it. This was too much for his persecutors, who executed him immediately.

Both Basil and Gregory were born in the city of Caesarea, but they met and became firm friends during their student days at the University of Athens.

Basil was far bolder than Gregory. A brilliant brain, he soon tired of lecturing at the University and decided to become a monk instead. For five years he tried to live alone as a hermit on the banks of the River Iris in Pontus, but so many people gathered round him to learn from his Christian wisdom that he was forced to set up a monastery for them. The rules he drew up for men who wished to live together as monks are still the basis of every monastic community in Eastern Christendom.

Realizing that Basil's brilliant preaching could convert many unbelievers to Christianity, Gregory persuaded him to leave the monastery. Basil was consecrated Archbishop of Caesarea. He gave away his money, and built a hospital for the poor but many pagans hated his boldness. The Roman Emperor sent a prefect who threatened Basil with deprivation, exile and even death. Basil replied that as he owned only a few rags for clothing and some books, deprivation was no threat. Neither was exile, since he lived as a stranger on earth, *en route* to the kingdom of God. As for torture and death, Basil admitted that his body was weak. But, he said, 'only the first blow will hurt me. As for death, that will benefit me, bringing me even closer to my God for whom I completely live.' So the prefect decided to leave him alone.

Basil arranged for Gregory to be made a bishop. Gregory hated this, believing himself unworthy, and he refused all pomp and ceremony. Countless people gathered to hear him preach. He continued to admire Basil enormously. 'His praise of the martyrs,' said Gregory, 'makes me despise my own bodily fears.' Basil died, aged only forty-nine, in the year 379. His friend died eleven years later, and today both are honoured as doctors of the Church.

Geneviève

Geneviève was only fifteen when the Bishop of Paris gave her the veil. The young girl loved to pray in church alone at night. One day a gust of wind blew out her candle, leaving her in the dark. Geneviève merely concluded that the devil was trying to frighten her. For this reason she is often depicted holding a candle, sometimes with an irritated devil standing by.

In later life the saint's bravery proved invaluable for the people of Paris. King Childeric of the Franks besieged the city, bringing its inhabitants to the point of starvation. Under Geneviève's leadership an intrepid band sailed out of the city and brought back boatloads of corn. Her bravery rallied the city a second time when Attila the Hun's army marched on the city. The citizens panicked, ready to flee. Geneviève persuaded them to stay. Her courage depended on complete trust in God, and as Attila and his army approached she encouraged the Parisians to pray in the hope that God would avert disaster. Attila's army turned away.

By the time she died King Clovis of the Franks had become a Christian, and had grown to venerate the saint. He interred her body in a great church he had built in the middle of Paris.

Elizabeth Seton

Elizabeth Ann Seton – the first American ever to be canonized – was born into a distinguished family on 28 August 1774. Although a stepbrother became Catholic Archbishop of Baltimore, most of her family were devout Protestants.

Elizabeth married at the age of twenty and became an active philanthropist. In 1797 she was one of the founders of a society designed to help poor widows with small children. Her own husband died in 1803, leaving her with five children.

Two years later Elizabeth horrified her Protestant relatives by becoming a Catholic. But the rector of St Mary's Seminary, Baltimore, asked her to start a school there. This marked the beginning of the Catholic system of parochial schools in America.

In 1809 Elizabeth invited four friends to found a new religious community, the Sisters of St Joseph. They opened a school for the poor close by Emmitsburg in Maryland. By 1812 the small community had grown to nineteen and was accepted as an official order, with Elizabeth Seton as its first superior. She took her vows as a nun in 1813. Her inspiration spread and when she died nearly two dozen sister communities had been founded.

St Elizabeth Seton

Simeon the Stylite

Balthasar, Caspar and Melchior

St Simeon the Stylite

As a shepherd boy, Simeon read the Bible and puzzled over it, especially the Sermon on the Mount, where Jesus speaks of the way suffering can bring great happiness. He decided to take these words to heart. He begged to be allowed to live in a monastery, working as the lowest of all the servants. The monks grew to love him, and he stayed over two years.

Soon he grew to believe that the life he had chosen was not rigorous enough and he moved to a stricter monastery. Simeon then decided to eat nothing in Lent. Fortunately he had told a priest what he was planning and the wise priest kept watch to make sure Simeon did not starve himself to death.

Simeon decided to live on the top of Mount Teleanissae near Antioch, in a small building that had no roof. By now he was famous. Many men and women came to disturb him. In 423 Simeon decided to escape interruption by building himself a pillar (hence his name 'Stylites', from the Greek word *stylos*, meaning 'pillar'). The pillar was about three metres high and the top was no more than two metres in diameter. He lived here for four years. Still the crowds came to disturb him, so he increased the height of this pillar first to six metres, then to twelve and finally to twenty metres. Altogether he lived in this way for thirty-seven years, preaching to visitors twice a day.

When Jesus was born in Bethlehem wise men came from the east, asking, 'Where is he that has been born king of the Jews, for we have seen his star in the east and have come to worship him?' The ruler at that time, King Herod, was worried by this. He told them to find Jesus and report back to him where the baby was. Herod planned to kill Jesus. The wise men followed the star, which led them to Bethlehem. There they found Mary, the mother of Jesus, her husband Joseph, and Jesus lying in a manger. They knelt before him and offered three gifts: gold, frankincense and myrrh. A dream warned them not to tell Herod anything, so they went home without reporting the whereabouts of Jesus to him.

Nowhere in the Gospel are we specifically told that there were *three* wise men; but Christians have deduced that this was so from the three gifts they brought. The Old Testament book of Psalms says, 'The Kings of Tharsis and the Isles shall offer presents; the Kings of Arabia and Saba shall bring gifts,' and – connecting the wise men with this prophecy – Christians decided that there must have been three kings.

These three are the first non-Jews to have worshipped Jesus. Very early in the Christian era they became favourite subjects of Christian art, painted on the walls of a catacomb in the early second century. Early in the next century they were given names, Balthasar, Caspar and Melchior. Artists began to paint one as a young king, another in his middle life, and the third as an old man. Later the artists reasoned that if they came from the east, at least one of them must have been a black man.

Soon Christians began to speculate on the significance of the three gifts. Gold obviously symbolized Jesus as a king himself – not only King of the Jews but King of the Gentiles too. Frankincense stood for the devotion of the wise men (and all the non-Jewish world) to Jesus. But myrrh was used to embalm dead bodies: and this gift foreshadowed Jesus's death on the cross, the means of our salvation.

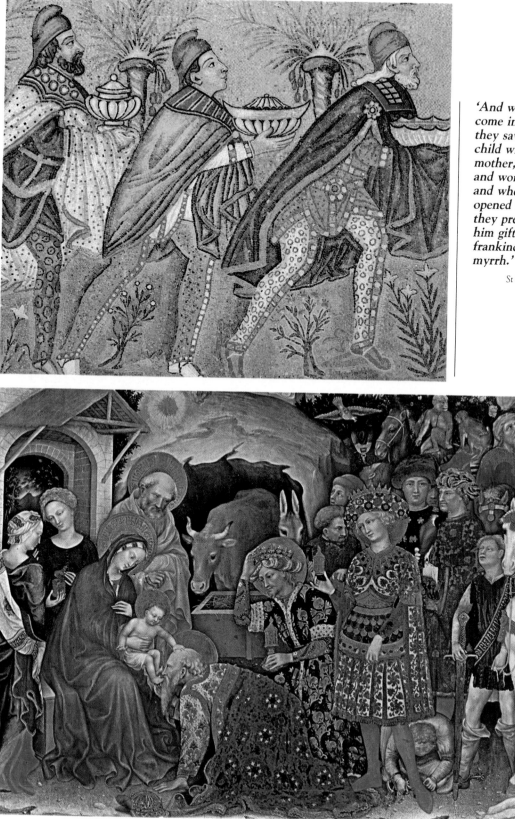

'And when they were come into the house, they saw the young child with Mary his mother, and fell down, and worshipped him: and when they had opened their treasures, they presented unto him gifts; gold, and frankincense, and myrrh.'

St Matthew's Gospel 2:11

Raymond of Penafort

Severinus of Noricum

St Raymond of Penafort

Raymond of Penafort was born in the year 1175, a relative of the Kings of Aragon, and endowed with a brilliant brain. Trained as a lawyer, he taught in the Universities of Barcelona and Bologna, until, in his forty-seventh year, he decided to become a Dominican monk, in part because he was growing extremely pleased with himself and desperately needed to learn some humility.

He asked those in charge of him in the monastery to prescribe some hurtful task in order to reduce his vanity. With great intelligence they decided to make use of his undoubted legal skills: Raymond was told to put together all the rules that the Church had worked out for dealing with men and women's sins. The collection of legal cases he made was a masterpiece and has never been forgotten.

The work also tamed Raymond's arrogant spirit. At this time his homeland, Spain, was besieged by the Moors, who were not Christian but Moslems. Raymond set himself to oppose the spread of the Moslem faith into Spain. But he insisted that Christians could only convert others if their own lives set an example of selflessness and godliness. He thought that even those who had been captured by the Moors could influence their enemy, provided that they continued to love them and did not abandon their own faith under persecution.

Raymond feared no-one. King James of Aragon was an immoral man, and Raymond said he would not live in the same place as such a sinner. In spite of the king's anger, Raymond sailed back to Barcelona. (A legend grew up that he boldly sailed across on his own cloak, with not the slightest fear that this quaint vessel might sink.) When honours came to him – he was made General of the Dominican order, Archbishop of Tarragona, and confessor to the Pope – he never boasted but regarded them as burdens he was obliged to bear. And the Pope used his legal talents by ordering him to make a collection of every church law. He died in 1275, at the great age of one hundred years.

Severinus was a Roman citizen who gave up all wordly goods to live in the deserts of Egypt. Here he was torn between the desire to live alone and the need to convert unbelievers. Eventually the second need triumphed: Severinus left Egypt to be a missionary in Austria.

The work was not easy. Many people simply ignored all he preached, but Severinus continued to found monasteries along the Danube, seeing these as oases of Christianity in an evil land. Men and women turned to him in need. During a famine, he discovered that a rich woman

had hidden away vast quantities of food which Severinus made her give to the starving. He could work miracles, it seems, and drove away a plague of locusts which threatened to bring another famine. Slowly many Austrians accepted his faith.

Yet Severinus never forgot his desire to live a solitary life; he would shut himself away for long periods to meditate on Jesus. Those who sought him out were astonished to discover that he lived in a room so low that a grown man was forced to stoop. Severinus never ate until the sun had set, and he wore no shoes, even in winter. Not everything he attempted was successful: he was saddened that he never managed to heal the sight of one of his greatest friends. But Severinus continued to trust in God. As he lay dying of pleurisy those around could hear him singing the words of the Psalmist: 'Let everything that has breath, praise the Lord.' So he died happily in peace and tranquillity.

Adrian of Canterbury

Marcian

When Archbishop Deusdedit of Canterbury died in the year 664 the Pope decided that the best man to succeed him was an African named Adrian who was already abbot of a monastery in Italy, near Naples. The English historian and monk, the Venerable Bede, records that he was 'very learned in the Holy Scriptures, very experienced in administering the church and the monastery, and a great Greek and Latin scholar.'

But Adrian did not want this high office. Bede tells us that when the Pope summoned Adrian and instructed him to go to Canterbury as archbishop, the abbot 'excused himself, saying that he was not fitted for such a great dignity, but that he would find someone else more suited for the task.'

The first substitute was too ill to become archbishop. Again the Pope urged the post on Adrian. Again Adrian begged permission to find someone else. At that time a monk from Tarsus named Theodore was in Rome. Adrian nominated Theodore to the Pope. Theodore was willing to become Archbishop of Canterbury, but only if Adrian agreed to come to England and help him. So on 26 March 668 Theodore was consecrated Archbishop of Canterbury, and two months later he and Adrian set sail for England.

They were a perfect team. Theodore appointed Adrian abbot of the monastery of St Peter and St Paul at Canterbury. Here the saint's learning and great virtues were employed to their best. Scholars came to the monastery from far away and Adrian taught there for thirty-nine years. His pupils could often speak Latin and Greek as well as they could speak their own languages, if not better. He knew an astonishing amount – teaching poetry, astronomy and maths (to calculate the church's calendar) as well as the Bible. Into the minds of his students Adrian 'poured the waters of wholesome knowledge day by day,' Bede records. The saint could convey happiness. 'Never,' asserts Bede, 'had there been such happy times as these since the English settled in Britain.' Adrian died in 710.

Marcian was a saint of Constantinople who modelled his life on that of Saint John the Baptist, always trying to serve God by fasting and praying. But unlike John the Baptist, he came of a rich family. Marcian gave away much money to the poor – secretly, so as not to gain the approval of his fellow men and women. At times he suffered persecution. One of his persecutors, threatening to kill Marcian, asked him, 'Why do you talk of life, if you wish to die?' Marcian replied, 'Because it is everlasting life I look for, not the life of this world.' Eventually people saw that this was an uncommonly good man, one who should be copied, not persecuted.

Many churches were in disrepair in Constantinople but Marcian restored them to their former beauty, and built others too. He was also inspired to write splendid hymns. So he used all his talents to bring people to worship Jesus.

One day when he was hurrying to the consecration of a new church he passed a miserable, nearly naked beggar. Saint Marcian gave him all his clothing. All he had left was a chasuble. The congregation, however, seemed to see a fine golden robe under Marcian's chasuble. Afterwards Patriarch Gennadius even rebuked the saint for dressing so ostentatiously. Marcian plucked off his chasuble and revealed that he was wearing nothing else.

Theodosius the Cenobiarch

Arcadius

A cenobiarch is a leader of monks. Theodosius, who was born in Cappodocia in 423, became one almost by accident. After a pilgrimage to Jerusalem, Theodosius put himself in the care of a holy monk named Longinus. Longinus soon saw that his charge was unusually committed to the ways of Jesus. Near to Jerusalem a rich woman had built a monastery and she needed someone to lead it. Longinus knew that Theodosius was the best man to do this, and he persuaded the saint to do so.

Theodosius longed to live alone. But although he retired from the monastery, many men and women flocked to listen to him and to become his pupils. In the end, Theodosius decided he had no choice but to look after them. He resigned himself to instructing anyone who came to him. Close to Bethlehem he built a large monastery, and attached to it three hospitals. One cared for the old; one for the physically sick and another for the sick in mind. Greeks, Armenians and Persians worked and prayed happily together. And no one was ever turned away without a meal and good hospitality – no matter how little the monks themselves had to eat.

At the beginning of the fourth century Christians in the Roman Empire were so viciously persecuted that Arcadius hid away in the countryside to avoid being forced to worship idols on pain of death. His absence was soon noticed by the persecutors. Worse, they caught one of his relatives, threatening him until Arcadius revealed where he was hiding. The saint would not allow anyone to suffer in his place and gave himself up to the Roman authorities. 'Release this innocent man,' he told the judge, 'since I have appeared in person before you and he did not know where I was hiding.'

The judge promised to release Arcadius too, if only he would offer a sacrifice to idols. Arcadius refused, though he knew he would now be tortured. 'Invent what torments you please,' he declared. 'Nothing shall make me betray my God. The fear of death will never make me fail in my duty.'

In a rage the judge decided that he would make Arcadius actually desire to die. As he boasted to the saint what tortures were now to be inflicted, all Arcadius would say was, 'Lord, teach me your wisdom.'

Usually Christians at this time were beheaded, if they refused to sacrifice to idols. At the place of execution, Arcadius was surprised that this did not happen. Instead, first his fingers were cut off, and then – bit by bit – his upper limbs. Next the torturers cut off his toes, his feet, his legs. Arcadius kept repeating, 'Lord, teach me your wisdom.' Eventually all that remained were his trunk and his head.

Then a remarkable thing happened. The dying saint looked round at all the pieces of him, hacked off and lying on the ground. He could still speak, and he cried out, 'You are happy, my members. Now you really belong to God. You have all been sacrificed to him.' His last words were addressed to all those standing by. 'Learn from my torments,' he shouted. 'Your gods are nothing. The only true God is the one for whom I am suffering and about to die. To die for him is to live.'

Hilary of Poitiers

Sava

Hilary of Poitiers was well advanced in years and a happily married man when his own reading of the Bible convinced him that Christianity was the true religion. He had no desire to be honoured by the Church and was at first unwilling to accept the bishopric of Poitiers urged on him by the Pope around the year 350. But once he did accept, he firmly resisted any attempt by the powerful unbelievers to impose their will on the Church.

The Emperor Constantius summoned him to a synod in Milan, called to condemn the teachings of Saint Athanasius. Hilary considered Athanasius to be right, and refused to attend. As a result the Emperor sent him into exile to Phrygia. Hilary went without complaint, and was so successful in arguing against the enemies of Christianity there that soon the Phrygians were begging the Emperor to send Hilary back to Poitiers. For three years he lived in exile, employing his time in writing fine books defending the faith.

In exile Saint Hilary perceived that his opponents used hymns to spread their false views. He decided that Christians could spread their religion in the same way, and he became the first Latin hymn-writer of the Christian church. Most of his hymns have been lost, but three survive: one about Jesus's temptations in the wilderness; another about Easter; and a third, on the Trinity, seventy verses long.

At the age of seventeen, Sava became a monk of Mount Athos in Greece. His father had been king, but he abdicated in 1196 and joined Sava in founding a new monastery on this sacred mountain, reserved for monks from Serbia, his own native country.

When he learned that his brothers (one of whom was now King of Serbia) were desperately at odds with each other, Sava returned home and succeeded in bringing peace and a new spirit to Serbia. Without his efforts the country would certainly have split apart and today Sava is venerated as the patron saint of Serbia.

All this was accomplished at the end of his long life. From seventeen to seventy Sava lived out of sight of the world. He had retired from the active life when he was summoned to serve as Archbishop of Serbia but with renewed energy he founded eight bishoprics and started schools throughout the country. Serbs, Greeks and Latin-speaking natives learned to live together under his leadership, they called him 'St Sava the Enlightener'. When he died his followers attributed to him all manner of wisdom. The most delightful is that he taught the Serbs that they could plough a field both ways, instead of dragging the plough backwards after each furrow to start again from the same end of a field, as they did before.

'Little children follow and obey their father. They love their mother. They know nothing of covetousness, ill-will, bad temper, arrogance and lying. This state of mind opens the road to heaven. To imitate our Lord's own humility, we must return to the simplicity of God's little ones.'

St Hilary of Poitiers

Paul the Hermit

Paul, the first well-known Christian hermit, never expected to enjoy life alone in the desert. His parents had died in the year 244, when Paul was only fifteen years old. Born in lower Egypt, he loved the culture of his native land and also knew Greek well. As a Christian he was in danger from the persecution of Decius. A pagan friend hid him in his house but his brother-in-law was about to betray Paul (so as to get his hands on Paul's inheritance), and for this reason the saint fled into the desert to hide in the caves there.

He grew to love the solitary life: dressed only in a garment made of palm leaves, he lived by a cool stream meditating on God. Until he was forty-three the fruit of the palm tree was all he had to eat. Then, so St Jerome tells us, a raven began to bring Paul half a loaf of bread a day.

This was a healthy life. A contemporary hermit was Saint Antony who, at the age of ninety, decided he would call on Paul. When the two saints met, the raven that had brought Paul half a loaf a day for sixty years incredibly brought a full loaf, to serve both men. The two saints took a long time to start eating, since Paul insisted that Antony, as his guest, should have the privilege of breaking the bread, whereas Antony insisted that Paul, as the older of the two, should act as host. Eventually they both broke bread simultaneously.

Paul was one hundred and thirteen years old when he died. Saint Antony again visited the saintly hermit and found him stretched out in prayer. For some time Antony prayed beside Paul before he realized that his fellow saint had died. For the rest of his own life, Antony cherished Paul's palm-leaf clothing, and wore it himself on important church feasts.

Marcellus I

Antony Abbot

When Marcellus became Pope times were dangerous for Christians in Rome. The papacy had remained vacant for three-and-a-half years. Marcellus himself reigned as Pope for only seven months and twenty days.

In the year 276 Antony's parents died, leaving him a wealthy man. Shortly after their death Antony listened to the story of Jesus telling a rich young man to sell all he possessed and give it to the poor. Antony did precisely that and retired to the desert to live a life of solitude.

Often he was terrified by strange noises or tempted by evil thoughts. But he put all this down to Satan who did not wish him to continue as a servant of Jesus. For many years he saw another human being only once every six months when a man brought him some bread. But he became so famous that he was obliged to found monasteries for all his disciples.

'Whoever sits in solitude and is quiet has escaped from three wars: hearing, speaking and seeing. Yet against one thing he must constantly battle: his own heart.'

St Antony Abbot

Marcellus was looked after by a devout Christian widow, named Lucina. In her home he opened an oratory as a place of prayer for those who still kept the faith. The Emperor Maxentius decided to torment the saint by making the oratory a stable, and worse: Maxentius forced the Pope to work there as a stable boy, cleaning it out as best he could. The old man's strength was not equal to this task, and he died (possibly in exile) in the year 309. His earthly remains were buried in the Roman cemetry of St Priscilla.

Maxentius was defeated in battle three years later by the Emperor Constantine, who embraced Christianity. The oratory became a regular place of worship, and in the sixth century the oratory was enlarged. Meanwhile the memory of Marcellus was preserved. After three hundred years his remains were placed under the high altar of the church that now stood where he had opened his oratory in 309 AD. Although the Church of San Marcello al Corso in Rome has been rebuilt many times since then, the saint's bones remain under its high altar to this day.

Margaret of Hungary

The daughter of King Bela IV and Queen Mary Lascaris of Hungary, Margaret was rich and beautiful. But her parents destined her for a nunnery – partly, it is said, because Hungary was under great external threat and they hoped that to offer their small daughter to God in this way would avert disaster.

Far from turning against her destiny, Margaret embraced it gladly. She chose the least attractive of the nuns' duties for herself. She would starve herself to keep her spirit humble. Yet her beauty seems to have remained unspoiled. King Ottokar of Bohemia longed to marry her. Margaret adamantly refused. The monastery was her life – though throughout Lent she scarcely slept or ate. She was only twenty-eight, when she died in 1270. Almost immediately many of her friends and acquaintances petitioned that she be acclaimed a saint. Among them was her own servant, Agnes, who rightly observed that this daughter of a monarch showed far more humility than any of the monastery's maids.

Marius and Martha

Marius and Martha (*below*) were a rich Persian couple, who gave all their wealth to the poor. The two Christians, along with their sons Audifax and Abachum, decided to visit Rome even though the Emperor Claudius was persecuting Christians. Claudius ordered his legions to gather Christians in the amphitheatre.

They were killed and then set alight. Marius and Martha, along with their two sons, gathered together the ashes and buried them. For this, the governor Marcian apprehended and tortured the whole family before putting them to death. Reverent Christians honoured the bodies of these martyrs with respect: they were buried on the Via Cornelia. Thirteen centuries later their bones were discovered and now lie honoured in churches as far apart as Rome, Cremona and Seligenstadt in Germany.

Wulfstan

Educated in English monasteries, Wulfstan became a monk at Worcester, and was made Bishop of that city just four years before the Normans conquered England in 1066. King William, the Norman conqueror, replaced every English bishop with one of his own men – save for one, the saintly Wulfstan. Yet Wulfstan was no weakling. He managed to put a stop to a slave trade based at Bristol, and rebuilt his cathedral. He remained a much-loved and respected bishop for thirty-two years and died in 1095.

JANUARY 20

Sebastian

The story of Saint Sebastian is that of a brave double-agent – a man who, though a Christian, kept his views secret during the persecutions of the Emperor Diocletian, not out of fear but in order to be able to comfort those who were daily being martyred for their faith. Born in Narbonne, France, he enlisted as a Roman soldier in the year 283, even though some of his duties seemed to cut across his Christian faith. Secretly, he encouraged Christians about to be killed not to waver in their beliefs. Even more boldly, he converted such noted pagans as a man named Nicostratus, who was in charge of the prisoners, and his wife Zoë.

Sebastian cured the prefect of Rome of his painful gout, and the prefect himself became a Christian, setting many godly prisoners free. Yet still Sebastian remained undetected. The Emperor Diocletian heard favourable reports of this young soldier and ordered that he be made a captain in the pretorian guards.

This could not last. First Nicostratus's wife Zoë was discovered to be a Christian. Hung up by the heels over a fire, she died in the smoke. Nicostratus and the converted prefect were captured, tortured and killed. Finally the faith of Sebastian was discovered. Diocletian is said to have been bitterly disappointed that one so close to him had been a believer in God. The saint was sentenced to be shot to death by arrows. In spite of his many wounds, he survived, to be nursed back to health by a widow named Irene.

But Sebastian now was determined to confront the great persecutor of his fellow-Christians. He publicly appeared before a startled Diocletian to attack the Emperor's cruelty to Christians. For a moment Diocletian could hardly speak. Then he sentenced Sebastian to be clubbed to death. The saint's body was cast into a sewer, but Christians rescued it, burying it on the Appian Way at the spot where the church of San Sebastiano stands today.

Agnes

'Christ is my bridegroom,' declared St Agnes. 'He was the first to choose me. I shall be his alone.' These fine words very much annoyed the young men of Rome in the early fourth century. Agnes possessed wealth and physical beauty. But she had no time for any of her suitors, and a number of them decided to try to force her into marriage by denouncing her as a Christian.

Their plan was to persuade her to renounce her religion and thus her allegiance to Jesus rather than to marriage. This was the time of the persecution under the Emperor Diocletian. Agnes was threatened with various savage tortures: again and again she replied, 'The Lord will guard his own.'

The Roman governor now decided that the best way to make this girl bend to his will was to submit her to the temptations of a brothel. Any man who wished would be allowed to abuse her. Unfortunately for his plan, the saint's meekness and purity impressed even those who wanted to harm her in this way. No-one would touch her.

All this deeply annoyed the Roman governor. The little saint was barely thirteen years old, but he determined now to kill her. The executioner tried to torment her, but she told him, 'Do not delay. This body draws from some a kind of admiration that I hate. Let it perish.' We do not know whether she was beheaded or stabbed in the throat. At any rate, Agnes meekly turned her neck to the executioner and died.

Her friends buried her near Rome, on the Via Nomentana. Her fame spread. When the Emperor Constantine wished to baptize his daughter, he did so near the spot where Agnes was buried. And a few years after her death the church of Sant' Agnese Fuori le Mura (which, much modified, still stands today) was erected over her grave. In Christian art, her emblem is a lamb.

Vincent of Saragossa

In the early years of the fourth century there seemed no limit to the brutality with which Christians were abused by their pagan persecutors. When Saint Vincent was ordained by the Bishop of Saragossa and ordered to minister in that part of Spain, the governor Dacian was doing his utmost to stamp out Christianity. He killed eighteen believers at Saragossa in the year 303. Then he arrested Vincent.

Vincent had no intention of giving up his Christian faith. Dacian banished the Bishop of Saragossa, but he decided to try to break Vincent's will. He ordered that Vincent's body should be stretched out on a rack, while other men tore the saint's flesh with great hooks. Then he had the saint laid out on a gridiron of heated bars. This did not kill the saint, who still refused to give up his faith or even to tell Dacian where he had hidden his sacred books.

The governor realized that he could not break the will of this saint and ordered his soldiers to give up the torture and throw Vincent into a foul prison. Some Christians came to care for him, cleaning his wounds and laying the saint on a soft bed. But he had suffered too much pain to go on living; he died, still praising Jesus.

Dacian's hatred of Vincent persisted after the saint's death. Not wishing anyone to give Vincent a decent burial, he ordered that the corpse should be flung into a bog. Dacian hoped that wild beasts would eat the mortal remains of this saint, but a raven seems to have decided that this corpse needed special protection. Whenever a wild beast or bird tried to attack the holy relics, the raven drove them away.

Ildefonsus

Francis de Sales

'Is there anything better on earth than gentleness? If there were, Jesus Christ would have taught it to us. But Jesus has given us only two lessons. "Learn from me," he said, "for I am meek and lowly of heart".'.

St Francis de Sales

'He is rich in spirit who has his riches in his spirit not his spirit in his riches; he is poor in spirit who has no riches in his spirit, or his spirit in his riches.'

St Francis de Sales

Saint Ildefonsus, Archbishop of Toledo, was sitting on the bishop's throne in his cathedral when he was granted a vision in which the Virgin Mary presented him with a chasuble.

The gift was a fitting one, for Ildefonsus adored the Virgin. He saw worship of Jesus as the supreme duty of a Christian; and he believed that one could do so by meditating on Jesus through the eyes, as it were, of his Virgin mother.

Ildefonsus's parents were from a noble Spanish family. He longed to become a monk. They opposed his wishes; but the saint nevertheless professed himself a member of a monastery at Agalia near Toledo. The other monks recognized his deep spirituality and wisdom by making him their abbot. About fifteen years later he was consecrated archbishop.

For nine years he governed the church wisely, until he died peacefully in 667. The grateful Spaniards dubbed him a Doctor of the Church and his memory is revered to this day.

Born in Savoy on 21 August 1567, Francis longed to devote himself to the Christian ministry, but his father wished him to take up more worldly pursuits. Francis obediently attended the University of Paris, as his father wished, but all the time his heart was set on the religious life. He learned philosophy and rhetoric, but he insisted on learning theology too.

These tensions made the young Francis miserable. For a while he even lost the certainty that God loved him. In his prayers he would admit that he feared God would desert him. 'Never let me curse you, my God,' he would cry. God heard his prayers and his doubts were lifted. But as a result, he learned to care for those who similarly doubted their salvation. His gentleness arose not from weakness but from his own experience of suffering.

Francis worked in Geneva, which was mostly Calvinist, and in 1602 he became Bishop of Geneva. He was the ideal person for this position, combining a deep commitment to the faith with a love of his fellow men and women. So great was his care for individuals that some of his converts set out his teaching in a *Treatise on the Love of God*, published in 1616. Just before his death a nun asked him to write down the virtue he most desired. He wrote one word: 'Humility'.

Conversion of St Paul

Saint Paul, originally named Saul, was born a Jew, in a place called Tarsus. He grew to hate the Christians, believing they were perverting the truths of his own religion. He came, says the book of the Acts of the Apostles, 'breathing threats and murder against the disciples of the Lord.'

The first Christian martyr, St Stephen, was stoned to death by a vicious crowd. Saul was present, and although he threw no stones, the book of Acts says he was 'consenting to Stephen's death.' After devout men had buried Stephen's body, Saul ravaged the church. He entered house after house where he supposed Christians lived or were hiding, and dragged them away to prison.

So great was Saul's anger against the early Christians that he went to the High Priest in Jerusalem asking for special

permission to seize the Christians of Damascus and bring them to Jerusalem for punishment. The High Priest gave him a letter with such orders, and Saul set off for Damascus. On the way there he was struck to the ground by a sudden flash of light from heaven and a voice cried out, 'Saul, Saul, why are you persecuting me?'

When Saul cried, 'Who are you Lord?', the voice replied, 'I am Jesus, whom you are persecuting.' Jesus then ordered Saul to journey on into Damascus, and visit a Christian named Ananias. Saul had been blinded by the flash of light, but he did as he was ordered by Jesus's voice, and Ananias, in spite of fearing what Saul might do to him, welcomed the persecutor. At Damascus he learned from the Christians about their faith. Then he amazed those who worshipped in the Jewish synagogues by telling them that he now believed Jesus to be the Son of God. Some of them decided to try to kill this convert to Christianity, but he escaped from Damascus by getting his new friends to lower him over the walls in a basket at dead of night.

As Saul perceived the truth about Christianity, his eyesight returned. And to symbolize his new life, he took a new name: Paul. His writings have had a major influence on Christian theology.

'Whatsoever things are true, whatsoever things are honest, whatsoever things are just, whatsoever things are pure, whatsoever things are lovely, whatsoever things are of good report; if there be any virtue and if there be any praise, think on these things.'

St Paul's Epistle to the Philippians

'Charity suffereth long, and is kind; charity envieth not; charity vaunteth not itself, is not puffed up, Doth not behave itself unseemly, seeketh not her own, is not easily provoked, thinketh no evil; Rejoiceth not in iniquity, but rejoiceth in the truth; Beareth all things, believeth all things, hopeth all things, endureth all things. Charity never faileth: but whether there be prophecies, they shall fail, whether there be tongues, they shall cease; whether there be knowledge, it shall vanish away'.

St Paul's Epistle to the Corinthians

Paula

St Paula

'If any person, because of his state of life, cannot do without wealth and position, let him at least keep his heart empty of the love of them.'

St Angela Merici

Paula, who was throughout her married life deeply content, was grief-stricken when her husband died in the year 379, when she was only thirty-two years old. She comforted herself through her children – her four daughters (Blesilla, Paulina, Eustochium and Rufina) and her son Toxotius. Then came a further blow to her earthly happiness: her eldest daughter Blesilla fell seriously ill and died.

Paula had by this time become the friend of Saint Jerome. She had coped with the death of her husband by devoting herself to God, giving up earthly treasures (though she was a rich woman), sleeping on sackcloth, eating little and indulging in nothing immoderately. But the death of Blesilla overwhelmed her.

Fortunately Jerome arrived at Bethlehem and learned all this. He wrote sternly to his dear friend. Paula was right to mourn her husband and daughter; but she ought also, said Jerome, to realize that they had entered a realm of greater happiness than this world can offer. Paula determined on a new life. With her third daughter Eustochium she left Rome for ever and met Jerome, who had now moved to Antioch. The three of them went on a pilgrimage to the Holy Land and finally settled at Bethlehem.

Paula and Eustochium were now content to live in a tiny cottage instead of the sumptuous Roman villa of their birth. They used their wealth to build a hospice, a monastery and a convent for women. Everyone dressed in exactly the same fashion, quite simply, showing that they were all equal in God's sight. When Paula first entered Bethlehem, she cried, 'I greet you, Bethlehem, the "house of Bread", for here was born that living Bread who came down from heaven.' The bread of heaven, she believed, satisfied all her needs. No longer did she and her companions care for fine food. In fact, she gave away so much money that towards the end of her life she and her companions were quite short of money. But nothing troubled them, and Paula herself died in peace aged fifty-seven on 26 January 404. She was buried near Jesus's birthplace.

Angela Merici

Angela was distressed that the children of the poor knew nothing about Christianity and were almost completely untaught in her part of Italy. She called on her fellow-Christians in the Franciscan order to start a humble school for local girls. It was a tremendous success. Angela became known for her zeal in the neighbourhood, and the Christians in nearby Brescia asked her to go to that city to start up another school for poor girls.

Once she dreamed of a group of young women climbing a great ladder into heaven. A voice told her that she one day would lead just such a group of dedicated women. She never forgot this vision, and in November 1535, while she was living at Brescia, she gathered together eight women companions who vowed to serve God unstintingly. They took as their patron saint the English queen and martyr, Ursula, calling themselves Ursulines.

Thomas Aquinas

The family of this brilliant intellectual were so much opposed to the idea that he should become a Dominican monk that they held him prisoner for fifteen months in the hope of dissuading him. They failed. As a monk Thomas met the greatest brains of the thirteenth century, studying in Paris and in Cologne and finally becoming a famous lecturer in Paris himself. So great was his influence that Thomas was also asked to teach at many Italian Universities; but Paris remained his spiritual and intellectual home until the year 1272, when he set up a great school at Naples.

St Thomas laboured to prove to the sluggish minds of human beings that God exists, that he is love and that in him is every possible perfection. His writings have long been recognized as intellectual masterpieces, even by those who disagree with them.

Thomas Aquinas was no dry and boring person although he was very shy. He loved to laugh; but he also wrote, 'I cannot understand how a person can even smile, if he is in a state of mortal sin.' He died in 1274.

Sabinian

In the third century a pagan named Sabinian became so disenchanted with the society and morals of his native island, Samos, that he journeyed to Gaul. At Troyes he was converted and baptized by Saint Patroclus who was later martyred *circa* 259. Saint Sabinian carried on the work of Patroclus for another twenty-six years or so. He preached and baptized in the region of the upper Seine, and many were converted. When Sabinian was brought to judgement before the Emperor Aurelian, he mocked the imperial threats and refused to renounce his Christian faith. Arrows and burning failed to kill him, however, and eventually he was beheaded at Rilly near Troyes in around the year 275.

Gildas

Born alongside the River Clyde around the year 500, Gildas travelled south and became a hermit at Llanilltud in Wales. Gildas lived a very varied life: he made a journey to Ireland to consult with the many contemporary saints of that land, and he lived for a time on an island in the Bristol channel. He married and was widowed. He made a pilgrimage to Rome, and on his way back founded a religious house at Ruys in Brittany where he died in the year 570. This monastery became the centre of his cult.

In all this time he grew increasingly disenchanted with the morals of the clergy and the great laymen of his age. Gildas decided to try to make his countrymen renew their way of life by writing a history of Britain from the coming of the Romans until his own time. As he reached the present his pen became more and more condemnatory. His, he said, was a chronicle of 'the miseries, the mistakes and the downfall of Britain'. Those who did not wish to hear his message claimed that he exaggerated the evils around him. And even to this day scholars do not know whether to take him at his word or to tone down his description of the evil doings of his time.

*'Word made flesh, true
bread Christ makes
By his word his flesh
to be,
Wine his Blood; which
whoso takes
Must from carnal
thought be free
Faith alone, though
sight forsakes,
Shows true hearts the
mystery.'*

St Thomas Aquinas

Martina

In 1634 Pope Urban VIII decided to rebuild an ancient church that stood under the Capital Hill in Rome, overlooking the Forum. The workmen discovered a Christian tomb containing the bones of a Roman lady and her two brothers. These were the remains of Saints Martina (*below*), Concordius and Epiphanius. Bernini created a magnificent bronze shrine for these relics and today, in the church of Santi Luca e Martino, Rome, lamps burn continually around the shrine. Although we know little about her, she remains one of the patron saints of the city of Rome itself.

Bathildis

Saint Bathildis was a woman whose life was one of rags to riches. An English girl, she was captured by pirates and sold as a slave to Erchinoald, major domo to King Clovis II of the Franks. So attractive and intelligent was Bathildis that Clovis eventually married her, and she bore him three sons, all of whom became king in turn. But she laboured all her life for the poor and desolate – building hospitals, banishing slavery and selling her own jewellery to supply the needy. Her last fifteen years were spent in one of the nunneries she herself had founded.

St Aidan

'Give as if every pasture in the mountains of Ireland belonged to you.'

St Aidan

St Martina

Aidan

Aidan, an Irish saint who died in the year 626, loved animals. His fellow Irishmen were fond of hunting them to death. Aidan so protected them that his symbol today in Christian art is a stag. Legend has it that as he sat reading in Connaught, where he was born, a desperate stag took refuge with him in the hope of escaping pursuing hounds. Aidan by a miracle made the stag invisible, and the hounds ran off.

Aidan came to Wales as one of many Irish missionaries, joining in David's monastic life, only differing from his fellow monks by bringing his own beer from his native land. The inspiration of Saint David caused him to return to Ireland, where he built his own monastery. There his great reputation for charity still survives, for he taught his monks to give their last victuals to those in need.

John Bosco

This day is also the feast day of John Bosco, who in the nineteenth century so successfully taught young Italian boys both religion and learning that his inspiration led to the foundation of the famous Society of St Francis de Sales – a world-wide organization dedicated to his own educational ideals. He died in 1888.

February

'To change your mind from good to bad is the height of absurdity. True goodness changes from evil to righteousness.'

'I thank my God that I am being allowed my share in the sufferings of his martyrs. He who gives me strength to endure fire will enable me to stand unmoved to the end.'

Polycarp (February 23)

Brigid

St Brigid

'We implore Thee, by the memory of Thy Cross's hallowed and most bitter anguish, make us fear Thee, make us love Thee, O Christ. Amen.'

Prayer of St Brigid

An Irish chieftain named Dubhthach fell in love with and married a serving girl at his court whose name was Brocca, and towards the middle of the fifth century their daughter Brigid was born. Very early in her life Brigid decided to become a nun, and when she was about eighteen she settled with seven other like-minded girls near Croghan Hill in order to devote herself to God's service. Then, around the year 470, she founded the first convent of Ireland's history, at a place known as Cill-Dara ('the church of the oak') and now called Kildare. Almost certainly this convent housed both monks and nuns, with the saintly Brigid presiding as abbess over both.

Even as a child Brigid showed especial love for the poor. When her mother sent her to collect butter, the child gave it all away. Her generosity in adult life was legendary: it was recorded that if she gave a drink of water to a thirsty stranger, the liquid turned into milk; when she sent a barrel of beer to one Christian community, this proved enough to satisfy seventeen more.

Brigid saw that the needs of the body and the needs of the spirit went hand in hand. Dedicated to improving the spiritual as well as the material lives of those around her, Brigid made her monastery a remarkable house of learning, producing exquisite works of art, copying and illuminating precious manuscripts and books, educating those who sat at her own feet and the feet of her followers.

During an important synod of the Irish church, one of the holy fathers announced that he had dreamed that the Blessed Virgin Mary would appear among the assembled Christians. When Brigid arrived the father cried, 'There is the holy maiden I saw in my dream.' So Brigid came to be known as 'the Mary of Gael'.

She died on 1 February 525. When the Danes invaded Ireland, her body was taken from Kildare to Downpatrick, to be buried beside the remains of St Patrick, who, like Brigid, is a patron of Ireland.

Joan de Lestonnac

Joan de Lestonnac lived to the age of ninety-six, and during her long life triumphed over ill-health and the evil plotting of a wicked woman. Born in Bordeaux in 1556 to a Protestant mother, she married Gaston de Montferrant and remained devoted to her husband, bearing him one son and three daughters. After only twenty-four years of deeply happy marriage, Gaston died.

Two of Joan's daughters had felt drawn to the life of a nun, and Joan herself now decided to enter a Cistercian monastery. The life did not suit her and she became seriously ill. Yet her wise superiors perceived what an exceptional woman Joan was and encouraged her to attempt a great service for God, by founding an order of women devoted to Our Lady. She gathered a band of young girls whose first task turned out to be bravely serving as nurses during a savage plague which struck the people of Bordeaux.

A number of priests had come to recognize the utter devotion of Joan, and with their help she persuaded the Archbishop of Bordeaux to support her religious order. In 1610 she became the mother superior. Seeking only the barest necessities for themselves, her sisters founded schools throughout the region, welcoming into them any girl who could come. But while this work prospered, one vicious sister named Blanche Hervé began to spread lies about Joan; the authorities believed them, and Joan was dismissed as superior.

Here her great meekness triumphed. She was beaten and humiliated, but she bore all so patiently that even Blanche Hervé was moved to confess her own maliciousness. Joan de Lestonnac no longer wished to work as mother superior, but she passed her last years highly honoured by her order, dying peacefully on 2 February 1640.

| FEBRUARY 3 | FEBRUARY 4 |

Blaise

Corsini

Blaise was Bishop of Sebastea. When the governor of Armenia began persecuting Christians, Blaise hid in a cave where the wild beasts grew to care for him, since he cared for them whenever they were hurt. His hiding place was discovered. As he was being brought to the governor, a poor woman appealed for help because a wolf had taken her pig and Blaise persuaded the wolf to release the pig unharmed. The governor decided Blaise must starve to death, but the grateful poor woman secretly brought him food.

Another woman brought him her son who was choking on a fish-bone. Blaise fished it out, the boy lived, and so the saint was known for curing sore throats, as well as the patron of sick cattle. When he discovered that Blaise was still alive, the governor ordered soldiers to rake away the saint's skin, and then Blaise was beheaded.

The Corsini family lived in Florence, devoted to God, but their son, Andrew, proved a wayward youth, spending his money on vice and carousing with evil friends. One day his mother told Andrew Corsini of her deepest fears. Just before his birth, she had dreamed that she was giving birth to a wolf and Andrew realized that he was indeed living like a wild animal. He slunk away to church, where he prayed, and became a new man.

Andrew Corsini decided to join the Carmelites. He became utterly devoted to his new life and was eventually made prior of his own monastery. The former ruffian was elected Bishop of Fiesole. Believing himself unworthy of this office, Corsini ran away and hid, but he was discovered and forced to accept the bishopric. The Pope sent him to Bologna, where the rulers and the people were quarrelling violently. Although both sides initially insulted Corsini, in the end he won them over and restored peace.

Andrew Corsini had been born into a rich family. He accordingly felt it good for him to find poor men and wash their feet every Thursday. He was seventy-one years old when he died and was immediately declared a saint by the people of Florence.

Ansgar

Saint Ansgar was renowned as a most successful missionary. He built the first Christian church in Sweden and became the first Archbishop of Hamburg. He asked, he said, for only one miracle: that God would make him a good man.

29

Agatha

St Agatha

Agatha lived in Sicily in the third century and must have been beautiful, since a consul named Quintian tried to force her to become his wife. When she refused he turned against her and decided to punish her by installing the pure girl in a brothel. She resisted all attempts to shame her.

Quintian therefore took his revenge by bringing her before the courts because she belonged to the outlawed Christian church. The accounts of her tortures are frightful. Even her breasts were cut off, and she was allowed no medicines or bandages. It is said that St Peter appeared to her in a vision, healing her wounds.

Agatha would pray passionately throughout all this: 'Lord Jesus Christ: you know what is in my heart and mind. Take me and all that I am and make me your own.' She was stretched on a rack. Then she was thrown naked onto burning coal. Naturally Agatha believed death would be a happy release, bringing her out of the reach of her tormentors into the arms of her Lord. They carried her broken body back to her prison, while she prayed for release. At that moment Agatha died.

A saint who bore such trials was greatly revered. Saint Gregory the Great, for example, took a church which the Goths had used in Rome, and reconsecrated it to the saint. The church of Sant' Agata dei Goti still stands, preserving the memory of this virgin martyr.

Dorothy

When Dorothy, who lived in Cappadocia, was imprisoned as a Christian she converted two women warders. This enraged Fabricius, the governor of Caesarea, who sentenced her to death. On the way to execution, Dorothy was cruelly baited by an onlooker named Theophilus. She believed she was going to paradise. He mockingly asked her to send him back some fruit and flowers. She took a napkin and placed in it three roses and three apples. Then she begged a child to take them to Theophilus. When he saw these gifts he himself was converted to Christianity, and later he too suffered martyrdom.

Before being killed, Dorothy was stretched on a rack. It is recorded that she was then still smiling, as she remembered the warders she had converted.

Amand of Maastricht

Amand of Maastricht was a hermit at Bourges in France for fifteen years before setting out to convert unbelievers. Amand was a tireless preacher, a wandering saint who worked as far afield as Flanders and among the Slavs of the River Danube. Although the saint was exiled, Amand continued his work and died, aged almost ninety, at the abbey of Elnone in the year 679.

Theodore the General

Theodore lived in Heraclea and was a general commanding one of the armies of the Emperor Licinius. A man of great political influence, Theodore also governed part of Licinius's territory.

His fellow-soldiers realized that their general had embraced the Christian faith when he refused to join them in pagan worship. For this the general was tortured by those he had once loyally served, and was then let out of prison on remand. He showed his scorn for the idol worshippers by setting on fire a temple dedicated to a pagan goddess, Cybele, at Amasea in Pontus. The authorities lost no time in throwing him into prison again and once more torturing him cruelly. The general was comforted by a vision of heaven, before perishing in a furnace. He was buried at Euchaita and is revered by the Eastern Church as a great soldier-saint.

Luke the Wonderworker

Luke the younger is known to the Greek Church as Saint Luke the Wonderworker. His parents were farmers in Thessaly. They often grew angry with their son, simply because his charity to those poorer than himself ran away with him. When sowing seed, for instance, Luke the Wonderworker spread at least half of it over the fields of the poor instead of over his parents' fields.

Later it was said that one of his legendary wonders was to make his parents' crops yield more than anyone else's, even though he had given away half the seeds. But at the time his mother and father were extremely angry. When he told them he wanted to enter a monastery, they tried to stop him. But Luke ran away. Unfortunately some soldiers caught him and for a time put him in prison, thinking he was a runaway slave.

In the end, Luke got his way. He built a hermitage on Mount Joannitsa near Corinth, and lived there happily for the rest of his life.

Jerome Emiliani

Jerome Emiliani is the patron saint of orphans and abandoned children. Born in 1481, he became a soldier and took charge of the fortress of Castelnuovo in the Italian mountains. The Venetians took the fortress and chained Jerome Emiliani in a prison, but he escaped, carrying his chains with him, and – thanking God for this in a church at Treviso – hung his chains on the church wall in happiness.

His gratitude inspired the rest of his life. He was ordained priest in Venice when the city was suffering an appalling plague. Jerome perceived that abandoned children were suffering particularly, since

starvation set them doubly at risk. Taking as many as he could into his own home, he fed and clothed them, nursed them back to health, and taught them the Christian faith. He caught the plague himself, but he was strong enough to recover.

Jerome Emiliani set up orphanages in half-a-dozen Italian towns and founded a society of priests whose principal work would be the care and instruction of abandoned children. He also built a hospital at Verona and continued to care for the sick, regardless of his own health, until 1537, when he succumbed a second time to the plague. This time it killed him.

Apollonia

Whenever Saint Apollonia is depicted in Christian art she either carries a pair of pincers of the sort used for pulling out teeth, or is shown with a necklace made of her own teeth.

The reason is that in the year 249 she was caught up in the midst of a bloodthirsty mob out to kill as many Christians as possible. Apollonia was an old woman, but she was as brave as the other Christians. First of all the mob smashed out all her teeth – hence the symbols of the pincers and the necklace. Then they dragged her outside Alexandria, where she lived, and lit a huge bonfire. They said that unless Apollonia cursed her God, they would fling her into the fire. Dionysius, Bishop of Alexandria, was there and witnessed the way this old lady foiled her persecutors. She clearly decided that in no way would anyone of them have the pleasure of throwing her aged body onto the fire. So she paused for a moment, as if deciding whether or not to curse. Expectantly, the mob let go of her and drew back. At this moment Apollonia jumped on the fire herself – to be honoured ever since as a fearless Christian martyr.

Miguel of Ecuador

On this day too is celebrated the feast of Miguel of Ecuador, the first person of that land to be canonized. Born in 1854, he could scarcely walk because of a deformity of his feet but he became a brilliant scholar. At the age of nine he went to a school run by the De La Salle Brothers, loved the life he discovered there and later joined the order himself. He wrote textbooks, poetry and works of Christian spirituality. He came to Europe to translate more textbooks from the French. 'I have my room, some books and a nearby chapel,' he wrote from Paris. 'That is complete happiness.' Miguel of Ecuador died in 1910 and was canonized in 1984.

| FEBRUARY 10 | FEBRUARY 11 |

Scholastica

Pascal

Saint Scholastica was the twin sister of Saint Benedict of Nursia, founder of the famous Benedictine order. She was as devoted to Jesus as her brother; and since he founded a community of nuns as well as monks, she was able to serve his great vision as an abbess.

According to Benedict's own rules, he and his sister were unable to enter each other's convents. They would meet once a year in a house outside the monastery Benedict had founded at Monte Cassino, praying together, and talking about the love of God.

In the year 543 Scholastica knew that she was very close to the end of her life. When her twin brother came for his annual visit, she wanted him to stay overnight, talking about heaven, where she hoped soon to be. This too was against the rules of Benedict's order, and he refused her request. Scholastica appealed to a higher authority; she knelt in prayer; a fearful storm arose, and Benedict was unable to leave. Saint Benedict upbraided his sister, but she laughed and replied, 'You refused my request when I asked you. When I asked God, he granted it.'

Three days later Scholastica died. In a vision Benedict saw her soul ascending to heaven. He placed her body in the tomb he had prepared for himself, and arranged for his own body to be placed there after his death. So, as Pope Gregory the Great wrote, 'the bodies of these two, whose minds were always united in Jesus, were not separated in death.'

Pope Pascal I loved religious art, though he lived at a time when many people in the Eastern Churches were breaking up pictures of Our Lord, his mother and the saints in the belief that these were idolatrous images. Fanatics would even murder those who supported the use of fine pictures to decorate Christian churches and foster the spirit of worship.

Pascal did his best to help Eastern Christians who were fighting to stop this destruction of great religious art. He sent his aides to try to secure the release of Abbot Theodore of Studius, who had been imprisoned for defending sacred pictures and icons. And he gave shelter to many Greek monks who had fled from the east in fear of those who were destroying what they held to be precious aids to the Christian life.

Alas, Pascal did not succeed in bringing this strife to an end. But the influence of Eastern artists can be seen in the work done between 817 and 824 while he was Pope to embellish his own city of Rome. Pascal rebuilt, for instance, the Roman church of Santa Cecilia in Trastevere, and made it into a fitting shrine for the bones of Saint Cecilia. This church has been considerably rebuilt since then, but another church in Rome, Santa Maria in Domnica, remains substantially as it was after Pascal had restored it and shows his deeply held beliefs.

'The heart is rich when it is content, and it is always content when its desires are set upon God.'

St Miguel of Ecuador

Julian the Hospitaller

Julian the Hospitaller committed by accident one of the worst crimes any man or woman could perpetrate. One day he returned to his castle and went to his bedroom. Unbeknown to him his parents had arrived unexpectedly, and being tired had got into Julian's own bed. Julian saw two figures there and not recognizing them under the bedclothes, he supposed them to be intruders and impetuously stabbed them both to death.

One suspicion in his mind had been that perhaps another man had been in bed with Julian's own wife. She, however, was at church. When she returned and found her distraught husband, he told her he was about to leave her, no longer fit to live with decent people. She refused to abandon him. Together they set out to try and make amends for his crime. They forsook their fine castle and journeyed as far as a swiftly flowing, wide river where they built a hospital for the poor. In addition to this work, they did penance for Julian's sin by helping travellers across the swift river.

After many years Julian was awakened one freezing night by a voice from the other side of the river crying for help. He got up, crossed over, and discovered a man almost frozen to death. Julian carried the man across the river and warmed him back to life in his own bed. The poor sufferer appeared to be a leper, but this did not deter Julian. And when the man recovered, he revealed himself to be a special messenger, sent from God to test the saint's kindness. 'Julian,' the leper said, 'Our Lord sends you word that he has accepted your penance.' Today Julian the Hospitaller is regarded as the patron of travellers and ferrymen.

Catherine dei Ricci

Cyril and Methodius

Catherine dei Ricci spent most of her life in the Dominican convent at Prato in Tuscany and became famous for the physical effects on her body of the visions she was granted of Jesus.

Once, in Lent 1542, she meditated so heartrendingly on the crucifixion of Jesus that she became seriously ill, until a vision of the Risen Jesus talking with Mary Magdalene restored her to health on Holy Saturday. For twelve years she went into a kind of trance each Thursday. Then her body would re-enact the sufferings of Jesus

from the time of his arrest in the garden of Gethsemane, through his scourging, his trial, his painful journey to Golgotha and his crucifixion. The following day the saint came to consciousness again.

All this would have been regarded by many people as bizarre, even foolish. But Catherine was a person of great self-control and stern, practical common sense – so much so that the nuns of her convent readily elected her as their prioress, convinced that she was able to administer their community better than anyone else. Catherine herself never regarded her trances as something to boast about. Together with her fellow-nuns, she begged God to put an end to them. Their prayers were answered in 1554, and the sisters once again began to live in peace, untroubled by crowds of curious visitors.

Cyril and Methodius lived in the ninth century and were brothers born in Thessalonika. Both rose to high positions in the world – Cyril becoming a leading philosopher at the University of Constantinople, Methodius becoming a governor of a colony in the Slav provinces. Both renounced the life of this world and went to live in a monastery on the Bosphorus.

In the year 861 the Emperor sent them deep into Russia to convert the Khazars. Both brothers were brilliant linguists and soon familiarized themselves with the Khazar language. They came back to their monastery after a successful mission, and were almost immediately sent by the Patriarch of Constantinople to convert the Moravians. The Moravians proved hard to convert.

In Rome the Pope had heard of the good work of these two men. Pope Nicholas I summoned them to meet him, but when they reached Rome he had died. His successor was so delighted and impressed by Cyril and Methodius that he determined that they should be consecrated bishops. Before this could happen, Cyril died. He was buried in the church of San Clemente in Rome. (His earthly remains were discovered in the lower part of the church in 1880 and now lie in a chapel dedicated to him and his brother, set off the right aisle of this church.)

Methodius struggled on alone, often in dangerously hostile lands. Although he was supported by the Pope, many German bishops resented his work among the Moravians. King Ludwig, urged on by the bishops, actually imprisoned him for two years in 870. The Pope secured his release. Finally Methodius returned to Constantinople to complete a translation of the Bible which he and his brother, that other heroic 'apostle of the Slavs' had begun together.

'. . . We pray Thee, Lord, give to us, Thy servants, in all time of our life on the earth, a mind forgetful of past ill-will, a pure conscience and sincere thoughts, and a heart to love our brethren; for the sake of Jesus Christ, Thy Son, our Lord and only Saviour.'

From the Coptic Liturgy of St Cyril

Sigfrid

Juliana

The patron saint of Sweden is an Englishman, Sigfrid, who reached Sweden as a result of a call from the King of Norway, King Olaf Tryggvason, who had been converted himself by another Englishman, Saint Alphege. He asked King Ethelred of England to send some missionaries to Norway and Sigfrid, a monk at Glastonbury, was chosen. After converting many pagans, Sigfrid carried on into Sweden. There he baptized King Olaf of Sweden and then built himself a wooden church at Vaxjö in southern Sweden.

During one of Sigfrid's absences he instructed his three nephews to carry on the missionary work. The Swedes cut off their heads and flung them in a lake. Sigfrid returned, recovered the three heads and claimed that they could still talk. He asked whether the crime would be avenged. 'Yes,' replied the first head. 'When?' asked the second. 'In the third generation,' answered the third. And so it was. The saint had brilliantly used the dead heads to terrorize his living enemies. Thenceforth he was invincible.

The saint became so renowned that the Germans claimed him as their own, insisting that he had been born either in Bremen or in Hamburg. He died in old age, and his bones rest beneath the high altar of the cathedral of Vaxjö.

In the paintings and stained glass of the middle ages Saint Juliana is frequently shown battling with a winged devil; usually she carries a chain in order to bind the beast. Her struggle with the devil was one of the favourite stories of the medieval church.

What still fascinates is its deep psychological meaning: for the devil is said to have appeared to the saint as an angel of light. His aim was to persuade her that what she

had renounced in this world was in fact good. On the face of it, the devil was right, for Juliana had turned against both her father and her suitor, a Roman prefect named Evilasius.

Her father despised her simply because she had become a Christian; her suitor simply because she refused to marry him. Her calling left her without a family of her own. Both men, failing to get their own way with this determined saint, treated her brutally: Juliana's father scourged and tortured her. Evilasius flung her into jail where she was seen to be fighting with the disguised devil, finally binding him and throwing him to the ground.

Juliana died a martyr's death. First she was partially burned in flames; then she was plunged into a boiling cauldron of oil; finally the long-suffering saint was freed from the torments of this world by the mercifully instantaneous act of beheading.

The Seven Servites

Simeon

In 1233 seven wealthy councillors of the city of Florence gave up the pleasures of this world in order to devote themselves to God through particular devotion to the Blessed Virgin Mary. Their lives till then had been by no means lax or undisciplined, even though Florence was then a city filled with factions and immorality.

At first they lived just outside the city gates, humbly obeying the dictates of the Bishop of Florence. But as their fame spread the seven moved further away to the wilder hills around Monte Senario. For seven years they lived there, eating little, fasting and praying and allowing no new recruits to their company. But in 1240 the bishop insisted that they must welcome others who wished to follow so rigorous a life, and gave them rules for their order. They were to adopt the black habit of Augustinian monks and to live as mendicant friars.

From that time they became known as Servites (or 'the Servants of Mary') because they meditated especially on the sorrows in the life of the mother of Jesus. So many joined the Servites that new groups were set up in neighbouring Tuscan

cities. In 1250, to commemorate the appearance of the Angel Gabriel to Mary, the seven founders built the superb church of Santissima Annunziata in Florence.

The Servite order continues to attract men and women, devoted to the Blessed Virgin and also, in many houses, to the education of children and the care of the poor and sick.

Not all of Jesus's relatives understood his teaching or recognized his divine self. One who did was Simeon, his first cousin. Some Christians believe that this Simeon was the same person as Jesus's disciple who was nicknamed 'the Zealot' because he belonged to a party of strongly nationalistic Jews. If so, Simeon was among the band of followers who, after the resurrection, devoted themselves to prayer in Jerusalem until the Holy Spirit blessed and inspired them all.

When the Jews rose against the Romans in AD 66, Simeon, aware that the Romans would strike back savagely, withdrew with many fellow-Christians to the city of Pella. His life was never free of danger and finally, during the persecutions of the Emperor Trajan, Simeon was caught, tortured and then put to death, like his Lord, by crucifixion.

Flavian

Flavian, the Patriarch of Constantinople, maintained that Jesus was fully human against those who taught that he had only a divine nature. In this Flavian was supported by Pope Leo the Great who sent Flavian a letter, which we now call the 'Tome of Leo', asserting that in Jesus Christ 'there was born true God in the entire and perfect nature of true man.'

But at a Council at Ephesus in the year 449 the soldiers of the emperor refused to allow Leo's letter to be read. Flavian was deposed and beaten, and died soon afterwards in prison.

Conrad

St Conrad

Conrad of Piacenza was born in 1290. He loved hunting. One day on Conrad's orders, his beaters set light to the undergrowth to drive out the game that their master wished to kill. The fire spread to neighbouring cornfields and even damaged several houses. Conrad and the beaters speedily returned home and said nothing. A poor man who had been collecting faggots nearby was unjustly accused of starting the fire and condemned to death. Conrad's conscience was stirred, and he confessed to being responsible for the fire, in order to save the poor man's life.

The compensation he had to pay for the damage caused by the fire was enormous. Conrad and his wife were virtually impoverished. But the experience had enriched him spiritually. It seemed to both of them that God was calling them to abandon a life devoted to selfish pleasures. St Francis and St Clare had established orders for those who voluntarily embraced poverty; Conrad became a follower of Francis and his wife joined the Poor Clares.

Nothing could keep away men and women attracted by the great austerity of the rest of Conrad's life. He withdrew more and more into solitude, finally reaching a grotto near Noto. Yet his prayers brought blessings to many, sometimes healing their diseases, and thousands flocked to find him. Even the Bishop of Syracuse travelled to seek his blessing towards the end of Conrad's life. He died in 1351, still praying for others, and was buried in the church of St Nicholas in Noto, and his tomb became the goal of many pilgrimages.

Eleutherius

Eleutherius was made bishop of Tournai, his native city, in 486, and many pagans and heretics were converted by his preaching. Once, a young girl fell in love with him. The bishop would have nothing to do with her. In response she fell ill, and then passed into a coma. Eleutherius told her father that he could restore her to health, but would do so only if the father promised to become a Christian. Once the girl was restored to health, her father reneged on his vow. At this Eleutherius is said to have brought a plague on the land — an action which soon forced the recalcitrant father to repent and believe. Eleutherius died in 532.

Bessarion

In the Eastern Church, this day is also the feast of Saint Bessarion, an Egyptian hermit and a disciple of Saint Antony. Bessarion lived in the open air, and often lost himself in the trackless desert. He always carried a copy of the four Gospels under his arm. One day he met a naked beggar. Bessarion himself had only one garment, but he gave it to the beggar and went about with nothing on, still carrying the Gospels under his arm. When the commissioner of peace saw the saint, he asked 'Who has stripped you?' Bessarion held out his book and replied, '*This* has stripped me.'

Peter Damian

Margaret of Cortona

Peter's parents died shortly after his birth in Ravenna in 1001. Peter's elder brother used the young lad as an unpaid servant until another brother found Peter tending pigs and rescued him, sending him to be educated at Faenza and at Parma. This brother was a priest and Peter took his Christian name – Damian – as his own surname. Peter Damian responded readily to his teachers and became a professor himself. But he longed to do more for his Lord. At the age of 34 he became a Benedictine monk. The monastery he joined – at Fonte Avellana – entirely suited his austere life. The brothers lived

as hermits in bare cells, utterly disciplined and given to constant study of the Bible.

In 1043 Peter Damian was elected abbot. His fame spread. Others were attracted to imitate his life, and Peter Damian founded five more religious houses for them. After a brief time as Bishop of Ostia, Peter Damian returned to his cell where he continued to write influential religious treatises. And he went on missions for the Pope – once even managing to persuade the King of Germany not to divorce his wife.

Peter Damian never considered his learning something to boast about. What counted, he said, was to worship God, not to write about him. What use was it to construct a grammatically correct sentence containing the word God, if you could not pray to him properly.

Margaret of Cortona ran away from home, to live with a rich young noble of Montepulciano. For nine years they lived together. She would ride arrogantly out of his castle, dressed in fine silks and despising the poor. She longed to marry the young man, but he refused, even when she bore him a son. One day after he failed to return to the castle, Margaret found his body in a pit where his murderers had thrown him.

In despair she returned to Cortona and publicly confessed her sins. Her father refused to let her come home again, but the Franciscans accepted Margaret as a member of their order. These wise monks tried to make the distraught woman modify her extreme grief and penances. Eventually Margaret's peace of mind returned. She began to experience the love of Jesus and to believe that her sins had been forgiven. Her son was educated at Arezzo and also became a Franciscan.

Margaret nursed the poor and in 1286 the Bishop of Arezzo gave permission for a whole community of women (whom she called the 'Póverelle') to develop her initiative. The town councillors gave money with which Margaret founded a hospital for poor people, dedicated to Our Lady of Mercy.

'Here they live in endless being: Passingness hath passed away: Here they bloom, they thrive, they flourish, For decayed is all decay.'

St Peter Damian
from his Hymn on the Glory of Paradise

Polycarp

Ethelbert

'God the Father of our Lord Jesus Christ, increase us in faith and truth and gentleness, and grant us part and lot among His saints.'

Prayer of St Polycarp

Polycarp, Bishop of Smyrna, was a disciple of Saint John the Evangelist. When the Emperor Marcus Aurelius was persecuting Christians, Polycarp utterly refused to make any sacrifice to idols. 'For eighty-six years I have served Christ and he has done me no wrong. How then can I blaspheme my king and saviour now?' he said.

The Roman proconsul threatened to throw him into a fire. 'You threaten me with a fire that will certainly die out. You know nothing of the eternal fire that is reserved for the wicked.' The men sent to kill him wanted to nail him to a stake, but Polycarp prevented this. Then, according to an eyewitness account which has survived to this day, the flames seemed to have so little effect on the saint that his pagan enemies had him killed with a dagger. As the saint had once written in his own letter to the Philippians, the Christian martyrs should be seen as our supreme models in the pursuit of our spiritual well-being.

When Saint Augustine of Canterbury arrived in England, he desperately needed the help of King Ethelbert of Kent. Ethelbert had married a Christian, but was still a pagan himself. Yet he was a man of great courtesy.

Fearing that perhaps Augustine and his followers were magicians, the king would not receive them indoors, in case he needed to make a speedy escape from their sorcery. He met the saint and his missionaries in the open air on the island of Thanet. Augustine and his followers approached, carrying a silver cross and the likeness of Jesus painted on a board. They prayed for the salvation of themselves and the English.

Reassured, Ethelbert responded courteously: 'Your words and promises are truly fine, but to me they are new and strange. I cannot accept them and give up the agelong beliefs of the entire English nation. But since you have come a long way and I perceive that you are sincere in your desire to teach us what you believe is true and excellent, I shall not harm you. I shall receive you with hospitality and supply all your needs. I shall not forbid you to preach and win as many persons as you can to your religion.'

Eventually Ethelbert accepted the Christian faith. Many of his followers, seeing this, also were baptized and the king persuaded neighbouring monarchs to embrace Christianity. He gave his kingdom a set of laws, the first of which decreed that any person who stole from the church or clergy must make immediate reparation. He built a cathedral at Rochester, dedicated to Saint Andrew, and another in London.

Pope Gregory the Great was delighted and sent Saint Ethelbert a number of presents. The pope wrote that 'by means of the good gifts that God has granted to you, I know he blesses your people as well.' He urged King Ethelbert to destroy the shrines of idols and to raise the moral standards of his subjects by his own good example. Ethelbert died on 24 February 616, twenty-one years after embracing the Christian faith.

Walburga

Walburga was born in Devonshire, the daughter of a West Saxon chief and his wife. They sent her to be educated at a monastery in Dorset, and she so liked the place that she professed as a nun there.

England in the eighth century was a great centre of missionary zeal. St Boniface called on English monks and nuns to help convert the Germans. Walburga and her brother Winebald answered the call. For two years Walburga preached at Bischofsheim, impressing the pagans also by her medical skills. Then Winebald started a monastery for men and women at Heidenheim. He appointed his sister over the nuns, while he ruled the monks. When Winebald died, the Bishop of Eichstätt (who happened to be another brother) had no hesitation in setting Walburga over the whole monastery, ruling both monks and nuns.

Walburga died in the year 779, and her fame spread throughout Europe. On 1 May her body was transferred to Eichstätt. Curiously enough, this day happened to be also marked by a pagan feast, and the saint's name has been incorporated into its title 'Walpurgisnacht' – a night given over to witchcraft and necromancy. Yet today this good Christian lady lies peacefully in her vault in the seventeenth-century Baroque church that bears her name, a symbol not of witchcraft but of Christian healing and mission.

Caesarius of Nazianzus

The feast of Caesarius, brother of Saint Gregory of Nazianzus, also falls on this day. Caesarius was a student so learned that he could have made a career as a philosopher or rhetorician or lawyer; but instead he chose medicine. Soon he was the finest, most celebrated doctor in Constantinople.

He became chief physician to the Emperor Julian. Julian renounced Christianity; but nothing could persuade Caesarius to follow suit, even though he continued to treat the emperor until 368, one year before his death.

Porphyry

Leaving his home in Macedonia at the age of twenty-five, Porphyry went to live as a monk in the Egyptian desert. After five years there he moved to a cave by the River Jordan. During his time there he developed a serious illness, and decided to spend the remainder of his life in Jerusalem, daily visiting the places made sacred by contact with Jesus. He would struggle round them each day, refusing any assistance because (as he said) 'I have come to beg pardon for my sins, and no-one must make this easy for me.' Miraculously, Christ cured him. Porphyry had been a rich man, but gave away so much to the poor that he himself was almost destitute. He then learned the trade of a shoemaker to keep himself. In the year 393 he was ordained priest, and only three years later he was consecrated Bishop of Gaza.

The year of his consecration was also marked by a drought at Gaza. Pagans blamed the Christians for bringing this new man into their midst, and locked the saint out of the city, when he and his supporters were in procession, supplicating God to send rain. At that moment the rain began to fall, and grateful citizens of Gaza re-opened the city gates and let their bishop in. By the time of his death he had either expelled or converted nearly every pagan in Gaza.

St Walburga

Possenti

Gabriel Possenti was born in 1838, the eleventh child of an Italian lawyer. A lover of the theatre, he was by all accounts a ladies' man who dressed flamboyantly, even with vanity.

Then he fell ill. Gabriel vowed that he should take up the religious life but when he recovered, he more or less forgot about his vow. He fell dangerously ill again, and this time his mind was changed: he asked to join the Jesuits. Gabriel was tempted by the world, but when a cholera epidemic took not him but his sister Gabriel Possenti fulfilled his vow.

He more than made up for his former lack of zeal; he prayed continually and gave freely to the poor. No penance was too much for the young man. Then he caught tuberculosis which was incurable in those days.

Baldomer

Saint Baldomer was a blacksmith in Lyons who specialized in making locks. He would make a lock for a poor family for nothing, and rarely had much money himself, since he gave most of it away to the needy. Eventually the reputation of this holy man reached the ears of Abbot Viventius of Saint-Just. He ordained Baldomer as a deacon, and the saint came to live for the rest of his days in a cell next to Viventius's monastery.

Hilarus

In the year 449 a church synod was convened at Ephesus which was so violent that the Pope, Leo I, called it the synod of brigands. The Pope's two legates were not allowed to speak. Flavius, the Patriarch of Constantinople, was knocked to the ground, and kicked and beaten to death. The papal legates, one of whom was Hilarus, managed to escape, retreating to safety in Rome.

Hilarus believed that only the special protection of St John the Evangelist had saved him so he built a chapel in the church of St John Lateran in Rome, inscribing there the words: 'To his liberator the blessed John the Evangelist, from Hilarus, bishop and servant of Christ.'

When Pope Leo I died in the year 461, Hilarus succeeded him. He was resolute in upholding the freedom of the Church and would publicly rebuke the highest in the land. The saint died in 468.

March

'My Lord and my God, remove
from me all that may keep me
from you. My Lord and my God,
give me all that I need to bring me
to you. My Lord and my God,
take me from myself and give me
to yourself.'

Nicholas von Flüe (March 21)

David

David, the patron saint of Wales, was born at the end of the fifth century at Henfynyw, Cardigan. His father was a prince named Sant; his mother was Saint Non. The legends of David frequently allude to the Holy Spirit in the form of a dove, and it was recalled that as he learned to read the psalms, a dove hovered at his lips, teaching him to praise God.

He is credited with founding twelve monasteries, after being educated at Ty Gwyn by Saint Paulinus. Elected abbot of the monastery of Ty Gwyn, he later moved to Mynyw, at the south west corner of Wales, where he set up a community who lived lives of incredible hardship – deliberately undertaken to discipline their souls. Only under extreme necessity were they allowed to speak. They never ate meat or fish – only bread, salt, and vegetables – and they tilled the land without the help of oxen. They stayed awake in prayer from dusk on Friday till day broke on Sunday.

Saint David may well have been present at a synod called at Brefi in Cardigan to condemn the heresy of Pelagius. Here not only is the Holy Spirit said to have alighted on his shoulder as he spoke; the earth too rose in a hillock, to ensure that all could see and hear him. David won a great victory over the Saxons, instructing the Welsh soldiers to wear a leek in their headgear for ease of recognition by their fellows on the battlefield.

At the synod of Brefi David is reputed to have been recognized as primate of Wales. Saint Dubricius resigned so that David could take his see and the saint's one condition in replacing Dubricius was that he could move the see from Carleon to Mynyw (now known as St Davids). There he died, saying to his fellow-Christians, 'Rejoice. Hold fast to the faith. And remember to fulfil those small tasks that you have learned while you were with me.'

MARCH 2	MARCH 3

Henry Suso

Cunegund

Henry Suso was born in 1295 or so. The son of a dissolute father named Von Berg, Henry preferred always to take his mother's name, Suso. At the age of fifteen he entered the Dominican monastery at Constance. Initially even great austerities could not quieten his unhappy spiritual state. He did achieve peace through mystical union with God, even though

outwardly his life was far from tranquil. He was a great preacher, made many converts, and also made jealous enemies. When a child accused him of theft and sacrilege, some preferred to believe the child. He took in an abandoned baby and was accused of being its father. He was accused of administering poison and of pretending to perform a miracle. One day, after he had seen a dog playing with a piece of cloth, he wrote:

'I thought: take note of it. This piece of cloth lets itself be maltreated by the dog as he likes. . . . Then I thought: you must do the same. Whether a person puts you up or puts you down, accept it with good grace. Even if someone spits on you, accept it.'

So he took the cloth and placed it on his chair in his little chapel, as a reminder of the goal of humility. He died at Ulm, Germany in 1365.

Duke Henry of Bavaria became Holy Roman Emperor in 1014, travelling with Saint Cunegund, his wife, to Rome to be crowned by the pope.

Pope Benedict was later to visit their lands, to consecrate the cathedral and open the monastery at Bamberg, both of which Cunegund persuaded her husband to found. She had longed to become a nun herself, and during an almost fatal illness, Saint Cunegund vowed that should she recover she would found a nunnery for Benedictines at Kassel. Her health was restored and she kept her vow.

The Emperor Henry II died before the nunnery was completed. In 1024, during the consecration, the Empress Cunegund took off her imperial regalia and replaced them with the habit of a nun.

'The dear Jesus did not say "Take my cross upon you"; what he said to each of us was, "Take up your cross". Do not try to imitate the austerities of the ancient fathers or even my own austerities. You should take on yourself only a portion of them, as much as you can reasonably practise with your infirm body, aiming to kill sin within yourself without shortening your life in the body . . . God has many kinds of crosses with which he chastens his friends. I leave it to him to lay a different sort of cross on your shoulders, far more painful than these austerities. When this cross comes to you, accept it with patience.'

St Henry Suso
(Letter of counsel to his
spiritual daughter and biographer)

Casimir

Saint Casimir of Poland is rightly known as the peacemaker. The year 1471 saw a powerful faction of the Hungarian nobility dissatisfied with the rule of Matthias Corvinus. They appealed to King Casimir IV of Poland, who decreed that his second son, Saint Casimir, should take possession of the kingdom. The teenage saint went so far as to lead an army to the borders of Hungary. But he learned that the pope was opposed to the adventure and as he had no wish to promote bloodshed he returned to Cracow. King Casimir was angry enough to confine his son in the castle of Dobzki near Cracow.

Saint Casimir's reluctance to fight was no sign of weakness. The Hungarian nobility continued to urge him to take their crown; but he was well aware that continued civil war only weakened the west which was beleaguered by the Turks. He was by no means unfitted for ruling others, and for some time acted as regent of Poland when his father was away. But he longed above all to pursue the life of prayer and caring for poor. He died in 1484 aged only twenty-six.

Eusebius of Cremona

Eusebius first met Saint Jerome in Rome when Jerome was acting as secretary to Pope Damasus and preaching a strict asceticism to all who would listen. Eusebius was so much attracted to the stern Biblical scholar that when Jerome decided

to leave for the Holy Land, he begged to accompany him. At Antioch they were joined by Jerome's other two great friends, the widow Saint Paula and her daughter Saint Eustochium. The four of them made a pilgrimage to all the places connected with the earthly life of Jesus, before deciding to make Bethlehem their home.

Jerome was much touched by the hundreds of pilgrims to Bethlehem, many of whom were extremely poor. Resolving to build a hostel for them, he sent Eusebius to Dalmatia and Italy, to raise money for the project. Saint Paula sold her Roman estate through him for this purpose and Eusebius also sold his own property at Cremona and gave the proceeds for the building of the hostel.

In the year 400 Eusebius returned to his native Cremona, where some sources indicate that he stayed until his death. Others suggest that he returned to Bethlehem to become spiritual director of one of the religious communities there. He may well be buried alongside Jerome in Bethlehem, where – in the crypt of the church of the Nativity – an altar is dedicated in his name.

Chrodegang of Metz

Chrodegang was a man of royal blood born in Brabant near Liège in the year 712. He was educated at the abbey of St Trond and then became chief minister of Charles Martel and Chancellor of France. Even then he went about in hair shirts and unostentatious clothing, fasting and praying, and great numbers of poor people depended entirely on his charity.

Shortly after the death of Charles Martel, Chrodegang was elected Bishop of Metz even though he was still a layman. So treasured was his advice by Charles Martel's son, Pepin the Short, that Pepin refused to allow the saint to be consecrated until Chrodegang had promised to continue as his chief minister.

As bishop the saint's zeal was outstanding. He persuaded his clergy to live together in communities and to follow a daily rule of life, drawn up by Chrodegang along the lines of Saint Benedict's rule. He converted the loosely organized canons of his cathedral into a community given to prayer. He founded or restored many monasteries; the abbey of Gorze, Italy, was his greatest foundation and became as famous as Metz for its sacred music. Chrodegang's support for the papacy was of inestimable value at a time when the Lombards had managed to force Pope Stephen II into exile. Chrodegang himself safely brought the pope over the Alps, and Pepin the Short welcomed him to France.

Fridolin

This day is also the feast of Saint Fridolin, the Wanderer (*right*), an Irishman who gained his nickname in the seventh century by his endless journeyings – through Gaul, Germany and Switzerland. An assiduous founder of monasteries Fridolin also found the body of Saint Hilary of Poitiers, which had been lost when the Vandals destroyed the monastery in that city. He started a school for young boys on an island in the Rhine and happily encouraged them to play many different sports.

Perpetua, Felicity and their companions

At Carthage in 203 six Africans were arrested for offering themselves as candidates for baptism. Two of them were women: Vivia Perpetua, the twenty-two year old wife of a local man of substance, who was suckling her young baby and a pregnant slave named Felicity. Their companions were four men: Secundulus, Saturninus, Saturus and another slave named Revocatus.

Remarkably we still possess Perpetua's own account of their sufferings, a story continued by Saturus and finished by someone whose name we do not know. This deeply moving account tells of Perpetua's fears for her baby and the difficult birth of Felicity's daughter.

None of the prisoners weakened before their judges. 'You judge us now,' they cried. 'God will judge you.' Perpetua was granted some exquisite visions of heaven – an old man milking sheep gave her curds; the elders before the throne of God told her to 'Go and play.' Perpetua observed: 'I was happy in the flesh. Now I am far happier.'

A leopard, a bear and a wild boar attacked the Christians. Perpetua and Felicity were gored by a wild cow, and comforted each other as they suffered. Finally a sword was thrust into the throat of each Christian.

John of God

After a devoutly Christian upbringing in Portugal, John of God led a wayward life as a soldier fighting in the Franco-Spanish wars and against the Turks; and as an overseer of Moroccan slaves. He was aged forty when he came to repent of his wasted life. He was so moved by a sermon by the famous preacher John of Avila that he roamed the streets screaming with sorrow for his sins. For a time he was so demented that the authorities decided to put him in a lunatic asylum.

John of Avila visited him and calmed him. In 1539 John of God left the hospital

and began to set up his own hostel for the poor. He sold wood to feed them and although he was constantly short of money, the work prospered. The Archbishop of Granada gave his support. John begged money from rich ladies. 'We receive here every kind of case,' he wrote to one of them: 'cripples, paralytics, lepers, the deaf and dumb, the insane, people with diseases of the skin, the old, children, pilgrims and vagrants.' The work attracted many devoted helpers, 'Brothers Hospitallers', who (after the saint's death) spread throughout Italy, Spain, France and Central Europe.

In 1550 he leapt into the River Ximel to rescue a drowning child. The shock brought on a fever which killed him. He was sixty-five years old.

Frances of Rome

From the age of eleven Frances had longed to enter a monastery, only marrying two years later in deference to the wishes of her parents. Her married life was subject to constant trials. When the troops of Ladislaus of Naples occupied Rome in 1408, they pillaged the family home. Later, during the disputes over the papacy, her husband, Lorenzo, was banished for a time, returning from exile in 1414 a semi-invalid. A plague carried off one of Frances's children, and a second died two years later.

Yet nothing disturbed either her faith or her determination to serve others in need. The recurrent plagues and the devastations of civil war gave ample opportunity for her efforts, and in 1425 Frances set up a group of women dedicated to the service of those less fortunate than themselves. Affiliated to the Benedictine monks of Monte Oliveto, these women lived in the bustle of the secular world, following Frances's example of selling their jewellery and fine possessions to give to the needy. At first known as Oblates of Mary, they later were called Oblates of Tor de' Specchi, from the house where they lived.

When Lorenzo died in 1436, Frances moved into the community herself, and spent the last four years of her life as its superior. She died in 1440, aged fifty-six.

Forty Martyrs

Around the year 320 the Emperor Licinius ordered every Christian in Cappadocia to renounce the faith. This reversed the policy of toleration which his brother Constantine had introduced in 313. The governor of Lesser Armenia, Agricolaus, published this decree before his army, but forty soldiers refused to obey. Agricolaus worked out a plan he considered certain to make them recant. Outside the city walls was a frozen lake. He ordered the forty Christians to strip and lie on the ice. At the edge of the lake a huge bathful of water was placed over a furnace, continually tempting the Christians to abandon their torment on the ice.

One of the soldiers broke, and jumped into the water. The intense contrast between the cold he had endured and the heat of the bath killed him.

Another soldier, seeing the faith of the other thirty-nine, stripped himself and joined them, accepting the fortieth place.

Soon almost all were dead. The youngest, a boy named Melito, was the last to die.

'A married woman, even when praising God at the altar, must when needed by her husband or the smallest member of her family, quit God at the altar and find him again in her household affairs.'

St Frances of Rome

Sophronius

Maximilian

St Sophronius

Saint Sophronius, who was elected patriarch of Jerusalem in the year 634, contended with two dangers to the Christian faith: one was heresy; the other the seemingly relentless advance of the Saracens.

The heresy is called Montheletism and basically consisted of denying that Jesus had two wills, one human, the other divine. In these early centuries of the Christian faith, men and women were still trying to work out precisely how someone could be, as Christians claimed of Jesus, both God and man. The whole question continued to be debated long after Sophronius's death, but he was the most vigorous defender of the view that eventually came to be accepted by the church: that Jesus had a divine and a human will. He sent letters to the pope and to the patriarch of Constantinople, begging them to give their weight to his side. So important was the question of right doctrine to Sophronius that he made his assistant, Bishop Stephen of Dor, stay in Rome for ten years in order to defend orthodoxy.

His second problem caused much pain. In the year 636 the Saracens took Damascus. They reached Jerusalem two years later. At Christmas Sophronius sadly comforted his flock, who were unable to leave the besieged city for their customary celebration of the birth of Jesus at Bethlehem. When Calif Omar took the city, Sophronius managed to win him to a greater tolerance of Christians by personally conducting him round the holy sites of the city.

In all this activity Saint Sophronius remained a disciplined monk. His early ambition had been to be a hermit, and he had lived in great friendship with a famous mystic called John Moschus in the monasteries of St Sabas and St Theodosius, making pilgrimages to monasteries and hermits in Egypt, reading philosophy and the Scriptures, practising great austerities. Saint Sophronius died around the year 638, soon after Calif Omar conquered Jerusalem.

In the year 275 a young man aged twenty-three was brought before the court for refusing to do military service in the Roman army. Although most Roman soldiers were volunteers, the sons of veterans were obliged to fight as conscripts. The young man's father, Fabius Victor, had become a Christian like his son Maximilian, and he supported Maximilian's stand against military service. The court assembled at Tebessa in Algeria under the public prosecutor Pompeian. A brilliant cross-examiner named Dion put the questions. The tension was heightened because the penalty for refusing military service was death.

'Other Christians serve our rulers as soldiers,' observed Dion. Maximilian answered, 'That is their affair, not mine. I too am a Christian. But I cannot enlist.'

Dion turned to Maximilian's father. 'You must put your son right,' he said. Fabius Victor replied, 'My son knows what he believes in. He will not change his mind.'

Dion tried to push matters forward. He ordered officers of the army to give Maximilian his badge of rank. 'I shall not take it,' cried Maximilian. 'If you thrust it on me, I shall deface it. As a Christian I must not wear that seal of lead around my neck. Already I carry the sacred seal of Christ.'

'If you do not accept military service, you will join your Christ immediately,' Dion threatened. 'That is the greatest thing I desire,' responded Maximilian. 'Dispatch me quickly. There lies my glory.' He added, 'I shall not die. When I go from this earth, my soul will live with Christ my Lord.'

'Since you will not perform military service, I condemn you to death for contempt of the army,' declared Dion. He read out the judgment of the court: 'Maximilian has impiously refused his military oath. He shall be beheaded.'

Almost instantly the saint was taken to the place of execution. His head was cut off. Fabius Victor went home rejoicing that his son had not weakened in preferring death to dishonouring his Lord.

Euphrasia

Matilda

The senator Antigonus was a relative of Emperor Theodosius I, and when his wife Eupraxia bore him a daughter named Euphrasia the emperor took a kindly interest in the girl. Following the custom of that time, he found her a future husband, a rich senator, when she was only five years old. When Antigonus died, his widow took her daughter (now aged seven) to Egypt and joined a convent at Tabenisi.

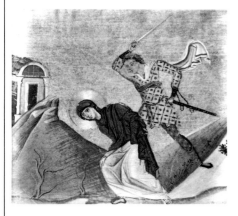

The little girl loved the life. At first the nuns supposed she would soon tire of the austerities. In those days some of the sisters would go without food for as long as a week at a time. Some of them tried to remain standing for a month, leaning against a wall to sleep. None of these burdens discouraged Euphrasia. And when the emperor summoned her to Constantinople to marry her senator, she wrote to him begging to be released. He agreed.

The nuns refused to accept any of Euphrasia's wealth. She therefore gave it to the emperor, to be distributed to the poor, and she freed all her slaves. For the rest of her life she lived in the convent.

Sometimes Euphrasia wondered whether she had missed some great pleasures by quitting the world. She dealt with these vain longings by taking on the least attractive jobs in the convent. She showed no resentment at slights, and died around the year 420, as humble as she had been as a child.

For twenty-three years Matilda lived happily as the wife of King Henry the Fowler of Germany, revered by the court.

After Henry's death she believed that of their five sons the second, Henry, was better fitted to succeed him than the eldest, Otto. Otto was elected. Henry (who was known as 'the Quarrelsome') tried to take the throne by force, but failed. Matilda managed to make peace and Henry was made Duke of Bavaria. Then Otto and Henry accused their mother of frittering away the wealth of the kingdom on the worthless poor. Otto's wife, Edith, managed to bring her husband to his senses. He begged his mother to forgive him and when he had to go to Rome to be crowned emperor, she looked after the affairs of state during his absence. But Matilda found greater consolation away from court, founding convents and monasteries, and she eventually retired to one she had built at Nordhausen. When the time came for her to die in the year 968, Matilda gave away everything. So she left this world, owning nothing.

Clement Hofbauer

A Czech by birth, Clement's original name was John. He had wanted to become a priest, but no-one could pay for his education so he started baking for the monks of the abbey at Buck.

John decided to live as a hermit. Hermitages were officially closed, so he became a baker again in Vienna. One day after mass, he struck up a friendship with two ladies who agreed to pay for him to study at the university. John adopted the name Clement, and in 1783 was accepted as a Redemptorist priest. The Redemptorists sent him to Vienna, but as the state authorities still opposed religious foundations he took over the German church of Warsaw and made it a centre of intense missionary activity. Five times a day he and those he gathered round him preached -- in Polish and in German. He opened an orphanage and a boys' school and also established the first Redemptorist house in Germany, at Jestetten near Schaffhausen in 1802. Napoleon closed down his Warsaw mission in 1808 and Clement Hofbauer was forced to return to Vienna. The saint never forgot the evil effects of state control in the activities of the church and for the last twelve years of his life he used all his eloquence and influence to diminish it.

Heribert

Heribert was appointed Archbishop of Cologne in the year 998. In the depths of winter he took off his shoes and walked into the city where he was consecrated on Christmas Eve 999, and from that time on he always wore a hair shirt underneath the rich robes of an archbishop.

He had been born in the city of Worms and sent as a boy to the monastery at Gorze in Lorraine. Heribert developed into

one of the strongest and most distinguished German statesmen of the age: by 994 he had become the emperor's chancellor. Even as archbishop these duties did not come to an end. As imperial chancellor, he was with the Emperor Otto III in Italy when Otto died. Saint Heribert brought the dead emperor back to Aachen for burial. And he incensed the ambitious men who wanted to succeed Otto by refusing to hand over the imperial insignia until a new emperor had been properly appointed. This man, Henry II, bore a grudge against Heribert for many years, but in the end came to acknowledge the saint's wisdom and probity.

At a time when many clerical statesmen forgot or neglected their spiritual duties under the pressure of serving the state, Heribert was a devoted chief pastor of his flock. As archbishop he was a rich man; but his entire income was divided between the church and the poor, save for the little that was absolutely necessary for his own needs. Saint Heribert died in 1021.

MARCH 17

Patrick

The patron saint of Ireland and the Jew who gave a tomb for the body of Jesus are both commemorated on this day.

Saint Patrick was born in Britain, of Roman stock, probably with the name Patricius Magonus Sucatus. When he was about fourteen, in the year 403, Irish raiders carried him to their own country as a slave, and there, near Ballymena in Antrim, he first learned to pray while looking after his master's herds.

The saint escaped in a ship taking dogs to Gaul and there he became a disciple of Saint Germanus of Auxerre, studying also at the monastery of Lerins. For fifteen years or so he lived abroad, but then he dreamed of Ireland and determined to return to the land of his slavery as a

missionary. Saint Germanus consecrated him bishop, and he returned to Ireland in the year 432. At Tara in Meath he confronted King Laoghaire with the Christian Gospel and confounded the druids. He converted the king's daughters. He threw down the idol of Crom Cruach in Leitrim. The saint wrote that he daily expected to be violently killed or enslaved again. But in 444 he established his bishopric at Armagh, and with this city as

his base placed the organization of the Irish church on a sure foundation.

'I bind unto myself this day the strong name of the Trinity,
By invocation of the same, the three in one and one in three,'

wrote Patrick in the hymn we call 'Saint Patrick's Breastplate'.

The saint died in the year 461 at Saul on Strangford Lough, Downpatrick.

Joseph of Arimathea

After the Crucifixion, Joseph of Arimathea (*above*) gave a place in his own tomb for the body of Jesus. Nothing is known about Joseph except what is written in the Gospels, but nearly four hundred years later the charming legend arose that he became an open (rather than secret) follower of the Risen Lord and travelled as a missionary to Britain. Here, it is said, he founded a church at Glastonbury in Somerset.

*'Christ be with me,
Christ within me,
Christ behind me,
Christ before me,
Christ beside me,
Christ to win me,
Christ to comfort and
restore me.
Christ beneath me,
Christ above me,
Christ in quiet, Christ
in danger,
Christ in hearts of all
that love me,
Christ in mouth of
friend and stranger.'*

St Patrick's Breastplate

*'Joseph of Arimathea,
an honourable
counsellor, which also
waited for the kingdom
of God, came, and went
in boldly unto Pilate,
and craved the body of
Jesus. . . And he
bought fine linen, and
took him down, and
wrapped him in the
linen, and laid him in a
sepulchre.'*

St Mark's Gospel 15: 43, 46

Frediano

Frediano, in spite of his Italian name, was an Irishman, the son of King Ultach of Ulster. He was trained in Irish monasticism and ordained priest. His learning was imparted by such flowers of the sixth-century Irish culture as Saint Enda and Saint Colman. He arrived in Italy on a pilgrimage and decided to settle as a hermit on Monte Pisano. Even when Pope John II persuaded him to accept the bishopric of Lucca in the year 566, the saint frequently left the city to spend many days in prayer and solitude.

His most famous miracle is certainly legendary. The River Serchio frequently burst its banks, causing great damage to the city of Lucca. The citizens called on their bishop for aid. He asked for an ordinary rake. Fortified by prayer, Frediano commanded the Serchio to follow his rake. He charted a new, safer course for the water, avoiding the city walls, as well as the cultivated land outside. Miraculously, the river followed him.

Joseph

Saint Joseph, the husband of Mary the mother of Jesus, was a carpenter of Nazareth. Saint Matthew's Gospel describes him as 'a just man'. When he discovered that Mary was pregnant, he did not wish to shame her publicly for bearing what he presumed was an illegitimate child. His plan was to allow her to bear the baby in private. But he was blessed with a vision of an angel of God, which appeared to him in a dream, saying 'Do not fear to take Mary as your wife. That which is conceived in her is of the Holy Spirit. She will bear a son and you will call his name Jesus.'

Saint Joseph bore the responsibilities of a father perfectly. He it was who learned from an angel – again in a dream – that King Herod planned to kill the infant Jesus. Joseph took Mary and Jesus away by night to Egypt and thus saved the life of the Saviour. He kept the child hidden from Herod's son, in case he too would have harmed Jesus.

Joseph was with Mary in the stable at Bethlehem when Jesus was born. He was looking after the mother and child when the shepherds and the Magi came to worship him. He took Mary and Jesus to Jerusalem to present him to God in the Jerusalem Temple. He shared Mary's anxieties for her son when Jesus was presumed lost, after their visit to the Temple when he was twelve years old.

After this no more is heard of Saint Joseph in the New Testament. He is not mentioned as being present at the crucifixion, a fact which persuaded many artists to portray him as an old man who had presumably died by the time Jesus was in his early thirties.

The notion of Joseph as the foster-father of Jesus fired the imagination of the medieval church. Saint John Chrysostom pointed to the anxieties of Joseph as a pattern of the trials of all Christians – relieved as they are by God's intervention. In the fifteenth century the French churchman Jean Gerson wrote twelve poems in his honour. Saint Teresa of Avila chose him as the practical saint who should be patron of her friars and nuns.

Cuthbert

Nicholas von Flüe

'My Lord and my God, remove from me all that may keep me from you. My Lord and my God, give me all that I need to bring me to you. My Lord and my God, take me from myself, and give me to yourself.'

St Nicholas von Flüe

Cuthbert, one of the greatest English saints and missionaries, became a monk of Melrose abbey on the River Tweed 'then ruled by Abbot Eata, the gentlest and simplest of men,' as the Venerable Bede observed. The prior of Melrose, named Boisil, taught Cuthbert the Bible and the pattern of a devout life, and when Boisil died, Cuthbert became prior in his place. He would preach throughout the surrounding countryside, riding many miles on horseback to win the erring for Christ. 'Cuthbert was so great a speaker and had such a light in his angelic face,' wrote Bede, 'he had also such a love for proclaiming his good news, that none hid their innermost secrets from him.'

But the saint preferred the life of a hermit and secured Eata's permission to live as one for eight years on the island of Farne. In the year 684 he was appointed, unwillingly, Bishop of Hexham. Cuthbert preferred Lindisfarne, where Eata was bishop, to Hexham and the two men exchanged bishoprics. He had two more years to live.

In 1481 the Swiss Confederation was on the verge of breaking up. The member states had defeated most of their enemies in battle. But they could not agree on how to divide the spoils. They were quarrelling too over whether or not to include Fribourg and Soleure in the Federation.

Counsel was sought from a sixty-four year old hermit who lived in a tiny cell alongside a chapel in the village of Ranft, Nicholas von Flüe. Though he could neither read nor write he had come to be regarded as the wisest person in Switzerland. On the saint's advice the delegates

of the contending parties hammered out the famous Compromise of Stans, which saved the peace and unity of the land.

Nicholas had been born on a rich plain known as the Flüeli, close by Sachseln in Unterwalden. A successful farmer, he did military service in the war with Zürich, and fought again for his canton as a captain fourteen years later. He married a religious woman named Dorothea Wissling, who bore him ten children. Nicholas retired to live as a hermit. For nineteen years he would pray and meditate for over half the night and day, reserving the afternoons for the countless men and women who flocked for his counsel.

Basil of Ancyra

The two saints commemorated on this day both suffered from the evil doings of the Arians, that is those who denied the true divinity of Jesus.

The Arians went so far as to kill Basil in the year 362. He was a priest who loyally supported his Catholic bishop against the heretics, even after the emperor had banished the bishop. The Arians tried to stop Saint Basil even from leading Christian worship. Basil's refusal to give way, under severe threats, led the authorities to claim that he was unfaithful to the emperor. He was hung up, first by the wrists, and then upside down from his ankles. His body was torn with rakes and finally he was slaughtered.

Deogratias of Carthage

Nearly a hundred years later, in the year 439, Arian Vandals seized Carthage and threw out its bishop. For fourteen years the city was without a chief pastor. Then the Arian leader Genseric relented and allowed the Christians there to make a priest named Deogratias their bishop. Two years later Genseric took Rome and removed from the city hundreds of captives.

Genseric and his dejected captives returned to Africa, where whole Christian families were split up and forced to work as slaves. Deogratias determined to free them. The only possible method was to ransom them. For this purpose the bishop sold everything he possibly could, including the rich gold and silver plate of the church and many precious ornaments. He managed to ransom so many families that there were not enough rooms in Carthage to house them. Undeterred, Bishop Deogratias gave them rooms inside his churches. Each day he made sure that they were properly fed, until they could once again look after themselves.

Many Arians resented the saint's work and a number tried – and failed – to kill him. Nonetheless he died, worn out by his enormous labours, after only three years as a bishop.

Gwinear

When Saint Patrick was attempting to convert Ireland in the fifth century, he came to the court of King Clito and was rejected with scorn. But the king's son Gwinear was more courteous than his father. Though not yet a Christian, he recognized Patrick's piety and rose to his feet to offer the saint his own seat. Later as he was hunting and at the same time meditating on Christianity, he was converted. Gwinear let his horse go free and began to live as a hermit. After King Clito's death, the saint returned home, but not to assume the throne. Instead he took seven hundred and seventy men and women (including his converted sister Piala) to spread the Christian faith in Wales and Brittany.

Among the celebrated miracles alleged to have been performed by the saint one – at Puvigner in Brittany – indicates his reputation for loving animals. Short of water the saint struck the ground and created not one fountain but three: one for himself, the other two for his dog and his horse.

The saint and many of his followers died as martyrs. The Cornish tyrant Teudar had long hated the Christians. He kept a lake filled with reptiles in amongst which he threw those he disliked. It is said that Teudar came upon a band of Gwinear's Christian friends 'from behind' and killed them.

Later Gwinear and some companions came across their bodies. The saint knew his own martyrdom could not be far off. 'Here brethren is the place of our rest,' he told his companions. 'Here God has appointed that we should cease from our labours. Come therefore and let us gladly sacrifice our lives for him. Let us not fear them that kill the body. Rather let us fear him who has power to cast both body and soul into hell.'

Shortly afterwards the saint was caught by Teudar and beheaded. A basilica was built in later years over his grave. And the Cornish village of Gwinear bears his name to this day. He is also still venerated in Brittany.

Catherine of Vadstena

St Catherine of Vadstena

Catherine was the fourth child of Saint Bridget of Sweden and her husband Prince Ulf of Nierck. Her parents sent her to the school of the Risberg Convent, and at the age of fourteen she married a man of German descent named Eggard von Kürnen. Catherine seems to have preferred the life of a celibate to that of a married woman and managed to persuade her husband to allow this.

She grew extremely sad when her father died and Saint Bridget went to live in Rome. For a time (as she herself told Saint Catherine of Siena) she never smiled. In the year 1349 Eggard von Kürnen allowed Catherine to pay a visit to her mother and while she was in Rome he died. Even now she was for some time still extremely unhappy, since Rome in the fourteenth century was a dissolute place and her mother would not let her go out.

In addition many men wished to marry the beautiful young widow. Some even lay in wait for her to carry her off. One was distracted when a hart ran by just as Bridget and Catherine passed. Others, it is said, were blinded. To try to repulse such suitors and also as an act of humility, Catherine always went about in the most ragged and threadbare clothing.

Soon she was her mother's devoted assistant, utterly reliable and constant until Bridget died in the year 1373, after a pilgrimage to the Holy Land. She had expressed a wish to be buried in the Swedish monastery of Vadstena, which she herself had founded twenty-nine years previously. Catherine took her mother's body home.

Now followed intense work to promote the Bridgettine Order which her mother had founded. Bound together in double monasteries, men and women pledged themselves to live in poverty, save for the right to buy as many books as they needed for study and devotion. She was in Rome and Sweden in the dark days of the papal schism, endlessly striving to get approval for the monasteries. Eventually Pope Urban VI gave his blessing. The saint died at Vadstena, in pain but in peace on 24 March 1381.

The Annunciation of Mary

'My soul magnifies the Lord,
and my spirit rejoices in God my Saviour,
for he has regarded the lowliness of his handmaiden.
For behold, henceforth all generations will call me blessed,
for he who is mighty has done great things for me,
and holy is his name.
And his mercy is on them who fear him
from generation to generation.
He has shown strength with his arm,
he has scattered the proud in the imagination of their hearts,
he has put down the mighty from their thrones,
and exalted those of low degree;
he has filled the hungry with good things,
and the rich he has sent empty away.
He has helped his servant Israel,
in remembrance of his mercy,
as he spoke to our fathers,
to Abraham and his posterity for ever.'

This song of the Blessed Virgin Mary, the 'Magnificat', filled as it is with references to the Bible of her people, the Jews, perfectly indicates both her piety and her humility. She was singing her joy at being chosen to bear the son of God.

'Hail, favoured one, the Lord is with you,' were the words of the angel Gabriel, announcing this. He told her not to fear, since she had found favour with God, would conceive and bear a son, to be called Jesus. Puzzled, Mary asked how this could be, since she knew no man. Gabriel replied, 'The Holy Spirit will come upon you, and the power of the Most High will overshadow you. Therefore the child to be born will be called holy, the Son of God.'

Mary answered, 'Behold, I am the handmaid of the Lord. Let it be to me according to your word.'

*'Virgin Mother of God:
may I bind myself to
God and to you, serve
your own Lord and
serve you too, obey
your own Son and so
obey you. May I
worship him as my
maker and you as the
mother of my maker.
May I venerate him as
the Lord of Hosts and
you as the handmaid of
the Lord. May I adore
him as my God and
you as the mother of
my God.'*

St Ildefonsus

Ludger

Although Ludger was born at Zuilen in the Netherlands, and had first been taught by Saint Gregory at Utrecht, he had gone to England as a pupil of Alcuin of York, and would have stayed there longer than four years or so had one of his fellow-countrymen not killed an English merchant and thus stirred up bad blood against the Netherlanders.

Ludger was sent to bring the Gospel to the Frieslanders. For seven years he built churches, destroyed idols and converted many pagans. Then the Saxon leader Widukind invaded, destroying Christian foundations and driving out all the missionaries.

Ludger made a pilgrimage to Rome and also visited the great Benedictine monastery on Monte Cassino. There he may have met Charlemagne. Three years later he returned to Frisia, and the emperor charged him with the spiritual care of five provinces. Ludger based himself on a place called Mimigerneford, which later became known as Münster because of the abbey he founded there. He turned down the bishopric of Trier, but in 804 agreed to be consecrated first Bishop of Münster. Although in some pain from his final illness, the saint continued to preach till the very end of his life.

Rupert of Salzburg

Rupert of Salzburg was not a German but a Frank and had been Bishop of Worms when the French King Childeric III suggested he go as a missionary to the people of Bavaria.

Childeric used his influence with the pagan Duke Theodo II of Bavaria to secure a welcome for the saint, and Rupert for his part decided that his first task was to convert the duke, and this he did. Many of the leading men and women of the land followed the duke's example and embraced Christianity.

Instead of knocking down pagan temples, as many missionaries did, Saint Rupert preferred to consecrate them as Christian churches. In this way he provided for worship at Regensburg and at Altötting. Where there was no suitable temple to be adapted, Rupert built churches, and soon the Christian work met with so great a success that many more helpers from Franconia were needed to serve the spiritual needs of Rupert's converts.

He was ably supported by his sister, Saint Erentrudis, who became the first abbess of a nunnery her brother founded at a place now called Nonnberg. Rupert also founded a monastery at another place known today as Mönchberg.

Rupert made the centre of his mission a decayed town called Juvavum, situated close by a valley profuse with salt springs. This ancient Roman town and the surrounding countryside were donated to Rupert by Duke Theodo. The saint saw that he could revitalize the place partly by developing salt mines in the area, and he renamed the town Salzburg. Here he founded a bishopric, and was the first to be consecrated bishop.

It was in Salzburg that he died, in about 715. He became so renowned that after his death countries such as Ireland claimed him as a native son, and in spite of the remarkable missionary successes which he did achieve he is said to have reached even further into pagan lands – notably into Pannonia – though there is not the slightest evidence for this.

John of Capistrano

Jonah and Berikjesus

In 1453 the Turks captured Constantinople and soon were threatening Christian Europe. John of Capistrano, deeply anxious about the possibility that the Turks might overrun western Christendom the way they had conquered the east, was already a famous preacher; but he failed to rally the princes of Austria and Bavaria to attack the invader.

By 1456 the Turks were threatening Belgrade. John sought an audience with the Hungarian general Janos Hunyadi. Hunyadi, inspired by the saint, rallied the Hungarian troops. John of Capistrano himself led the left wing of the forces. The Turks were beaten off, and western Europe reprieved.

Saint John of Capistrano had spent his early life vigorously engaged in secular affairs. He had read law at the University of Perugia and been made governor of that city. At the age of thirty he took a wife. During the war with the supporters of Malatesta, he was flung into a foul dungeon. There he experienced a conversion which made him repent of his past sins and seek the life of a friar. He was dispensed of his marriage vows and became a Franciscan.

Such an experienced man was welcomed as a papal emissary. As apostolic commisary he was sent to Milan and Venice, to France and the Holy Land.

But his chief skills – once used as a legal orator – were those of a preacher. Hundreds and thousands came to hear him preach as he travelled throughout Italy. Soon he was asked to preach abroad, in Bavaria, in Saxony, in Poland.

He was also made a papal inquisitor. When the Emperor Frederick III begged the pope to send someone to try to counteract the activities of the Hussites, John was chosen. He regarded these men and women with implacable hostility, as heretics. (So great was the reaction of later Protestants to John's vehemence towards the Hussites that in 1526, the Calvinists threw his relics down a well.)

In 1456, shortly after the Battle of Belgrade, John of Capistrano died of plague.

In the year 327 the Sassanian King Shapur II began a vicious persecution against the Christians in Persia. He cast many into prison, and two brothers of the city of Beth-Asa decided, in spite of the danger, to visit and comfort them in their last hours of torment and death.

The two men were arrested for this, and brought to trial. The judge told them they must venerate the King of Persia and also the sun, the moon, fire and water. They answered him that only a fool would worship a mortal man rather than the immortal king of heaven.

The two saints were then barbarously put to death. After hideous tortures Jonah's mangled body was placed in a wine-press, and the saint was crushed to death. Berikjesus was treated with equal brutality. Hundreds of reeds were cut into sharp splinters and inserted into his flesh. Then Berikjesus was rolled along the ground, so that the long splinters pierced him deeply. As he endured the hideous pain, the judge called out that he could still save himself. Berikjesus replied, 'God, the maker of this body, will restore it; and he will judge you and your king.' And so he joined his brother in death.

St John of Capistrano

John Climacus

Acacius

'Rule your own heart as a king rules over his kingdom, but be subject above all to the supreme ruler, God himself.'

St John Climacus

'We venerate our God because he made us; we did not make him. He as our Master loves us, for he is also our Father. Of his goodness he has rescued us from everlasting death.'

St Acacius

'Climacus' is the Latin version of the Greek word for a ladder. John Climacus's fame derives from a book he wrote towards the end of the sixth century, which he called 'The Ladder of Perfection'.

A Syrian, he joined the monastery of Mount Sinai when he was only sixteen years old. For forty years he spent most of his life living almost completely alone as an anchorite, studying the Scriptures and the lives of the fathers of the church. He would return to the monastery to meet other monks only for the celebration of the Eucharist.

At the request of the Abbot of Raithu he wrote his 'Ladder of Perfection', taking the notion of a spiritual ladder to heaven which would have thirty rungs – one for each year of Christ's earthly life up until his baptism.

Acacius, Bishop of Antioch, led a devout life and was much revered by his flock, who nicknamed him 'Agathangelus', which means 'good angel'. During the persecution of Christians under the Emperor Decius not a single Christian in his diocese is said to have denied his faith.

Around the year 251 Decius's representative in Antioch, whose name was Martian, summoned the bishop for cross-

examination. Acacius appeared and first of all insisted that his whole flock was entirely faithful to the emperor. Martian responded that the saint should prove this by making a sacrifice to the emperor as a god. The bishop adamantly refused.

Instead of instantly sentencing Acacius to death, Martian continued to cross-examine him. They discussed the nature of angels. They spoke about the myths of the Greeks and the Romans. They philosophized together about the nature of God. Martian then asked the saint to provide him with the names of other Christians. The bishop would give him only two names: his own, Acacius, and his nickname, Agathangelus. The emperor's representative was so impressed by Acacius that he sent a transcript of the whole cross-examination to Decius himself. Decius smiled when he read it, promoted Martian to a higher post, and pardoned Bishop Acacius.

April

'Whenever you think God has
shown you other people's faults,
take care: your own judgment
may well be at fault. Say nothing.
And if you do attribute any vice
to another person, immediately
and humbly look for it in yourself
also. Should the other person
really possess that vice, he will
correct himself so much the
better when he sees how gently
you understand him, and he will
say to himself whatever you
would have told him.'

Catherine of Siena (April 29)

Hugh of Grenoble

When Hugh of Grenoble (*below*, *right*) was born at Châteauneuf, the French churchmen were very undisciplined. Hugh himself, though a layman, was made a canon of Valence Cathedral, and set out to reform the church. The Bishop of Die soon saw the young man's zeal and appointed Hugh to his household. This bishop was particularly keen to stamp out simony (that is sale for personal gain of positions in the church).

In 1080 the bishop took Hugh to a council at Avignon. One of the purposes of this council was to try to sort out disorders that had arisen in the diocese of Grenoble, whose bishop had just died. To Hugh's surprise, the members of the council decided that he was by far the best person to be consecrated bishop. He protested that he was only a layman. Nevertheless the bishop ordained him and then took him to Rome where the Pope consecrated Hugh as bishop.

Hugh discovered the diocese of Grenoble to be in a far worse state than he had imagined. Although the clergy had taken vows of celibacy, many of them lived more or less openly with women.

Influential laymen had seized most of the property of the church. Hugh manfully set about putting matters right. Several times he despaired and went to live as a monk. Each time the Pope insisted that he must take up the struggle again. Each time Hugh obeyed. He gave land to a group of monks who built there the famous monastery of the Grande Chartreuse. He sold jewels and ornaments to raise money and gave it to the poor. For fifty-two years he laboured as Bishop of Grenoble, dying in 1132 aged seventy-nine, having restored the diocese both financially and morally.

Mary the Egyptian

About the year 430 a holy man named Zosimus who had lived in a monastery in Palestine for fifty-three years decided to join a community with stricter rules near the River Jordan. As he journeyed there through the desert he saw in the distance a white-haired lady. He walked towards her, but she backed away, crying out, 'Throw me your cloak to cover me, for I have no clothes.' Zosimus did so, and then she told him her story. Born in Egypt, she had gone to Alexandria at the age of twelve and there lived shamelessly as a prostitute. After seventeen years of this sinful life, she joined a group of pilgrims who were setting out for Jerusalem – not because she felt pious but simply out of curiosity. In Jerusalem, in front of an icon depicting the Blessed Virgin, Mary the Egyptian suddenly realized the enormity of her sinfulness. Straight away she went across the Jordan into the wilderness. There she had lived, completely alone, for forty-nine years, seeing no-one until Zosimus came.

During these years she had suffered from drought and from cold. Sometimes she had been tempted to return to her life of sin, but always she prayed to Mary for strength to resist the temptation.

Mary made Zosimus promise to tell no-one of these things until she had died. He also promised to return to the same spot on the Thursday before Easter to give her holy communion. He did so, bringing also dates, figs and lentils. But after she had received the sacrament, Mary would take from him no more than three lentils. She thanked him and begged him to return the following year. When he returned, he found her there, dead. Zosimus took back his cloak, which he cherished for the rest of his life, and then he reverently buried Mary the Egyptian. She had written in the sand, 'Bury the body of Mary the sinner here.'

Sixtus I

Isidore of Seville

St Sixtus I

'O most merciful
  Redeemer, Friend, and
Brother,
May we know Thee
  more clearly,
Love Thee more dearly,
Follow Thee more
  nearly:
For ever and ever.
  Amen.'

Prayer of St Richard of Chichester

After the death of Pope Alexander I when the Emperor Trajan ruled the Roman Empire, it was virtually certain that anyone who succeeded the pope would suffer martyrdom, for this was an age when Christians were savagely persecuted. Sixtus I took the office knowing this, and survived as pope for ten years or so, before being killed by the Roman authorities.

As well as displaying great bravery, Sixtus I was also much concerned with the liturgy of the church. At the Eucharist when the priests came to the words 'Holy, holy, holy Lord, God of power and might; heaven and earth are full of your glory. Hosanna in the highest', Sixtus insisted that all the people in the church should join in as well.

Sixtus I was killed by the pagan Romans in the year 127.

Richard of Chichester

Richard was born poor and even as a student in Paris is said to have lived with two fellow-students, the three of them having only one tunic and one cloak between them. When two of them went to a lecture, the other had to stay at home.

Eventually Richard became first of all Chancellor of Oxford University and then chancellor to the Archbishop of Canterbury. When Richard was appointed Bishop of Chichester in 1244, he was in exile in France. King Henry III did not approve of the pope's choice, and confiscated the goods of the bishopric. Eventually Richard was allowed to take possession of his see; but his early poverty and his recent experiences made him eschew riches. Whenever he heard of any fire or damage to his property, Saint Richard would say to his stewards, 'Do not grieve. This is a lesson to us. God is teaching us that we do not give enough away to the poor. Let us increase our almsgiving.' He died in 1253.

Although Isidore of Seville became one of the most learned men of his age, as a boy he hated his lessons. He was taught by his elder brother, Leander, who later became Bishop of Seville, and Isidore succeeded him. Aware by now of the great boon of education, he founded schools throughout Spain. He thought that students should be taught law and medicine, Hebrew and Greek, as well as the classics. For centuries Isidore was known as 'the schoolmaster of the middle ages', because he wrote a kind of twenty-volume encyclopedia of everything that was known in seventh-century Europe.

Isidore also longed to convert the Spanish Goths. He rewrote the services of the church for their use, never wearying in all his thirty-seven years as a bishop of preaching and teaching those in error. His own writings included a summary of all the events in the world since the creation until his own time; a book giving the stories of every great man and woman mentioned in the Bible; a history of the Goths; new rules for monasteries; and a book about astronomy.

This extraordinary man loved to give to the poor, and towards the end of his life scarcely anyone could get into his house in Seville, crowded as it was with beggars and the unfortunate from the surrounding country.

Vincent Ferrer

William Ferrer, an Englishman, married a Spanish woman named Constantia Miguel, and in 1350 she bore him a son named Vincent. These were difficult times for the church, since for many years two men claimed to be Pope. One was a friend of Vincent, Pedro de Luna, who in 1394 set up a papal court at Avignon in the palace built by previous antipopes (as they are known) and called himself Benedict XIII. For many years Vincent maintained his friendship with Pedro, but he came to believe that his friend's claims were false. In spite of Vincent's entreaties, the antipope refused to resign. Reluctantly Vincent was obliged to abandon de Luna, persuading King Ferdinand of Castile also to reject the antipope's false claims – a course which in the end led to the deposition of 'Benedict'.

Pedro de Luna had even offered to make Vincent a cardinal. Although Vincent refused this title, he had continued as the antipope's confessor. In 1398 he relinquished his duties at de Luna's court and decided to become a missionary preacher, inspired by the examples of St Dominic and St Francis of Assisi. Throughout France he preached to enormous crowds. Many people at this time believed that the world would end in the year 1400, and this made Vincent's words about the Last Judgment all the more terrifying. Sometimes his audiences were so frightened that many of them fainted. Others wept bitterly and determined to lead new and better lives. Thousands followed him wherever he went. From these Vincent organized a group of helpers who would continue his missionary work in one place after he had travelled on. Soon he was in Switzerland and then Italy, still converting many to Christianity. He may even have visited Britain and certainly preached in Holland. At Grenada in Spain the saint is said to have converted eight thousand Moors. He was almost seventy when he died at Vannes in France in 1419.

Vincent's favourite saying was, 'Whatever you do, think not of yourselves but of God.'

William of Eskill

John-Baptist de la Salle

John-Baptist de la Salle was destined for the priesthood at ten years of age, and was actually made a canon of Rheims cathedral eleven years before he was ordained. Soon, however, he decided to devote himself to the education of poor boys. John-Baptist gave up his family inheritance, and his canonry, and began to train laymen as teachers. He called the young men he gathered together 'the Brethren of the Christian Schools'. In 1688 he took over a free school in Paris and started teacher-training colleges in Rheims, Paris and Saint-Denis.

John-Baptist believed that to teach the poor in Latin (as was the custom) was absurd. They needed to be taught to write and read their own language. Many believed he was misguided to teach the poor anything save manual labour. In 1702 his enemies managed to get him dismissed, but all his teachers threatened to leave with him, so John-Baptist managed to keep control of his brethren. He taught the children of those who had come into exile in France with the deposed King James II of England. He set up a school for delinquent boys at Dijon and even taught prisoners. Today, over 17,000 of his brothers are still teaching throughout the world.

Eskill is the British equivalent of Eskiloë, a Danish town which once housed an abbey. William was born in Paris around the year 1125. He had already made his mark in France when the Bishop of Röskild, Denmark, invited him to become abbot of Eskiloë.

His early experiences stood him in good stead in Denmark. After being educated by the monks of Saint-Germain-des-Prés in Paris, he became a canon of the church of Sainte-Geneviève-du-Mont. But his fellow-canons were lax, and frequently mocked their new recruit for his disciplined life. They so disliked him that William was forced to resign and take a living at Épinay outside Paris. Fortunately Pope Eugenius III visited Paris, perceived the laxity of the canons of Sainte-Geneviève-du-Mont, and replaced them with more devout men. William rejoined the canons and became their sub-prior.

These early trials fitted him for reforming the abbey of Eskiloë. William first of all expelled two monks, setting about the reformation of the rest. His enemies tried to overcome his zeal by appealing to powerful lords, but for thirty years William unflinchingly persisted, in spite of inner strain and painful illnesses.

Perpetuus

Perpetuus became Bishop of Tours in the mid-fifth century. The poor, it is recorded, were his heirs: he left them pastures, groves, vineyards, houses, gardens, water-mills, gold, silver and his clothing. He also venerated his great predecessor St Martin, the soldier who had sliced his cloak in two and given half to a beggar. Martin was buried in a basilica at Tours and Perpetuus rebuilt this fine

building to house the countless pilgrims who flocked to his tomb.

Perpetuus decreed that all the people in his diocese should fast on Fridays and Wednesdays, save at a few church festivals. He also decreed several Mondays in the Christian year as fasts. So great was Perpetuus's influence, that these fasts were still being observed in the diocese of Tours over a century after his death. And so powerful was his memory that, thirteen centuries after his death, some unknown forgers drew up a fake will for the saint, declaring: 'You, my dearly beloved brothers, my crown, my joy, that is to say, Christ's poor, needy, beggars, sick, widows and orphans, you I hereby name and decree to be my heirs.' Though the will was a fake, the true spirit of Saint Perpetuus shines through it.

Waudru

The family of Saint Waudru, who is the patroness of Mons in Belgium, was amazingly saintly too. Both her parents were canonized; her three children were also declared saints and so was her husband. He was the Count of Hennegau, and one of the courtiers of King Dagobert I. After their children were born both he and Waudru longed to live lives totally devoted to meditation and prayer. He retired to an abbey he had founded at Haumont. Waudru built for herself a tiny home and, giving away her possessions, lived there alone. Though she clung to her solitude, her great wisdom and piety meant that countless men and women pressed on her for advice. Eventually Waudru had so many followers that she was obliged to found her own nunnery at a place called Châteaulieu. She dedicated this convent to the Mother of Jesus, and around it grew the present town of Mons. By the time of Waudru's death in the year 688 she had become famous not only for her charity but also for her miraculous powers of healing.

Fulbert of Chartres

Guthlac

*'Ye choirs of new
 Jerusalem,
Your sweetest notes
 employ,
The Paschal victory to
 hymn
In strains of holy joy.'*

Fulbert of Chartres

Fulbert was born in Italy in the mid-tenth century of humble parents. Because of his promise as a student he was sent to study at Rheims. There he became the favourite pupil of a celebrated philosopher and mathematician named Gerbert (later Pope Sylvester II) and Gerbert took Fulbert to Rome with him. After Gerbert's death, Bishop Odo of Chartres made Fulbert chancellor of the cathedral.

Fulbert's vigour and brilliance soon made Chartres the finest centre of learning in the whole of France. Scholars came from the length and breadth of Europe to study

S. FULBERTUS
EP.

there. Inevitably in time Fulbert was called to be Bishop of the city. He remained extremely humble, and used to describe himself as 'the very tiny bishop of a very great church'. Almost as soon as he was consecrated bishop, his cathedral burned down. He rebuilt it splendidly, and although today much of the cathedral is of a later date, Fulbert's Romanesque steeple still dominates the city.

Fulbert's pupils loved him. Shortly after his death in the year 1029 a pupil from Liège named Adelman (who later became Bishop of Brescia) wrote: 'With what dignity of spiritual interpretation, with what weight of literal sense, with what sweetness of speech did he expound the deep secrets of philosophy'.

As a young man Guthlac had been a soldier, fighting for Ethelred, the King of Mercia. At the age of twenty-four he renounced both violence and the life of the world and became a monk in an abbey (inhabited by men and women) at Repton and ruled by an abbess named Elfrida. Even in these early years his discipline was of an extraordinary kind. Some of the monks in fact disliked him for refusing any wine or cheering drink. After two years in the monastery it seemed to him far too agreeable a place. He found a wet, remote, unloved spot on a bed of the River Welland in the Fens, and there lived for the rest of his life as a hermit, seeking to imitate the rigours of the old desert saints.

His temptations rivalled theirs. Wild men came out of the forest and beat him up. Even the ravens stole his few possessions. But Guthlac said we should be patient, even with wild creatures. Bit by bit the animals and birds came to trust him as their friend. A holy man named Wilfrid once visited Guthlac and was astonished when two swallows landed on his shoulders and then hopped all over him. Guthlac told him, 'Those who choose to live apart from other humans become the friends of wild animals; and the angels visit them too – for those who are often visited by men and women are rarely visited by angels.'

Zeno of Verona

Martin I

Zeno was born in Africa, but in 362 was made Bishop of Verona in Italy. He loved fishing in the River Adige, and his symbol today is a fish. He also chose to live in great poverty. His example fired the zeal of many fellow-citizens in Verona, who used to throw open their homes to the poor. This inspiration proved vital when the Goths overcame the neighbourhood and took many captives. The people of Verona were foremost in offering all they possessed to ransom these prisoners.

The bishop was a trained orator, and ninety-three of his sermons still exist – the earliest collection of Latin homilies we possess. He preached often to a group of nuns who lived in a convent he himself had founded. Whenever Zeno preached, so many people thronged the church that he was obliged to build a bigger one.

The body of the saint lies today in one of the most beautiful Romanesque churches of Italy, San Zeno Maggiore in Verona. In the tympanum over the great west doorway is sculpted the saint, who is trampling down the devil, and his tomb is in the huge crypt.

Martin I was the last pope to suffer martyrdom. He was an Umbrian, born in the Italian town of Todi, had risen rapidly in the church and had served his predecessor, Pope Theodore I, as papal nuncio in Constantinople.

At this time a good number of Christians were stating that Jesus, though divine, did not have the will of a human being. As soon as Martin became pope, he called a council to condemn this notion. This was a brave act, since the wrong ideas were supported by the Emperor Constans II. The emperor speedily took his revenge. Though a sick man, the pope was brought by force to Constantinople. For three months he lay in prison. Then at a trial at which he was not allowed to defend himself, he was sentenced to death.

The dying Patriarch of Constantinople pleaded with the Emperor to spare Martin's life. Although the emperor heard the Patriarch's plea he merely banished Martin to Kherson in the Crimea; such a sick man could not be expected to survive such cruelty and he died in 656.

Tiburtius and Valerian

St Tiburtius and St Valerian

According to the legend of Saint Cecilia, Valerian was a young pagan when she was betrothed to him, not by her own wish, but by the decision of her parents. Cecilia had determined not to marry, so as to devote herself entirely to God. On their wedding day, she told Valerian of this vow. So persuasively did Cecilia speak of her faith that she converted her new husband to Christianity. He went to the home of his parents and succeeded in converting his brother, Tiburtius.

The two brothers now set about displaying the virtues of Christian charity. One of these was especially dangerous. It consisted of gathering together the broken bodies of Christian martyrs and giving them a decent burial. Tiburtius and Valerian were caught at this work. The prefect Almachius demanded that they sacrifice to pagan gods. Both Tiburtius and Valerian refused and so they were taken outside Rome, beaten and then beheaded.

Caradoc

Caradoc had been employed as a musician (chiefly playing the harp) at the court of Prince Rhys ap Tewdr of Wales. He also looked after the prince's greyhounds. One day these escaped, through no fault of Caradoc's. The ill-tempered prince was so angry that he threatened to mutilate Caradoc. The saint replied, 'If you so lightly regard my long and laborious service, I shall from now on serve a Prince who rewards a small service bountifully and who does not prefer greyhounds to men.' He went to the Bishop of Llandaff who received him as a monk.

After some time in a monastery at St Teilo, Caradoc lived as a hermit close by an abandoned church of St Cenydd in Gower. He still loved animals, and could quieten the wildest beasts. But he also suffered much from his fellow human beings, once being carried off by Norwegian pirates. At another time a ruthless marauder named Richard Thanehard stole his cattle. But Caradoc never despaired, dying peacefully in 1124.

Basilissa and Anastasia

St Basilissa and St Anastasia

These two women lived in Rome and were converted to Christianity by the teachings of Saint Peter and Saint Paul. Both apostles were put to death by the Roman authorities. The two women secretly found their bodies and gave them a Christian burial.

This infuriated the authorities. They discovered who had buried the apostles and cast the two women into jail, eventually bringing them before the tribunal of Nero. Neither Basilissa nor Anastasia would renounce their Christian faith. In consequence both were sentenced to be savagely mutilated, and then they were beheaded.

Paternus

Paternus was born in Brittany to devout parents named Patran and Gwen. His father sought Gwen's permission to go to live as a hermit in Ireland, and she brought up their son to be pious and godly.

The boy cherished the memory of his father. When he grew up he sailed to live as a hermit himself, landing in Wales. He met the great Welsh saints, and humbly learned from them. One day Saint Samson summoned Paternus when he had just put on one boot. Without delaying to put on the other boot the saint hastened to answer Samson's summons.

Instead of leading a solitary life, Paternus was called to found a great monastery. He chose a spot in Cardiganshire which was later known as Llanabarn Fawr, which means 'the church of the great Paternus'. Over a hundred and twenty monks joined Paternus at Llanabarn Fawr.

He was a bold opponent of the pagan kings of the region, never tiring of preaching in the hope of their conversion. Once the evil King Maelgun accused the saint of stealing much royal treasure. Paternus is said to have proved his innocence by plunging his hand into boiling water and taking it out completely unharmed.

Bernardette

Marie Bernardette Soubirous was born in 1844 and her father, a miller, could not afford her education.

On 11 February 1858 she was collecting scraps of wood on the bank of the River Gave, near Lourdes, when she was granted a vision of the Virgin Mary. She showed people the cave in which Mary had appeared. Most of them mocked her but from 18 February until 4 March Bernardette continued to see and talk with the Blessed Virgin each day. Crowds gathered, drawn by her reports and by the mysterious appearance of a spring. Then on 25 March another vision of Mary told Bernardette that she must build a chapel at the place where the appearances took place.

Today this spot is one of the most famous places of pilgrimage in the world for the waters of the spring seem to have miraculous healing properties. Bernardette's lifelong ambition had been to become a Carmelite nun herself, but for many years her general ill-health, particularly her asthma, prevented this. Then, in 1866, she joined the sisters of Notre Dame at Nevers. She refused to return to Lourdes, even in 1876 when the great basilica there was consecrated.

Anicetus

Towards the end of the reign of the Emperor Antoninus Pius, Anicetus was elected Pope. For eight years or so he laboured to defend the faith against those who said, first that the physical life of Jesus was really illusory, and secondly, that the Jewish background to Christianity was dangerous and needed to be shed completely.

During his reign as Pope a further anxiety arose because Christians had begun to quarrel about determining the correct date of Easter. Anicetus died about the year 166, worn out by these troubles which he had been unable to bring to an end. Some say he died a martyr's death.

Stephen Harding

Stephen Harding was born in Dorset and educated at Sherborne Abbey. After visiting Scotland, Paris and Rome, he joined some hermits at Molesmes in Burgundy. Their leaders were Saint Robert of Molesmes and Saint Alberic. Soon the three men left Molesmes to found a yet stricter monastery at Cîteaux.

Twenty monks came with them, and Robert was appointed abbot, Alberic prior and Stephen sub-prior. Later, when Saint Robert returned to Molesmes, Stephen succeeded Alberic as prior and Alberic took Robert's position. When Alberic died in 1109, Stephen Harding took his place, and remained abbot of Cîteaux until 1133, which was a year before his death.

Stephen's stern austerity was set out in the 'Charter of Charity' he drew up, which was to become the basis of Cistercian monasticism. But for a time his severity repelled many. The movement and the house at Cîteaux seemed destined to peter out, when Stephen's monks were joined by the man who was to achieve fame as Saint Bernard of Clairvaux. Thenceforth Cistercian monasticism flourished and by the end of the twelfth century there were no fewer than five hundred Cistercian monasteries throughout Europe.

Apollonius

Leo IX

St Leo IX

'O Lord Jesus Christ, give us a measure of Thy spirit that we may be enabled to obey Thy teaching to pacify anger, to take part in pity, to moderate desire, to increase love, to put away sorrow, to cast away vain-glory, not to be vindictive, not to fear death, ever entrusting our spirit to immortal God, who with Thee and the Holy Ghost liveth and reigneth world without end.'

St Apollonius
(Prayer adapted from part of his defence before Perennis)

'I enjoy my life,' said the martyr Apollonius, when brought before the Roman authorities. 'But because I love my life, it does not make me frightened of death. There is waiting for me something better: eternal life, given to the person who has lived well on earth.'

Apollonius was on trial before the Roman prefect Perennis in the year 185. He was a Roman senator and a very learned man. He read the philosophy of the pagans. He also read the Old Testament and the writings of Christians, and under their influence had become a Christian himself. One of his slaves denounced Apollonius as a Christian to the authorities and the saint was brought before Perennis and told he must give up Christianity or die.

Apollonius pointed out that everyone must die and that it was better to die for the sake of true belief and the true God than to die of some ordinary disease. Saint Apollonius then took the opportunity to give the whole court a reasoned explanation of his Christian faith. He remained steadfast in his refusal to renounce Christianity and in his belief in eternal life. His legs were crushed, and then he was beheaded.

Pope Leo IX curiously combined the life of a holy man with that of an army commander. Born in Alsace in the year 1002, he was a deacon in the church when the Emperor Conrad II invaded Italy. In spite of his holy orders, Leo readily joined the emperor's army and fought valiantly.

For twenty years he was Bishop of Toul, which lies on the left bank of the River Moselle. Leo was a stern bishop, disciplining lax priests and bringing order into the monasteries of his diocese. Then in 1048 he was elected pope. What had been done on a small scale in the diocese of Toul Leo now attempted to apply to the whole church. He tirelessly travelled western Europe to enforce his reforms, and became known as the pilgrim pope. Wherever he went he called together the bishops and clergy in councils, inspiring them to follow his lead.

Leo IX decided to consolidate the material position of the papacy by adding parts of southern Italy to his territories, but this proved to be his undoing. The Normans invaded these new territories; the warrior pope himself led an army in their defence – an action which caused even St Peter Damian to criticize him. Unfortunately too, the Normans defeated him. Pope Leo IX was captured at Civitella and imprisoned at Benevento. Although his captors declared themselves to be the pope's loyal subjects, they did not release Leo for several months. In prison he began to learn Greek, in an attempt to understand better the teachings of the Eastern church, which was now split from Rome. But his health was breaking down. On his release, the pope ordered his bed to be placed in St Peter's, Rome, next to a coffin. There in 1054 he died.

Agnes of Montepulciano

Born in the little village of Gracchiano-Vecchio in Tuscany, Agnes persuaded her parents to place her in the nearest convent, at Montepulciano, when she was only nine years old. But already she was a remarkably impressive girl. A new convent opened at Procena, and the sisters there asked the nuns of Montepulciano to send them a mother superior. The sister offered the post would go only if Agnes were allowed to come to help her. Soon many other girls joined the convent at Procena simply because they knew

Agnes was there. By the time she was fifteen the nuns had elected her their superior.

The saint's self-discipline became legendary. She lived on bread and water for fifteen years. She slept on the floor with a stone for a pillow. It was said that in her visions angels gave her Holy Communion and once she had a vision in which she was holding the infant Jesus in her arms.

The sisters at Montepulciano built a new convent and Agnes came to be its superior. The convent grew, as did Agnes's fame. When she knew she was dying, she told her grieving nuns that they should rejoice, for, she said, 'You will discover that I have not abandoned you. You will possess me for ever.'

Anselm

The son of a landowner in Lombardy, Anselm wished to enter a monastery at the age of fifteen. Because his father disapproved, Anselm led a worldly and undisciplined life for several years. But in 1059 he joined a monastic school at Bec in Normandy which was run by a fellow-Italian, Lanfranc. The lives of the two men were to run curiously parallel. First Anselm succeeded Lanfranc as prior of Bec, and though many of the monks greatly resented the appointment of a young man over them, Anselm's firmness combined with gentleness won them over. His work as prior brought him to England, where the monks possessed lands and earned revenues. Lanfranc had been consecrated Archbishop of Canterbury in 1070. On his death the English clergy had come to respect Anselm enough to ask him to succeed Lanfranc as archbishop. Anselm agreed, but for many years was kept out of England because the king was improperly interfering in the rights of the church.

In exile Anselm wrote his most famous work of philosophy: *Cur Deus Homo?* It was an attempt to explain why God had been obliged to become man in Jesus. Anselm argued that if God had merely forgiven men's sins, his mercy would have conflicted with the demands of justice. To reconcile mercy and justice an offering was needed greater than men's disobedience. Only God *could* make such an offering, argued Anselm, but only man *ought* to. Therefore only a God-made-man could and should make it – as Jesus did on the cross.

'O Lord our God, grant us grace to desire thee with our whole heart; that, so desiring, we may seek, and, seeking, find thee; and so finding thee, may love thee; and loving thee, may hate those sins from which thou has redeemed. Amen.'

St Anselm

Soter

George

St Soter

After the death of Pope Anicetus in the mid-second century, Soter was elected to this dangerous office. His influence was widespread, partly because of his charity, his personal kindness and especially his care for those who had been persecuted for their faith.

This kindliness did not mean that Pope Soter looked kindly on error. During his pontificate, a number of Christians, known as Montanists, were preaching that the heavenly Jerusalem would soon descend near Pepuza, a town in Phrygia. These Montanists condemned their fellow-Christians as far too lax: they did not fast enough, it was alleged; they should never marry again if one partner had died; they did not prophesy enough, for they lacked the gift of the Holy Spirit.

The movement was dividing the church and causing violent quarrels among the faithful, and Soter did not hesitate to condemn its leaders, sending round an encyclical outlining their errors. He died – possibly martyred – in the year 174.

Epipodius and Alexander

Epipodius and Alexander were young men, still unmarried. They lived at Lyons, as good Christians, and tried to avoid capture by the pagans by hiding with a widow who lived just outside the city. When they were captured the judge mocked Epipodius, saying, 'We worship the gods with revels and jollity and festivity. You worship a crucified man with fasts.'

Epipodius said nothing in reply, and the judge ordered him to be killed by the sword. Two days later his friend Alexander was flogged and then crucified.

The legend of St George tells how this Cappadocian knight was riding through Libya and came to a city called Sylene. In a swamp by the city lived a huge, fearsome beast which terrorized the citizens unless they fed it. As all their sheep had been eaten by this beast, they were obliged to feed it human beings. These were chosen by lot, and as George rode up the king's daughter was about to be sacrificed.

George promised to slay the dragon if the whole city would accept Jesus as Lord and be baptized. The citizens agreed, and the saint killed the beast with his lance. Four ox-carts were needed to carry its dead body away. And fifteen thousand persons or more were baptized.

So strange are the legends that have gathered round the name of St George that sceptics have argued even more that he never existed at all. It is very likely that he was a Roman soldier at the end of the third and the beginning of the fourth century. He is said to have been raised to the rank of military tribune of the imperial guards. Once when the emperor was present, heathen priests were consulting the entrails of animals to foretell the future. Those Christians among the guards made the sign of the cross on their foreheads. The emperor was extremely angry and ordered them to be flogged and dismissed. He then sent out an edict ordering the Christian clergy to make sacrifices to pagan gods. Seeing a copy of this edict posted on the door of the emperor's palace, George tore it down. He was imprisoned, tortured and put to death.

Even this story is a considerably embroidered one. But we can be reasonably certain that George did suffer martyrdom around the year 303, and a strong tradition says that this took place at Lydda in Palestine.

Ivo

Mark

'And they brought young children to him, that he should touch them: and his disciples rebuked those that brought them. But when Jesus saw it, he was much displeased, and said unto them, "Suffer the little children to come unto me, and forbid them not: for of such is the kingdom of God."'

St Mark's Gospel 10: 13–14

Ivo was a Persian bishop who enjoyed great honour and luxury in his own land but he yearned for a more disciplined and arduous life, and, together with three companions he came to England.

They settled in remote, wild fenland in Huntingdonshire. There they died, and would have been forgotten had not a holy well sprung up, at which many miracles were performed.

Fidelis of Sigmaringen

Fidelis of Sigmaringen was martyred as a result of the religious fanaticism created by the Reformation. Born in Prussia, he became a lawyer and, in spite of his very high qualifications, his practice at Ensisheim was at the service of those who could scarcely pay him. He became known as 'the lawyer of the poor'.

His religious convictions soon persuaded the saint that he should become a Capuchin monk, and his qualifications took him to be head of the mission to Zwinglian Protestants in the Grisons, Switzerland where he met his death. One assassin's bullet missed him on 24 April 1622, but a second killed him as he was returning home later that day.

Many scholars think that the second Gospel in the New Testament was actually the first of the four Gospels to be written. If this is so, then its author, Mark, was an exceptionally brilliant Christian, since he was the first person to write a Gospel and must be said to have invented this remarkable form of religious writing.

Ancient tradition says that although Mark had not been one of Jesus's own disciples, he was the mouthpiece of St Peter. This means that Mark's gospel must reflect the views of this great apostle, probably more than any of the other three. This ancient tradition is supported by a phrase in the first letter of Peter, when the writer speaks of 'my son Mark'.

A Mark also was a companion of St Paul. Paul and Barnabas both worked with Mark, but for a time Paul grew to distrust their fellow-missionary and did not wish him to come on a second journey with them. Barnabas, for this reason, left Paul and went to Cyprus with Mark. Paul and Mark must have become friends again, for we know that when Paul was a prisoner in Rome, Mark supported him and stayed with him.

Mark's Gospel starkly sets out the demands of Jesus on his followers. Jesus had suffered, says Mark. His followers will suffer similarly. Indeed, Jesus had explicitly warned the disciples about this. But it is also clear that those who can endure such sufferings will be greatly rewarded, for what Mark claims to be bringing is 'good news' (this is the meaning of the word 'gospel'): 'the gospel of Jesus Christ, the Son of God', as he states in the very first verse of his Gospel.

Anacletus

Zita

St Zita

Anacletus was elected pope in the year 76, second successor to St Peter, and like Peter fated to be a martyr. He divided Rome into twenty-five parishes, and was put to death under the Emperor Domitian around the year 91.

Stephen of Perm

Stephen of Perm, one of the great Russian missionary bishops, had been born in 1345 among the Zyrian people, who lived west of the Ural mountains, and he longed to convert his own folk to Christianity. After about twenty years in a monastery at Rostov preparing himself for a missionary life, he set out on a preaching mission among them.

Soon Saint Stephen of Perm realized that he needed to make a translation of the Liturgy into their tongue. Since the Zyrians at that time did not possess even an alphabet, Stephen invented one, using for letters parts of the traditional elements of Zyrian carvings and embroidery. He set up schools to teach this alphabet to his converts and in 1383 he became the first Bishop of Perm. He died in 1386.

Zita, the patron saint of servants, was a servant herself, sent at the age of twelve to work in a rich household in the Tuscan city of Lucca. Her own parents were extremely poor, but they had brought up their daughter to know right and wrong and taught her to pray. She also knew that – poor as they were – other people were worse off. As a servant she ate well, for her employers fed her properly; but Zita gave away most of what she was meant to eat to beggars and to the impoverished of Lucca.

At first her fellow-servants laughed at her piety and kindness. Zita cared not at all about this, and in the end they grew to admire her. But her master was often deeply irritated that she gave away so much. During a local famine she secretly gave away much of the family supply of beans. When her master inspected the kitchen cupboards, to Zita's relief the beans had been miraculously replaced. Another time, as she went to church on a freezing Christmas Eve, he lent her his cloak, warning her to look after it and bring it back. Zita lent it to an old man outside the church. After the service he had disappeared with it. Her master was extremely irritated, until the poor old man appeared at his door to return the cloak. People later decided he must have been an angel in disguise, and so the door of the Church of St Frediano, Lucca, where he first appeared, is called the Angel Portal.

As time passed, Zita became a trusted member of the household in Lucca. She could calm her master even when he fell into the most terrible fit of anger. Her duties were lightened, but she spent her free time caring for the sick and visiting prisoners. In her last illness, the family that employed her longed to feed her with luxuries, but these the saint refused, dying at the age of sixty on 27 April 1278.

Vitalis

There are two second-century saints called Vitalis, but the one who is commemorated on this day was a rich man who lived in Milan. He was happily married with at least two fine children. His only crime was that he became a Christian. Another martyr was to be executed and Vitalis stood by him, urging him not to lose his faith in the face of this final trial. The authorities were enraged. They stretched Vitalis on a rack and then buried him alive. His wife too was attacked by vicious pagans and died of her wounds. All this·took place just outside Milan when Marcus Aurelius was Emperor.

Vitalis is shown on the extreme left of the picture below.

Peter Chanel

Peter Chanel had been born, the son of a peasant family, at Belley in France in 1803. He worked for a time as a shepherd boy before setting his heart on becoming a priest.

In 1822 a missionary society was set up in Lyons called the Society of Mary. After working in a country parish for a time, Peter Chanel joined the Marists in 1831. Some years later he was sent to Futuna, an island in the New Hebrides. Here he gained the reluctant confidence of the island chief, a man named Niuliki. ·

But when the chief discovered that Peter Chanel had converted and baptized his son, he became enraged. He arranged for Peter Chanel to be clubbed to death. The year was 1841.

Catherine of Siena

Pius V

Although Catherine of Siena frequently saw visions of Jesus and experienced mystical ecstasy, she was also one of the most down-to-earth of women. Her visions were not always beautiful. At times she was made miserable by images of foul demons and gross temptations. But at other times sweet visions of her Saviour entranced her.

Catherine loved working amongst the sick. Unlike most other volunteers, she would care for those with the most repellent diseases, such as leprosy, which was then virtually incurable. She gathered around her many friends, and when a fearful plague broke out in Siena she led them boldly amongst those who had caught it – sometimes even digging graves and burying the dead herself.

Catherine also took part in some of the wider events of the church. At this time the papacy was tragically weakened by contested elections, pope and antipopes denouncing each other. Catherine supported the true Pope Urban VI against his opponents; but he was a somewhat graceless man, and her letters to him never hesitated to reprove the pope for this fault, while remaining entirely loyal to him.

Pius was born Antonio Michael Ghislieri in 1504, and he taught philosophy and theology in Dominican schools until made a bishop in 1556. When Pius IV died in 1565, Michael Ghislieri seemed by far the best person to succeed him.

Immediately he showed the sort of man he was. Instead of feasting at his elevation as pope, he sent money to the poor convents of Rome. He insisted that bishops and clergy should no longer live miles from their flock, to the neglect of their rightful work, but should live and work in their sees and parishes. Pius V stopped bull-fights and bear-baiting in the streets of Rome. He insisted that Sunday be hallowed. And once a month he held a special court for any persons who felt they had been treated unjustly.

Western Christendom at this time was seriously threatened by Turkish invasions and the Catholic states that ought to have driven them out were ridiculously divided. Pius V realized that he alone could unite them. He managed to form a Catholic League, which defeated the Turkish fleet at the battle of Lepanto. All this Pius V accomplished in only six years as pope.

May

'All of us are naturally frightened of dying and the dissolution of our bodies, but remember this most startling fact: that those who accept the faith of the cross despise even what is normally terrifying, and for the sake of Christ cease to fear even death. When he became man, the Saviour's love put away death from us and renewed us again; for Christ became man that we might become God.'

Athanasius (May 2)

Sigismund of Burgundy

Gunebald, ruler of the kingdom of Burgundy in the early sixth century, claimed to be a Christian but denied the divinity of Jesus Christ. His son and heir, Saint Sigismund, under the influence of the Bishop of Vienne, accepted the true faith.

But although intellectually he had become a Christian, his temper and savage ways remained those of a pagan. He had been king for scarcely a year when his son Sigeric fell out with his stepmother, Sigismund's second wife. The king took the stepmother's part. So great became his rage during the quarrel that he would hear any slander against Sigeric and eventually ordered his officers to strangle the prince.

When Sigismund's temper had abated, he was appalled at what he had ordered to be done to his son. He strove to make amends. He founded anew the decaying monastery of St Maurice at Agaunum, bringing there enough monks to make sure that the voice of praise was silent at no time of the day or night.

The king became a lover of the poor, liberally distributing his goods in their service. But still he felt he had not properly made amends for the murder of Sigeric. Only some great calamity, he felt, could atone such an action; and in his prayers Saint Sigismund welcomed anything that might happen to him by way of punishment.

Gunebald had killed the grandfather of three royal sons of Clovis, King of the Franks. They decided not only to take revenge by attacking Sigismund; they also aimed at overrunning Burgundy too. The three men conquered Sigismund in battle. For some time Sigismund escaped their swords, by living as a hermit close by the monastery of St Maurice. But he was eventually captured and taken to Orleans for execution. His corpse was flung down a well.

MAY 2

Athanasius

Athanasius's life as Bishop of Alexandria was anything but peaceful. He had been consecrated in the year 328, at a time when the church was split almost to breaking point. His enemies accused him of all sorts of crimes – even of murder – and the emperors believed them. Again and again he was driven into exile, returning when he could to take up his see once more.

Shortly before his consecration the church had established Christian orthodoxy at a great council held at Nicea. Athanasius wrote brilliant works defending this council and its teachings, insisting that Jesus was truly God and fully man, defining the Holy Spirit also as God.

As Bishop of Alexandria Athanasius also took responsibility for the welfare of the desert monks and fathers. He wrote a life of Saint Antony and was the person who introduced monasticism to the west. The desert fathers also protected Athanasius, after some of his enemies had broken into his church, killed and wounded worshippers and forced the saint into exile for six years.

Athanasius wrote splendidly about the work of Jesus Christ. 'It was his task to restore the corruptible to uncorruption,' he declared, 'and to maintain the honour of the Father before all. . . . He alone was able to recreate everything and to be ambassador for all men with the Father.' Jesus, says Athanasius, was born, lived as a man, died and rose again, 'that, whithersoever men have been lured away, he may recall them from that place, revealing to them his own true Father: as he himself said, "I came to seek and to save that which was lost".'

Although he did not write what is usually called the Athanasian Creed, almost certainly it was compiled using his ideas and from his own writings. He died on 2 May 373, happily restored to his bishopric in Alexandria.

Philip

Philip, who was born in Bethsaida in Galilee, was called to be an apostle by Jesus himself. Immediately he began to convert others, finding his friend Nathanael and telling him that Jesus of Nazareth was the one of whom Moses and the prophets had written.

He had the gift of raising issues that were in everyone else's mind, even if it made him seem foolish or doubting. When Jesus was about to feed the multitude on only five barley loaves and two fishes, Jesus turned the tables on Philip, by asking him 'How are we to buy the bread so that the people may eat.' The Gospel writer (John) adds that Jesus was here testing Philip, since he already knew what he would do.

Later, when Jesus made difficult statements about himself and God the Father, Philip was bold enough to say 'Lord, show us the Father and we shall be satisfied.' Jesus replied, 'Have I been so long with you, Philip, and still you do not know me? He who has seen me has seen the Father.'

James the Less

James the Less is not called by this nickname because he was a less important apostle than the other one – known as James the Great. He was in fact a relative of Jesus, and is called the less simply because he was younger than his namesake. After Jesus's ascension into heaven, this James became head of the church in Jerusalem. He was martyred about 62.

St Philip

Pelagia

Two saints who both died in the year 304 are commemorated on this day. They lived many miles apart, during the persecutions of the Emperor Diocletian. Pelagia, the daughter of pagan parents, is even said to have caught the eye of Diocletian's son. She, however, had no desire to marry. On the pretext of visiting her old nurse, she sought help and counsel from a Christian bishop.

Under his inspiration, Saint Pelagia became a Christian herself, and the bishop baptized her. At this point not only did the emperor's son turn against Pelagia; so did her own mother. Both reported her to the emperor, no doubt hoping that her faith would weaken under the threat of torture. Diocletian himself is said to have personally interviewed her – the legend alleges that he was as attracted to her beauty as was his son – but completely failed to change Pelagia's mind.

A singular torture was now prepared for the beautiful girl. A hollow bull was made out of bronze. Pelagia was put inside it and then roasted to death. The bishop is said to have buried her relics.

Florian

While all this was happening in Tarsus, an officer of the Roman army was serving Diocletian in Noricum in Austria. The governor of Lorch on Diocletian's instructions ordered the army to look for Christians. The officer, whose name was Florian (carrying a staff in the picture), had been secretly converted, but now decided he no longer wished to conceal his faith. He went to Aquilinus, the governor, and confessed his faith. Even under torture he remained firm. He was beaten twice. Then his skin was slowly peeled from his body. Finally, instead of being executed by the sword and thus afforded a soldier's death, Saint Florian was weighed down with heavy stones and flung into the River Enns.

Some of Saint Florian's relics later reached Poland, so that he is much venerated there as well as in Austria.

Hilary of Arles

Hilary of Arles was an impetuous bishop, zealous in charity and zealous in asserting the rights of his episcopate. In the latter he twice went too far and was censured by the pope. But each time Saint Hilary, even though he had defended himself, submitted to the superior authority; and after his death in the year 449, Pope Leo the Great wrote of his 'blessed memory'.

Perhaps Saint Hilary's impetuous zeal arose because he was still a young man, barely thirty years old, when he became Bishop of Arles. Already he had been groomed for the post by his predecessor, Bishop Honoratus, to whom he was related. Honoratus was abbot of Lérins when Hilary was a young man. He welcomed the youth into his monastery and regarded Hilary as a favourite son. Hilary for his part gave away all that he possessed to the poor, before being professed as a monk. Then in the year 426 Honoratus was consecrated bishop, and he insisted that Hilary join him as his personal assistant.

The saint still lived as if he were in the monastery, observing the regular monastic hours of prayer, and he humbly continued this pattern of life after his consecration as bishop.

Edbert

When Saint Cuthbert, Bishop of Lindisfarne, died in the year 687, he was succeeded by Saint Edbert in the see. Edbert, wrote the Venerable Bede, was 'a man noted for his knowledge of the Holy Bible and for his obedience to God's commandments, and especially for his generosity.'

Bede tells us that Saint Edbert every year 'obeyed the law of the Old Testament by giving one tenth of all his cattle, his crops, his fruit and his clothing to the poor.'

Eleven years after Cuthbert's death, his coffin was opened and the body was found to be still incorrupt. Edbert caused a new coffin to be made for the saint's remains. He kissed the clothing that had covered the saint's body and then ordered that new garments be put on the saint. The coffin, he said, must be given a place of honour. And he instructed his monks to leave a space under it for his own grave.

Edbert imitated his predecessor in other acts of godliness, spending forty days in solitary meditation twice a year, and building fine churches for the worship of God. He lies, like Cuthbert, in Durham Cathedral, for the bodies of both saints were carried there after many years of being moved around to escape the marauders from Scandinavia.

Petronax

Just as the English monks suffered the depradations of marauders, so the monastery of Monte Cassino had been grievously ruined when Lombards invaded that part of Italy in the year 581. Scarcely a stone stood on another in 717 when Petronax made a pilgrimage to Benedict's tomb. A few desolated monks still lived there.

Petronax determined to raise Monte Cassino to its old glory. From Pope Zachary he obtained the rule of the monastery, written in Saint Benedict's own hand. The pope also gave him the monastery's old measure for bread and wine. Before Petronax died in the year 747, Benedict's monastery on Monte Cassino was reborn, its old vigour restored.

John of Beverley

Peter of Tarentaise

St John of Beverley

Beverley Minster in Humberside is finer than some of England's great cathedrals. It owes its fame and the wealth that built and enriched it to John of Beverley.

John founded a monastery here on the site of a small church dedicated to Saint John the Evangelist, and on his death in the year 721 chose to be buried here. According to the Venerable Bede, John of Beverley possessed the gift of healing. He cured a youth of dumbness, even though the boy had never uttered a word. Bede tells how the saint patiently taught the boy the alphabet. He also cured a woman of a pain so grievous that she had been unable to move for three weeks. Several persons who seemed in imminent danger of death were saved by the saint's prayers.

After John of Beverley's death, such miracles continued around his shrine, which became a famous object of pilgrim-

age. The manner of his earthly life amply justified his canonization in 1037. Born in a little Yorkshire village called Harpham, he had trained for the priesthood and monastic life in Kent. But he returned to Yorkshire to become professed as a monk in the abbey at Whitby.

Soon he was appointed Bishop of Hexham and then Bishop of York. Not until old age had tired him out did he resign as Bishop of York, to spend the last four years of his life in the peace of his beloved monastery.

Few bishops have both been so successful as Peter of Tarentaise and so unwilling to take up the office. His one true desire was to be a Cistercian monk. He had entered a Cistercian monastery when he was twenty, persuading his parents and brothers and sister to follow him into the religious life. Before he was thirty he became abbot of a new Cistercian monastery, at Tamié in the desolate Tarentaise hills.

Here he was entirely happy. He struck up a fruitful friendship with Count Amadeo III of Savoy. Together they built a hospital for the sick – a place which also served as a guest-house for strangers passing from Geneva to Savoy over the mountain pass. Peter of Tarentaise liked nothing better than to join in conversation with those staying in this hospital, humbly joining the servants in looking after them.

But in the year 1142 he was elected Archbishop of Tarentaise. The whole Cistercian order decided that whatever the saint wished, they must accept. Peter's predecessor had been so incompetent and lax that he had been deposed. The diocese was in complete disorder. Reluctantly Peter set about its renovation, refusing to let his personal feelings hamper the work. Only once did he give way. After thirteen years as archbishop, he ran off and secretly offered himself as a lay member of a Cistercian house in Switzerland.

Of course he was found, but not until a year had elapsed. The reluctant archbishop was forced to return to his see. Again he set to work with a will, founding travellers' refuges on the Alpine passes, instituting soup and bread for the hill-farmers during the lean months of the year.

Uncompromisingly Peter supported the true pope against his false rivals – even though the antipope Victor was supported by no less than the Emperor Frederick Barbarossa. A man so honest before even the highest in the land could be trusted to intercede between the warring kings of England and France. In 1174, at the pope's request, he met both sovereigns but Peter did not succeed in reconciling them, and he died near Besançon as he returned from this mission of peace.

Pachomius

Antoninus of Florence

'It is very much better for you to be one among a crowd of a thousand people and to possess a very little humility, than to be a man living in the cave of a hyena in pride.'

St Pachomius

About the year 310 a young man named Pachomius (*centre above*) was forced unwillingly to enlist in the Theban army. When they reached Thebes the officers in charge, knowing the feelings of their reluctant recruits, locked them up. They were taken down the Nile as virtual prisoners with scarcely an earthly comfort; but some Christians took pity on them and fed the prisoner-soldiers.

This kindness set Pachomius enquiring about the faith of the Christians, and after his release from the army, he was baptized. He heard of an old desert father named Palaemon, and joined him as a disciple. Palaemon would not use wine or oil in his food, even on Easter day, so as not to lose his understanding of the meaning of Christ's sufferings. He forced Pachomius to collect briars barefooted; and the saint would often bear the pain as a reminder of the nails that entered Christ's feet.

Eventually Pachomius founded a monastery at Tabennisi on the Nile. Palaemon helped him to build his cell, but preferred the solitary life. Saint Pachomius's distinction is to have been the first person to bring monks and nuns together to live under a holy rule. Six other monasteries and a nunnery (on the opposite side of the Nile) were established by the saint, and before he died up to a thousand monks lived under his rule. The monks learned the Bible by heart, worked at their trades, and came together for daily prayer. The austere saint died about the year 346.

Antoninus of Florence (*opposite page*) is best remembered today by the exquisite 'Cloister of St Antoninus' with its wide arches and beautiful ionic capitals, designed in the saint's lifetime by Michelozzo for the monastery of San Marco, Florence, which the saint restored, helped by the wealth of Cosimo de' Medici, in 1436. In the lunettes of the cloister Bernardino Poccetti and others painted scenes from Antoninus's life. And when Giambologna restored and altered the church of San Marco in 1588, he built for the saint's body a superb chapel.

Antoninus was a fellow-monk of the Florentine artist Fra Angelico, and it was partly under his inspiration that the frescoes of San Marco, Fra Angelico's masterpieces, were painted. And in addition to this, the saint's chief literary work, the *Summa Confessionis*, is generally thought to have laid the foundation for modern moral theology.

Antoninus's father, Niccolo Pierozzi, had been a noted lawyer, notary to the Republic of Florence. He called his son Antonio, but because the saint was both small and gentle people called him by the affectionately diminutive 'Antonino' all his life. For forty years or so he served with distinction and humility in Dominican convents throughout Italy. He assisted popes at their councils, was prior of several monastic houses and became an expert in canon law as well as a historian. Then Pope Eugenius IV appointed him Archbishop of Florence and he was consecrated in 1446. During the plague which wreaked havoc in Florence in 1448, Antoninus spared himself no effort and avoided no danger in caring for the sufferers. During the earthquakes of 1453 he was similarly self-giving. He died, loved by the whole city, in 1459.

Walter of L'Esterp

Walter of L'Esterp was abbot of L'Esterp Abbey in France for thirty-eight years, until his death in the year 1070. Even when he went blind in 1062, the saint's fellow-monks begged him to continue in office. So wise were his judgments that Pope Victor II granted the abbot the power even to excommunicate those whom he considered were insufficiently penitent for their sins.

Yet he was also gentle. One day, it is recorded, the monks of L'Esterp to a man forgot that it was Friday and cooked meat for their midday meal. When they remembered the rule about abstaining from meat on the day in the week that Christ was crucified, they were horrified. Walter told them that they would be forgiven. To show that he genuinely believed this, he himself then sat down and ate some meat, which relieved them greatly.

Albert of Bergamo

Albert of Bergamo, like Walter of L'Esterp, was frequently rebuked, though in Saint Albert's case the criticism came from his wife and other relatives who hated his habit of giving away money to the needy.

Having been an Italian farmer, Albert became a tertiary member of the Dominicans. Tertiaries, though closely associated with the monks, lived in the world. Saint Albert was able to make pilgrimages to Compostela (no fewer than eight times), supporting himself on each journey by means of his own labour. He also managed to reach Jerusalem, and made many journeys to Rome. He finally made his home at Cremona. The saint died in the year 1279. After his death numerous miracles were attributed to this farmer-saint, and his generosity to the poor became legendary.

Nereus and Achilleus

These two men (shown here with Domitilla), soldiers in the pretorian guard, became Christians and decided that they must give up fighting. They escaped from the guard, but were discovered and sent in exile to the island of Terracina. There in the reign of Emperor Trajan both saints were beheaded.

The vault in which these men were buried later became the cemetery of Domitilla, situated on the Via Ardeatina. Later Christians erected a church over the spot, and towards the end of the fourth century Pope Damasus inscribed a tombstone in honour of the martyrs. It read:

> 'Nereus and Achilleus the martyrs joined the army and carried out the cruel orders of the tyrant, obeying his will continually out of fear. Then came a miracle of faith. They suddenly gave up their savagery, they were converted, they fled the camp of their evil leader, throwing away their shields, armour and bloody spears. Professing the faith of Christ, they are happy to witness to its triumph. From these words of Damasus understand what great deeds can be brought about by Christ's glory.'

Dominic of the Causeway

Far less important in the eyes of the world was the humble life of Saint Dominic of the Causeway. He too is venerated on this day. A Basque, he failed to join the Benedictines, who turned him down as a member of their order in spite of his repeated attempts to offer himself. All the saint could achieve in following his vocation to live as a monk was to become a hermit near Rioja. He later moved his hermitage to one of the routes taken by pilgrims visiting the shrine of Saint James at Compostela. There he had the simple extremely useful notion of building a road, a bridge and a hospice, solely to ease their journey. He died in the twelfth century

Andrew Hubert Fournet

Matthias

During the French Revolution the parish priest of Maillé, Poitiers, Fr. Andrew Hubert Fournet, went into exile in Spain. After five years he grew ashamed of this ministry in exile and clandestinely returned to serve his parishioners. Often he was almost discovered by the authorities, as he ministered illegally to his flock. Once as government officers arrived at a house where the saint was visiting, he leapt onto a bed. The lady of the house covered him with a sheet, lit candles around the bed, knelt down to pray, and the officers retired thinking somebody had died. At another time a parishioner treated him as a lazy servant and not a faithful priest, beating Saint Andrew over the head as the officers appeared.

Once in fact Saint Andrew Fournet was caught by the authorities. They put him in a carriage to carry him to prison. The saint, insisting on walking, observed that his Saviour had not ridden to his much greater punishment.

Curiously enough, this saint had not wished to become ordained. As a student of law and philosophy at university, he was idle and simply enjoyed himself. He did not even learn to write properly. Only when his parents sent him to stay with an uncle who was parish priest of an extremely poor village did Andrew Hubert Fournet come to his senses and follow his true vocation in life.

When Napoleon allowed the church back openly into France, Andrew once again was officially parish priest at Maillé. With the help of a saintly woman named Agnes Bichier he founded a group of teachers known as the Daughters of the Cross. By the time Andrew Fournet died in 1834, over sixty convents of these sisters had been formed in Poitou, caring for the sick and teaching girls the Christian faith.

After the disciple Judas Iscariot had betrayed Jesus, the other eleven apostles decided to make their number up to twelve again. There were two candidates: a pious, just man named Joseph Barsaba, and Matthias. Jesus's followers gathered together, prayed, and then drew lots to choose the new apostle. The lot fell on Matthias.

This is all we learn of the saint from the New Testament. For some time a Gospel, said to be by Matthias, circulated in the early Christian world, but this has now been lost, apart from a few sentences quoted in other writers. What we know for certain, as St Peter put it when Matthias was chosen as an apostle, is that he was 'one of the men who accompanied us during all the time that the Lord Jesus went in and out among us, beginning from the baptism of John until the day he was taken up from us.' Matthias, says Peter, was 'a witness to Christ's resurrection.'

Isidore the Farm-Labourer

Brendan the Voyager

'I fear that I shall journey alone, that the way will be dark; I fear the unknown land, the presence of my King and the sentence of my judge.'

The dying words of St Brendan the Voyager to his sister, Abbess Brig

Brendan sailed in skin-covered coracles, from Ireland to Scotland, then to England and Wales. His most famous voyage, in search of the promised land, was described in a famous saga known as the *Navigatio*, which indicates that Brendan reached Greenland or even North America. It is still possible to construct a coracle according to the instructions of the *Navigatio*, and to sail it from Ireland to Newfoundland.

Brendan was born near Tralee on the west coast of Ireland, and he was brought up by a saint called Ita, who taught him three things that God truly loves: 'the true faith of a pure heart; the simple religious life; and bountifulness inspired by Christian charity.' (She added three things that God hates: 'a scowling face; obstinate wrong-doing; and too much confidence in money'.)

Brendan founded several monasteries, the most renowned being at Clonfert, a centre famous for missionary work, where he is said to have directed three thousand monks. He died in 578.

In the year 1070 a poor man and his wife in Madrid bore a son, who became a labourer on the great estate of a rich landowner, named John de Vergas. The boy's parents had given him the name of their patron saint, Isidore of Seville. He grew to be such a fine and hardworking ploughman that John de Vergas treated him as a brother, allowing him to worship in church daily – though Isidore took care that this never interfered with his work.

Many used to say that to make up for the time he spent in prayer, angels and other heavenly helpers would assist his ploughing. Isidore had no truck with such suggestions. 'I work alone,' he insisted, 'looking only to God for my strength.'

Although he remained poor, he gave whatever he could to the poor. The tale is recounted that one winter he was carrying corn to be milled when he saw that the birds could find nothing to eat. He gave them half of his corn – though the sack is said to have been miraculously refilled by the time he reached the mill.

Paschal Baylon

Venantius

From the age of seven until he was twenty-four Paschal Baylon was a shepherd. His parents lived on the borders of Castile and Aragon, and their flock of sheep was their most valuable possession. They were too poor to send their son to school. Paschal learned to read and then to write of his own accord, using as text-book the only volume he had, a prayer-book containing the Hours of the Blessed Virgin Mary. He was a conscientious shepherd, though sometimes the sheep would damage neighbouring vineyards (perhaps during those times when their guardian was kneeling in prayer). Then Paschal insisted on paying for the damage out of his own poor wages.

At the age of eighteen he had tried to join some local Franciscan friars, but his application was at first scorned. When he was finally allowed to join the order, he surpassed all of the rest in his devotion to his duties, in his mortification, in his love of the poor and sick, and in his upright commitment to the truth.

Little is known about the Venantius celebrated on this day in the Christian year. Legend has it that he died in 257, a martyr at the age of seventeen. The story is filled chiefly with an account of the savagery of his persecutors, who scourged him, burned him with flaming torches, hanged him upside-down over a fire, knocked his teeth out, broke his jaw, threw him to lions (who merely licked his feet), tossed him over over a high cliff and finally cut off his head.

Dunstan

Dunstan, nephew of the Archbishop of Canterbury, spent a privileged youth at the court of King Athelstan and eventually became abbot of Glastonbury.

English monastic life had almost totally disappeared as a result of the Viking invasions. Dunstan set about vigorously reviving it. He founded monasteries at Bath, Exeter, Malmesbury, and elsewhere, drawing up new rules for their good order. He installed monks in Winchester, in Chertsey, Surrey, and Milton Abbas, Dorset and restored the old abbey of Abingdon.

After a period of exile King Edgar recalled him to be Archbishop of Canterbury in the year 960. There he founded an abbey to the east of the city, along with three churches dedicated to St Mary, Saints Peter and Paul, and St Pancras. As a skilled metalworker, scribe and bellfounder himself, he stimulated the revival of church art and illuminated manuscripts. He also loved to play the harp and wrote several fine hymns.

St Bernardino of Siena

'Jesus, crucified for me, with the nails of your love fasten my whole self to you.'

St Bernardino of Siena

Bernardino of Siena

At the age of seven Bernardino, the son of the governor of Massa Marittima in Italy, was orphaned. An aunt took charge of him until at the age of seventeen he joined a confraternity of the Blessed Virgin. Three years later he took charge of the hospital of La Scala, Siena, at a time when a deadly plague had killed most of the staff and many of the patients.

After the plague was over Bernardino decided to join the Franciscans, and in 1303 became a member of the convent at Colombaio. He had delayed entering the order to nurse his aunt in her last bed-ridden illness. Now he virtually retired from the world for twelve years.

Suddenly a new calling came to him. He left the convent for a time to become a fiery mission preacher. First he preached at Milan, attracting huge crowds. He travelled throughout most of Italy on foot, preaching for up to three hours at a time. He would castigate vice and then hold up a placard with the sign of the name of Jesus, I H S, written on it, urging the congregations to turn to the one symbolized by those letters. Once a man whose livelihood came from making playing cards complained that Bernardino had so successfully preached against gambling that the trade was ruined. Bernardino gave him a new, even more profitable trade, printing cards with the sign I H S.

So powerful was the saint's preaching that some complaints were made to the pope. But once Bernardino's life was examined, he was completely exonerated. The pope told him to preach whatever he wished.

Later Bernardino was offered the bishoprics of Siena, of Ferrara and of Urbino. He turned them all down, preferring to continuing as a preacher. But in 1430 he did accept the post of vicar general of his religious order. He reformed it, swelling its ranks from three hundred to over four thousand members. He resigned to start missionary work again in 1442, dying two years later on the way to preach in Naples.

Andrew Bobola

Humility

Andrew Bobola was a Polish aristocrat who joined the Jesuits in 1611 when he was twenty. At first he worked as a parish priest in Vilna, Lithuania, but in 1630 he was made superior of the Jesuit house at Bobrinsk just as a dreadful plague broke out there. Andrew's kindness to the dying and his care for the dead, in spite of the great personal danger of catching the disease, impressed many.

In 1636 this brave man set out as a missionary, travelling in Lithuania for more than twenty years. He was so successful at converting men and women that his enemies called him the 'thief of souls'. Deep religious divisions were in those days made worse by intolerance and by marauding Russians, Cossacks and Tartars who continually raided Poland and tormented the Christians there. In 1652 Andrew Bobola took charge of a house in Pinsk where fleeing Jesuits could be sheltered. He ran it for five years, before being captured in a Cossack raid on the city. He was tortured and then killed by the sword.

Humility was born to wealthy parents in Faenza, Italy, in the year 1226, and baptized Rosanna. She longed to enter a convent from her earliest years, to model herself on St John and the Blessed Virgin who stood by Jesus on the cross. But her parents insisted instead that she take a husband and forced her to marry a nobleman of Faenza named Ugoletto. He was apparently frivolous and uncaring, mocking his bride's spiritual ways. Her sorrows were increased when the two boys she bore Ugoletto died not long after being baptized.

What brought Ugoletto to decency was a dangerous disease, nine years after his marriage. He barely escaped death. Chastened, he agreed to allow Rosanna to enter a convent. They chose a mixed monastery, that of St Perpetua at Faenza, where he went to live as a brother and she became a nun, taking the name Humility. Soon she decided that she needed even more discipline than the rules of the nunnery demanded. One of her relatives built for her a cell, against the wall of the church of St Apollinaris. A hole was cut into the wall, so that she could follow the services inside the church. Then she was bricked into her cell. Her spiritual welfare was in the care of Vallombrosan monks. Each day she ate only bread and water and sometimes a few herbs. She slept on her knees, her head resting against the wall.

After twelve years of this life, she was persuaded to leave her cell by the master general of the Vallombrosan order, who begged her to become abbess of the first Vallombrosan nunnery. She helped to found this nunnery at Faenza, before becoming abbess of a second one in Florence. And in spite of her heroic fasting and savagely austere life, she was eighty years old when she died.

St Humility

Desiderius

David of Scotland

David I of Scotland (*below, left*) was the son of Margaret of Scotland, queen and saint, and was born in 1084. In 1113 he married Matilda, the widow of the Earl of Northampton, on whose behalf he waged a long war – unsuccessfully – against King Stephen for the throne of England.

As King of Scotland from the year 1124 he was much more successful, ruling with firmness, justice and liberality. He also learned the spirit of Cistercian monks from Ailred of Rievaulx, who for a time was David's steward. Scottish monasticism began to flower from the start of David's reign and countless almshouses, leper-hospitals and infirmaries were set up.

The monasteries established under David's patronage were superb architecturally as well as spiritually. The king refounded Melrose Abbey on the main road from Edinburgh to the south, and it remained one of the richest houses in Scotland. David also founded Jedburgh Abbey (in the year 1138), filling it with monks from Beauvais in France. At Dundrennan in Dumfries and Galloway he founded in 1142 a splendid abbey and staffed it with Cistercians from Rievaulx. The monks were so well managed that they even started their own shipping line and traded from the Solway Firth a mile and a half away.

Born at Autun in Gaul in the mid-sixth century, Desiderius rose to be Bishop of Vienne. This was a time of much laxity among the clergy and the new bishop set about reforming them. He was ready to rebuke the highest in the land for their immorality. One of these was Queen Brunhildis. Desiderius found the behaviour of her courtiers shameful, and said so. The Queen appealed to Pope Gregory the Great, accusing the bishop of being too much interested in the writings of pagans. In fact the bishop was merely teaching such subjects as Latin grammar.

For several years the bishop was banished but eventually Gregory the Great came to see that he was innocent of Brunhildis's charges and restored him to Vienne. Desiderius also attacked the queen's grandson, King Thierry of Burgundy, whose life was as immoral as his grandmother's. Thierry found a new false accusation against the bishop, alleging that Desiderius had an immoral relationship with a lady named Justa. As he was being taken into detention, three hired murderers set on him (at a place now called Saint-Didier-sur-Chalaronne) and cruelly put him to death.

Madeleine Barat

Madeleine Sophie Barat was born in Burgundy, France, ten years before the French Revolution of 1789. Her father owned a small vineyard and also worked as a cooper. Her elder brother acted as Madeleine's godfather, and he determined to give her an education at least as good as that of any boy of the time. Madeleine loved her lessons and her Latin and Greek, her mathematics and science and history, gave her enormous pleasure. For a while the brother was imprisoned during the Revolution, but he escaped and took his sister to Paris, where she studied religion.

A group of French priests decided to establish a society of women devoted to teaching girls. Their leader heard of Madeleine, and in 1800 received her and three companions as nuns, commissioning them to found a society to educate girls. They started their first school at Amiens in 1801.

Madeleine was scarcely twenty-three years old, younger than any of her companions, but unanimously they elected her their superior. She ran the order for the next sixty-three years. Times were not always easy. The July Revolution of 1830 banished the sisters for a time to Switzerland. But Madeleine was glad to travel, opening schools outside as well as inside France. By 1865 her society had founded over a hundred houses and schools in twelve countries, including the United States of America.

'Hard work, dangerous for an imperfect soul, brings a great harvest for those who love the Lord.'

St Madeleine Barat

Philip Neri

Augustine of Canterbury

'A joyful heart is more easily made perfect than one that is cast down.'

St Philip Neri

Philip Neri was a layman until, in 1550, one of his friends insisted he should be ordained. He lived in a community of priests in the church of San Girolamo della Carita, and more and more disciples (including some of the highest dignitaries of the church) came to confess to him and seek his counsel. He became rector of the church of San Giovanni in 1564 and there installed five young priests to share a common table and common worship. They would summon others to prayer in their room or 'Oratory' and gradually became known as Oratorians. Soon Philip was being called 'the apostle of Rome'. Prayer and sermons, pilgrimages and music, the liturgy and godly conversation marked the daily life of this company, which continued to grow well after the saint's death.

In the year 596 Pope Gregory the Great sent the prior of St Andrew's monastery in Rome, along with forty monks, to preach to the English. By the time they reached southern France the company had heard so many stories about the fierce English that they wanted to turn back. Gregory refused to hear of it. 'It is better never to

undertake any high enterprise than to abandon it once it has started.' he wrote, adding, 'The greater the labour, the greater will be the glory of your eternal reward.'

Gregory persuaded some French priests to aid the mission and Augustine with his party landed in England in 597. He found a welcome from King Ethelbert, a pagan whose wife Bertha was the daughter of the King of Paris and already a Christian. Soon Ethelbert was baptized. Augustine was consecrated archbishop of the English, and he established his see at Canterbury. The saint was able to found two more bishoprics – at London and Rochester, and many came to learn from him; but much of the land still lay outside his jurisdiction at the time of his death seven years after he first reached England: some bishops in Wales and the south-west held fast to their Celtic practices.

Germain of Paris

The oldest and greatest of the medieval abbeys of Paris, Saint-Germain-des-Prés, was in fact founded in the saint's own lifetime – in the year 558 by King Childebert I. Saint Germain consecrated it to St Vincent and to the Holy Cross. When Germain died on 28 May 576, at the age of eighty, he was buried in this abbey, in a sumptuous tomb which the French revolutionaries destroyed; and when he was canonized in the year 754, Saint-Germain-des-Prés was reconsecrated in his name.

That King Childebert I should have founded such a place of Christian learning is a tribute to the influence of Saint Germain. Born near Autun in the year 496, he had been ordained there in 530 and ten years later was elected abbot of the monastery of St Symphorien in his own city. He was in Paris when the bishopric fell vacant and was appointed both bishop and archchaplain to Childebert.

In no way did the great office affect the saint's pattern of life. Always austere, he was continuously pestered by the poor and never repulsed them. When he died in 576, the great poet Venantius Fortunatus wrote a eulogy of his life which, in spite of its many incredible miracles and legends, fittingly thanks God for a vigorous and noble saint.

Joachim

Joachim, an Italian abbot, is reputed to have been extremely vain in his younger days, and to have conquered this by great austerities. The story is told that the Empress Constance summoned him to her palace at Palermo, seeking to be shriven by the abbot one Good Friday. Saint Joachim found Constance on a lofty throne, set up incongruously in her prayer-room. She motioned him to sit on a lowly stool beside her. Joachim responded: 'As I now occupy the place of Christ and you that of the penitent Mary Magdalene, get down, sit on the ground and confess your sins honestly to me. Otherwise I shall not listen to you.' The empress humbly obeyed the abbot's apostolic authority.

Theodosia

Theodosia lived in Constantinople in the mid-eighth century when the emperor was destroying all pictures of Jesus, his mother and the saints. One image of Christ was greatly loved by Theodosia. The emperor sent one of his officers to smash it to the ground. When he climbed a ladder to reach the icon and perform this sacrilegious act, Theodosia shook it so hard that he fell off and was killed.

Not content with this, Theodosia led a group of women to stone the palace of the heretic Patriarch of Constantinople, who was supporting the destruction of icons. The authorities took their revenge. All these warlike Christian women were punished, but Theodosia, who had inspired their rebellion, was viciously tortured and killed.

Joan of Arc

Petronilla

St Petronilla

When England and Burgundy joined forces against the French, Joan, though barely thirteen, believed she had received visions urging her to save France. She failed to persuade the French commander, Robert de Vaucouleurs, that her visions were genuine. She therefore prophesied that the French would be defeated near Orleans and in February 1429 this happened. Now Joan was granted an audience with the Dauphin. He appeared in disguise and was astonished when the maid recognized him. A group of theologians decided that Joan was divinely inspired, and she was granted permission to lead the French army against the British. Wearing white armour and carrying a banner inscribed 'Jesus, Maria' and with the symbol of the Holy Trinity, Joan led the French to Orleans and routed the English. She won a second victory at Patay and the third at Troyes. She brought the Dauphin to a sense of responsibility, and on 17 July 1429 he was crowned King Charles VII.

Then, on 24 May 1430, the armies of Burgundy captured Joan near Compiègne and sold her to the English. Accused of witchcraft and heresy, she was burned to death in the market place at Rouen in 1431.

In the cemetery of Domitilla, Rome, is a fresco dating from the fourth century which shows Saint Petronilla about to be put to death. She had refused to marry a nobleman named Flaccus, preferring to devote herself totally to her Saviour.

Amongst the legends connected with Petronilla is the notion – no doubt derived partly from her name – that she was the daughter of Saint Peter. Most scholars do not accept this; but it is certain that around the middle of the third century a young virgin of this name was martyred because of her steadfast Christian faith.

Cantius, Cantianus and Cantianella

Two brothers, Cantius and Cantianus, along with their sister Cantianella, were members of a noble Roman family the Anicii. They were left as orphans but their guardian, a man named Protus, happened to be a Christian.

He brought up his three charges in the faith. When the persecution under the Emperor Diocletian started, the three orphans and their guardian decided on flight. Before leaving Rome they sold their home and possessions. Apart from what they needed for their journey, they gave the proceeds to the poor.

Then the fugitives escaped to Aquilea. They were pursued and captured at a place called Aquae Gradatae. Although all four knew that the penalty for holding fast to Christianity would be death, not one agreed to make a sacrifice to the pagan gods. On 31 May in the year 304, Cantius, Cantianus, Cantianella and their guardian Protus were all beheaded.

June

'Finally, all of you be likeminded, compassionate, loving the brethren, tender-hearted, humbleminded, not rendering evil for evil, or reviling for reviling, but instead paying back with a blessing. You are called to do this, so as to inherit a blessing yourselves.'

Peter (June 29)

Justin Martyr

St Justin Martyr

'Is this not the task of philosophy to enquire about the divine?'

St Justin Martyr

Justin's parents were Greek pagans, living at Flavia Neapolis in Samaria. Justin made a long study of philosophy, finding that the teachings of Plato, though by no means identical with Christianity, led him to embrace the teachings of Jesus. He became a bold defender of Christianity, trying to show that faith was compatible with rational thought. Thus Justin can be regarded as the first great Christian philosopher.

At a time when Christians were continually subject to persecution by the state authorities, his first open defence of Christianity was addressed to the Emperor Antoninus Pius, along with the emperor's three adopted sons. His second great public defence, written about the year 161, was addressed to the Roman Senate itself.

Justin did not believe that everything he had learned before becoming a Christian must necessarily be untrue. 'Those who have been inspired by the creative word of God, see through this a measure of the truth,' he wrote. 'We are taught that Christ, the first-born of God, is the word of which the whole human race partakes, so that those who before him lived according to reason may be called Christian, even though accounted atheists.' Justin wanted to embrace people like the Greek Socrates and the Jewish father Abraham into the fold of Christianity.

Twice he visited Rome, but his public writings made him suspect to the authorities. A rival philosopher named Crescens denounced him, five other men and a woman, about the year 165. Rusticus, the prefect of Rome, asked if they would sacrifice to idols. Justin replied, 'No right-minded man forsakes truth for falsehood,' and so all seven were beheaded.

Erasmus

Erasmus (*left, opposite*) – popularly known as Saint Elmo – was a Syrian who may well have been consecrated Bishop of Formiae, Campagna, Italy. When Christians were being persecuted by the Emperor Diocletian, Saint Erasmus took refuge on Mount Lebanon, living alone on what ravens brought him.

Captured by his enemies, he was brought before Diocletian and beaten with clubs weighted with lead and with whips. When it was perceived that he was still alive, the saint was rolled in tar and set alight; but still he survived. Thrown into prison with the intention of letting him die of starvation, Erasmus managed to escape.

He was recaptured in the Roman province of Illyricum, after boldly preaching and converting numerous pagans to the Christian way. This time his tortures included being forced to sit in a heated iron chair. Finally he was killed, about the year 303, when his stomach was cut open and his intestines were wound around a windlass.

Since sailors use a windlass to wind up the anchor of their ships, Erasmus became the patron saint of seafarers. Sometimes after a storm blue electrical discharges appear at a ship's masthead, and this is still known as 'St Elmo's fire'.

Pothinus and Companions

Pothinus and his companions, who are also specially venerated on this day, were martyrs at Lyons in France in the year 177. Pothinus, who was bishop, was ninety years old. He and forty-seven of his followers were put to death under the decrees of the Emperor Marcus Aurelius. The bishop himself died after merciless handling by a savage mob. A slave girl named Blandina, racked until she perished, kept repeating the simple words, 'I am a Christian.' Two men, Maturus and Sactus, were roasted to death on an iron chair. All forty-eight martyrs suffered tortures of equal viciousness. Not one wavered in the faith.

Martyrs of Uganda

King Mwanga of Uganda took as chief steward a young Christian named Joseph Musaka Balikuddembe. Joseph disliked the king's debauched ways, especially how he tried to corrupt other young men of Uganda, and the steward tried to protect them. Mwanga distrusted foreign visitors, fearing they might report his evil ways to the British government, which had given him his power. In October 1885 Mwanga ordered his followers to kill an Anglican missionary, Bishop James Hannington. The Catholic steward Joseph protested at the murder of a fellow Christian. The following month Mwanga had him burnt alive. 'A Christian who gives his life for God is not afraid to die,' Joseph proclaimed. 'Mwanga has condemned me without cause; but tell him I forgive him from my heart.'

Six months later Mwanga's savagery was even worse. He discovered that a fourteen-year old page had been receiving instruction in the Catholic faith. Denis Sebuggwago, who had been teaching the page, was killed with a butcher's cleaver. The king then ordered every Protestant and Catholic living in the royal enclosure to be put to death. That night the master of the pages baptized five of them including his son Kizito. Next day Mwanga raged at the Christians, but scarcely anyone gave way out of fear. Thirty-two Catholics and Protestants were led to a place called Namugongo to be burned to death. Some were killed on the way. One of these, a district judge named Matthias Kalemba, declared, 'God will rescue me. But you will not see how he does it, because he will take my soul and leave you only my body.' He was cut in pieces and left to die slowly by the roadside.

The rest of the martyrs were taken to Namugongo and forced to lie down on reed mats. Wrapped up in the mats and tightly bound, they were laid side by side. Fuel was poured over them, and they were all set alight. As their executioners sang barbarously, the martyrs died confidently praying to their Saviour.

Francis Caracciolo

In 1588 a priest of Genoa, John Augustine Adorno, decided to start an association of priests who would combine their pastoral duties with the strictest possible discipline. He sent a letter to a friend named Ascanio Caracciolo. By error it was delivered to Francis. Francis was so drawn to the idea that he decided God must have misdirected the letter to him. He offered his help to Adorno.

The Pope so approved of their ideas, he wanted them to set up a similar association in Spain. At first the Spanish authorities simply refused but later the saint managed

to form associations in Alcala, Valladolid and Madrid. And when Adorno died young, Francis was elected first general of the new order of priests.

When, at the age of twenty-two, he had almost died of a severe illness, he had devoted his life to serving others as a priest, giving all he had to the poor. These ideals he carried over into the new association of priests until he died in 1608 aged only forty-four, crying, 'To Heaven, to Heaven!' Francis Caracciolo is on the right in the picture above.

Boniface

Norbert

On the peak of Mount Gudenberg at Geismar in Germany, grew a huge oak, which the heathen venerated as sacred to the god Thor. Boniface arrived at Geismar and announced that he was about to cut it down. A huge crowd of pagans gathered, in the belief that their god would strike him dead. But Boniface had hardly begun to strike at the tree with his axe when it split into four and crashed to the ground. The pagans were astonished. Many of them became Christians; and Boniface built a chapel dedicated to Saint Peter out of the wood of Thor's tree.

Boniface had been born around the year 680 at Crediton in Devonshire, England. Educated at monastery schools near Exeter and at Winchester, he decided to become a missionary to the continent. Pope Gregory II made him a regional bishop in Germany. Boniface started a monastery at Ohrdruf in Thuringia. He brought English monks there as missionaries. Then he moved to Bavaria, founding missionary monasteries at Reichenau, Murbach and Fritzlar. In the year 735 he and his disciple Sturmius founded the most famous of all these monasteries, at Fulda. In 747 the pope made him supreme bishop of Germany, and then papal legate to Gaul.

The son of a count, Norbert exploited the church for his own profit until he had an experience akin to that of St Paul on the way to Damascus. As with Paul, Norbert heard the commands of his Lord. Jesus said, 'Turn from evil and do good; seek peace and pursue it.'

Norbert was a changed man. Ordained priest in the year 1115, he became a monk. But his new austerity was too much for some of the lax canons at Xanten. They resented the attempts of the former playboy-courtier to persuade them to reform their own lives. In 1118, at the Council of Fritzlar, they denounced Norbert as a hypocrite who preached without any proper commission.

Norbert travelled barefoot in the snow to meet the pope at Saint-Gilles in the Languedoc. Resigning his canonry, giving all his remaining goods to the poor, he begged to be allowed to carry on preaching. Pope Gelasius II told him to preach wherever he wished throughout France. Soon Norbert became the most famous missionary of his time. In 1120, Norbert and thirteen followers formed the first group of monks known as Premonstratensian Canons. He died in 1134 at Magdeburg in Germany.

St Norbert

Meriadoc

William of York

St William of York

'Poverty is a remover of cares and the mother of holiness.'

St Meriadoc

Meriadoc, though venerated especially in Cornwall and northern France, was a Welshman who lived in the fifth or sixth century. He came to Cornwall and founded several churches, one of which at Camborne was once dedicated to him. He became renowned in these parts and a miracle play in Cornish still survives, recounting his legendary exploits.

He then crossed over into Brittany, where his memory is still strong. In the sixteenth-century church at Plougasnou is a reliquary containing what may well be part of Meriadoc's skull. At Stival is preserved what purports to be his bell. Placed on the heads of the deaf and those suffering migraine, it is said to heal them. Some documents state that Meriadoc even became Bishop of Vannes at a time when it was one of the most important cities of Brittany.

Meriadoc had been a rich man. Before becoming a hermit he gave all his money to poor clerics, distributing his lands to the needy. So great became his reputation for sanctity that he feared he would become vain and retired even further from the world. Instead of the silks and purple that he once wore, Meriadoc now dressed in rags, eating simple food, living in complete poverty.

When his relatives tried to make him leave his new life and return to the world, he told the Viscount of Rohan who had come with these relatives that he would be better engaged extirpating the thieves and robbers of the neighbourhood. The viscount took the saint at his word, and a great evil was removed from Brittany.

Although Meriadoc was unanimously elected Bishop of Vannes, he took the bishopric reluctantly. After his consecration he continued a life of abstinence and love for the poor. He died kissing his brethren and crying, 'Into your hands, Lord, I commend my Spirit.'

William had impressed many as canon and treasurer of York Minster and in 1142, after the death of Archbishop Thurstan, he was elected archbishop in turn by a majority of the cathedral chapter.

At this point the smooth running of William's life ended. Cistercian monks in the diocese of York claimed that he had paid to be elevated to the archbishopric. Others said that his friendship with King Stephen gave him an improper influence in securing election to the see. The Archbishop of Canterbury was reluctant to consecrate William under such a cloud of accusation. For a time even the pope hesitated, before finally agreeing to support William. Henry of Blois, who was both Bishop of Winchester and King Stephen's brother accordingly consecrated William and he took up his duties as archbishop.

Matters soon became difficult again. William failed to receive the official 'pallium', symbol of the pope's authority, before the pope who sent it had died. The papal legate took the pallium back to Rome. The new pope was a Cistercian and sided with the archbishop's opponents. William visited Rome to persuade the pope of his credentials. But the pope suspended him. To make things worse, a group of his followers now violently attacked some of the monks of Fountains Abbey, itself a Cistercian foundation, and set fire to the monastery farms. The Abbot of Fountains had been William's rival for the see of York in the first place.

A council held at Rheims in 1147 now deposed William. He went to stay with Henry of Blois, and spent several chastened years living as a monk at Winchester. Only when both the pope and the Abbot of Fountains were dead was he able to make a successful appeal to Rome and return in triumph to York. Enormous crowds gathered on a bridge over the River Ouse as William arrived. The bridge collapsed. Fortunately no-one was injured, and this was taken as a sign of good things to come. William, however, had reached the end of his life; he died a month after his return to York in 1154.

Columba

Landry of Paris

Columba (*below*) was born in County Donegal, Ireland, and spent fifteen years preaching to his native Irish and founding monasteries – the greatest of which were at Derry, Durrow and Kells.

In 563 Columba sailed to the Scottish island of Iona, there to found a monastery that for centuries was the most famous in the west. Iona became the heart of Celtic Christianity. Daughter houses sprang up in England and on the Scottish mainland. The next thirty-four years of Columba's life were spent in missionary service.

On 8 June 597 Columba was copying out the psalms. At the verse, 'They that love the Lord shall lack no good thing,' he stopped, and said that his cousin Baithin must do the rest. He died the next day.

Landry was consecrated Bishop of Paris in the year 650, and he soon perceived that some proper institution was needed to care for the many sick poor of Paris. Close by his cathedral he built the first major hospital in the city, and dedicated it to Saint Christopher. So great was the need for this hospital that even Landry's munificence scarcely cared for those who, through no fault of their own, needed care and attention. The Parisians used to say that here in every single bed was a sick person, a dying person and a dead body. The hospital later changed its name to the Hôtel-Dieu, and still today, north of Notre Dame, you can see the modern successor of Landry's great foundation.

'Alone with none but
    Thee, my God,
  I journey on my way;
What need I fear when
    Thou art near,
  Oh King of night and
    day?
More safe am I within
    Thy hand
  Than if a host did
    round me stand.'

Attributed to St Columba

'We know for certain that Columba left successors distinguished for their purity of life, their love of God, and their loyalty to the rules of the monastic life.'

The Venerable Bede

Barnabas

St Methodius

The Acts of the Apostles describes Barnabas as 'a good man, full of the Holy Spirit and of faith'. His parents had called him Joseph, but when he sold all his goods and gave the money to the apostles in Jerusalem, they gave him a new name: Barnabas, which means 'son of consolation'.

He was one of the first to welcome St Paul, the former persecutor of the early Church, and he persuaded the Christians of Jerusalem to accept Paul's claim that he was now a believer in Jesus. He, John Mark and Paul went together on the first missionary journey of the Christian church. They landed at Cyprus, and for this reason Barnabas is honoured as the founder of the Cypriot church.

Barnabas was a man of considerable determination and courage. He was with Paul when they preached for the first time to non-Jews, and when both of them were taken for pagan gods at Lystra in Lycaonia. Once Paul fell out with John Mark. In spite of Paul's extremely forceful character, Barnabas took Mark's side. The Book of Acts says, 'There arose a sharp contention between them. Barnabas took Mark with him and sailed away to Cyprus.' Paul chose a new ally, Silas, and went elsewhere to strengthen the churches.

Leo III

Leo III succeeded Pope Hadrian I on 26 December 795. Hadrian's two nephews were both enraged at the election, since both hoped to be made pope themselves. In 799 they incited a gang of young nobles to attack Leo. On St Mark's day Leo was riding in a procession when these roughs dragged him from his horse, tried to cut out his tongue and attempted to blind him. Leo escaped to the monastery of Erasmus with the help of the Duke of Spoleto, and there recovered.

Leo enlisted the help of the most powerful layman of the age, Charlemagne, who sent troops to guard the pope as he journeyed from Paderborn in Germany back to Rome. Charlemagne appointed learned commissioners to examine whether any fault in Leo could account for the attacks made on him. They found none.

The following year Leo crowned Charlemagne as Holy Roman Emperor in St Peter's Rome. He and the emperor now worked side by side to resolve quarrels throughout the Holy Roman Empire, and to combat the spread of Islam through the depredations of the Saracens, and to Charlemagne's bounty can be attributed the churches Leo restored both in Rome and Ravenna. The saint died two years after his great ally, Charlemagne, in the year 816.

Antony of Padua

Antony of Padua was small in stature and even chubby. In statues he often carries the child Jesus and a lily. Yet he was one of the most powerful preachers of the thirteenth century, had a voice that could carry for leagues, it seems, and could by his brilliant personality overwhelm the sinful and make them turn to God.

Until the age of twenty-five he lived a quiet life as a canon in Portugal, where he had been born in 1195. It was his ambition to convert Moslems to Christianity, but the moment he arrived in Morocco Antony fell so ill that he had no choice but to return home.

The ship he was travelling in was blown off course and landed in Sicily. For a while he lived as a hermit near Forli. One day some Franciscans arrived for an act of worship, but no one had prepared a sermon so Antony stood up and preached and his remarkable talent was discovered. Antony was commissioned by the head of his order to preach the Gospel throughout Lombardy. From then on his skills were used to the uttermost by the Church. Occasionally he took another post, as a teacher, for instance, at the Universities of Montpellier and Toulouse, but always he was recalled to missionize in Italy.

By the time he died, aged no more than thirty-six, on 13 June 1231, his fame was assured. He was canonized within a year. His body was enshrined at Padua, and a great basilican church was begun in 1232. Fittingly for one who had hoped to work in Morocco, the building has domes and a bell-tower built like an Arab minaret. Antony's tomb lies behind the altar of his chapel in the north transept of this Basilica di Sant'Antonio, with nine superb reliefs lining the walls.

Methodius

Methodius, who was born in Syracuse at a time when many people in the Eastern Church were engaged in destroying all images of God, Jesus and the saints, courageously defended the attempt of Christian artists to inspire the faithful by means of beautiful icons.

He had first gone to Constantinople intending to be a courtier of the Emperor, but a holy monk so much impressed him that he decided to retire from the world. He built a monastery on the island of Chios, intending to stay there for the rest of his life. But the Patriarch of Constantinople, St Nicephorus, wanted Methodius by his side. Both men stood out against the destroyers of icons, but Nicephorus was deposed and sent into exile. Methodius too was forced to flee, but in the year 821 returned to Constantinople with a letter from the pope demanding the reinstatement of Nicephorus. Instead the emperor ordered Methodius to be scourged and exiled himself. For seven years he was kept in a dungeon with three thieves, one of whose corpse after death was left to rot in the dungeon alongside the three living prisoners.

In 842 the emperor died and his widow Theodora took control of the empire as regent for her small son. Happily, she supported those who defended icons. In 843 Methodius became Patriarch of Constantinople.

He had five more years to live. Speedily he summoned a council to declare icons lawful in the church. An annual 'feast of Orthodoxy', still observed in the Eastern Church, was instituted to mark this victory for reason and devotion. The saint died of dropsy on 14 June 847.

St Antony of Padua

'Consider every day that you are then for the first time – as it were – beginning; and always act with the same fervour as on the first day you began.'

St Antony of Padua

Vitus

No-one is certain *when* Saint Vitus lived; we are certain that he *did* live, probably during the reign of the Emperor Diocletian. Tradition has it that Vitus was born in Sicily and secretly became a Christian at a very early age, probably about seven years old. His tutor and his nurse accompanied him on his journeys about Sicily, when his godliness and (some say) power to work miracles came to the notice of the Roman authorities, who tried to convert the saint back to paganism.

Various tortures to which the saint was submitted have been transformed into miracles. For instance, when thrown to a hungry lion, the saint found that the beast merely licked him affectionately.

Vitus's relics were transported first to Paris and then to Saxony. They were reputed to possess many healing properties, especially when epileptics prayed before them. So Vitus (*left of picture*) is the patron of epileptics, as well as of those suffering from chorea (which is still popularly called 'St Vitus's dance'). He is said to be able to avert poisoning by dog or snake bite, and is also invoked as the patron saint of dancers and actors.

Cyricus and Julitta

At the beginning of the fourth century, when persecution was raging against Christians under the Emperor Diocletian, a wealthy and pious woman named Julitta was widowed with a three-year-old son named Cyricus.

As a Christian Julitta decided that life in her native Iconium in Lycaonia was too dangerous. Taking Cyricus and two maids, she fled to Seleucia and to her alarm found that the governor there, Alexander, was savagely persecuting Christians. The four fugitives journeyed on to Tarsus. Unfortunately Alexander was paying a visit to that city when the fugitives were recognized.

Julitta was put on trial. She brought her young son with her to the courtroom. She refused to answer any questions about herself, save to say that she was a Christian. The court pronounced sentence: Julitta was to be stretched on the rack and then beaten. The guards, about to lead Julitta away, separated Cyricus from his mother. The child was crying, and Alexander the governor, in a vain attempt to pacify him, took Cyricus on his knee. Terrified and longing to run back to his mother, Cyricus kicked the governor and scratched his face. Alexander stood up in a rage and flung the infant down some steps, fracturing the boy's skull and killing him.

Cyricus's mother did not weep. Instead she thanked God. Her son had been granted the crown of a martyr. This made the governor even angrier. He decreed that her sides should be ripped apart with hooks, and then she was beheaded. Both she and Cyricus were flung outside the city, on the heap of bodies belonging to criminals, but the two maids rescued the corpses of the mother and child and buried them in a nearby field.

Rainerius of Pisa

As a young man in Pisa, Italy, Rainerius lived dissolutely. But one day his aunt introduced him to a monk of the monastery of St Vitus, who persuaded Rainerius that there is more to life than dissipation and self-indulgence.

So great was Rainerius's sorrow at his wasted life that his parents feared for his sanity. A changed man already, Rainerius visited those places connected with the earthly life of Jesus. In a dream he discovered that his purse was filled with scalding, burning tar. Only water finally extinguished the flames. Rainerius decided that it signified that only water – not strong drink – could put out his burning bodily desires. From then on he drank only water. He also gave up luxuries, eating only on Sundays and Thursdays. Often he went about barefoot. And on his return to Pisa, he decided to live a humble life in monasteries – though he never became officially either a monk or a preacher, nor was he ordained priest.

He died in the monastery of St Vitus in the year 1160. Today he is the patron saint of Pisa, known in that city as San Ranieri. Twenty years after Rainerius's death the architect and sculptor Bonnano Pisano built a superb entrance to the cathedral of Pisa, with twenty-four panels showing scenes from the life of Christ. He called it the doorway of San Ranieri.

St Cyricus

Gregory Barbarigo

Romuald

When Gregory Barbarigo was born in Venice in 1625, Catholics and Protestants in Europe had been waging a vicious war against each other for seven years, a war that was to last for thirty years. Gregory Barbarigo was in his early twenties when the Venetians chose him to go with their ambassador to Münster, where in 1648 the Treaty of Westphalia was drawn up, bringing peace to Europe. At the conference was the papal representative, Fabio Chigi. He found Gregory Barbarigo to be a quite exceptional young man, and they became friends. When Fabio Chigi became pope he did not forget the impression the Venetian had made at Münster in 1648: he made Gregory Bishop of Bergamo. Three years later he created Gregory a cardinal, and in 1664 he consecrated him Bishop of Padua.

Gregory set about improving the training of the clergy, endowing an excellent college for them, building up its library, setting up its own printing press, appointing teachers who knew the writings of the church fathers and who were devoted to the Scriptures. Altogether this saintly man served the diocese of Padua for thirty-three years.

About the year 970, when Romuald was twenty years old, his father quarrelled with a fellow-citizen of Ravenna in Italy, and Romuald was horrified when his father killed his opponent. Just outside Ravenna stands the monastery and church of Sant'Apollinare in Classe and Romuald sought refuge there as a monk.

After three years he asked an austere hermit named Marinus if he might join him as a disciple outside Venice. Romuald's early experience in his family made him exceedingly stern against those who pursued their public careers violently. Peter Orseolo, the Doge of Venice, had reached that office by murdering his predecessor. Romuald and Marinus, helped by the Abbot of Catalonia, persuaded Peter Orseolo to repent and resign the office he had gained with blood.

Eventually the emperor appointed Romuald head of the monastery where he had first sought refuge from the evils of the world. But after two years he went to live as a hermit again. He spent his last years founding monasteries and hermitages in Italy, dying on 19 June 1027 at Val di Castro in Piceno. Romuald is shown below on the right.

Adalbert of Magdeburg

Aloysius

At the age of seventy Princess Olga of Kiev became a Christian. The last woman to rule Russia for many centuries, this remarkable lady asked the Emperor Otto the Great to send a missionary from Germany to convert her subjects. Otto chose Adalbert, a monk of St Maximin's monastery at Trier, to lead a small group of courageous missionaries. They had scarcely begun their work when Princess Olga's pagan son Svyatoslav deposed his mother and set the heathen to kill the Christians. Adalbert alone managed to escape.

Otto appointed Adalbert abbot of an important monastery at Weissenberg. He held that part of a monk's duty was to record the history of God's world, and so we still possess a chronicle of Adalbert's age, written by his followers at Weissenberg.

Many of Otto's subjects were ready to revolt whenever they thought insurrection might succeed. Otto therefore decided to found a new, fortified city, Magdeburg, to dominate Saxony. He wanted it to be a centre of Christianity as well as a fortress, so he set up a new abbey and persuaded the pope to create an Archbishop of Magdeburg. In 968 Adalbert was the first to be given this office.

Born on 9 March 1568 into a noble Lombardic household, Aloysius Gonzaga was destined by his father for the life of a soldier. But Aloysius was revolted by the violence and loose morals of the society for which he was destined. He longed to become a Jesuit. His father would hear none of it. From 1577 to 1579 he sent his son as a page to the court of Francesco de' Medici in Florence.

A serious disease of his kidneys made it difficult for the saint to eat normal food for the rest of his life. Aloysius Gonzaga used his sickness as an excuse to spend more time at his prayers. Even when forced to act as courtier to the Empress of Austria he never allowed his duties to interfere with his spiritual exercises.

At last Aloysius's father could resist no longer. The young man returned to Italy and in 1587 entered a Jesuit house for novices. He proved a perfect candidate, seeking only to discipline himself, to deepen his understanding of the faith, and to serve wherever his superiors sent him. In 1591 the plague devastated Rome and many other regions of Italy. The Jesuits opened a hospital for the sick and dying, caring for them when others fled. Aloysius Gonzaga was foremost in this, but he caught the disease himself and died.

John Fisher and Thomas More

'These things, good Lord, that we pray for, give us Thy grace to labour for.'

St Thomas More

'It is a shorter thing, and sooner done, to write heresies, than to answer them.'

St Thomas More

John Fisher, made Bishop of Rochester in 1504, was a man of great distinction. He had been a friend of the famous humanist Erasmus, a Catholic of high ideals, a learned Cambridge teacher, and Chancellor of the University. When King Henry VII died in 1509, Fisher preached his funeral sermon.

He met his death because he resolutely refused to accept Henry VIII's claim to be head of the church. 'I do not condemn any other men's consciences,' he declared. 'Their conscience may save them, and mine must save me.'

A subtler man than John Fisher, Thomas More, Lord Chancellor of England, declared that no-one matched the Bishop of Rochester 'in wisdom, learning and long approved virtue.' Thomas More did not wish to die. 'I am not so holy that I dare rush upon death,' he declared; 'were I so presumptuous, God might suffer me to fall.' But he could not accept that Henry VIII was supreme head of the church. He resigned rather than be seen to support the king's divorce.

The saint spent fifteen months imprisoned in the Tower of London. Nine days after John Fisher's death, Thomas More was declared guilty of treason and condemned to death. He died, he said, 'the King's good servant, but God's first.'

St Thomas More

Etheldreda

Twice Saint Etheldreda (who is also called Saint Audrey) married, released from these unwelcome ties first by the death of her husband after five years and secondly after she managed to persuade her second husband that they should live as brother and sister, a relationship that led him to release the saint after twelve years.

At last she was able to fulfil her life's desire. In between her two marriages she had lived in solitude for five years on the island of Ely. Now she founded a nunnery and a monastery about the year 672, ruling this double house as abbess.

Etheldreda was a woman of noble birth, the daughter of King Anna of East Anglia. But from now on she ceased to wear clothing of fine linen and dressed only in woollen garments. Except at Easter, Pentecost and Epiphany, she washed only in cold water. Only when she was ill or on great church festivals did she eat more than one meal a day. Seven years after the foundation of the double monastery, she died of a plague. The year was 679.

Bede tells how the body of the saint was exhumed. When she died, she had a tumour on her neck. She attributed this to divine punishment because she was once vain enough to wear a costly necklace. When her coffin was opened sixteen years later, the tumour had healed. Thus Etheldreda became the patron saint of those suffering throat and neck ailments.

'Now Etheldreda shines upon our days,
Shedding the light of grace on all our ways.
Born of a noble and a royal line,
She brings to Christ her King a life more fine.'

The Venerable Bede

John the Baptist

The Virgin Mary's cousin Elizabeth was married to a priest of the Jerusalem Temple named Zechariah. Both had hoped for a child, but grew old. When Zechariah was in the Temple, an angel appeared and promised that Elizabeth would bear his son. The angel said:

'He shall drink no wine nor strong drink,
And he will be filled with the Holy Spirit,
even from his mother's womb.'

The angel added that the son of these two aged Jews would prepare people for the Lord. Elizabeth conceived a child. Many of her neighbours wanted him called after his father, but she called him John, and Zechariah agreed.

To prepare people for the coming of Jesus, John went to live in the desert on locusts and wild honey. He wore clothing made of camel hair, and a leather belt. Many Jews came to him, confessed their sins and were baptized in the River Jordan.

John warned them that the wicked would be cut down. 'Even now the axe is laid to the root of the trees,' he cried. 'Every tree that does not bear good fruit is cut down and thrown into the fire.' He told them about Jesus: 'I baptize you with water, but he who is coming after me is mightier than I, whose sandals I am not worthy to carry. He will baptize you with the Holy Spirit and with fire.'

When Jesus came, he persuaded John the Baptist to baptize him in the river, even though John was reluctant to do this, arguing 'I need to be baptized by you.' Jesus said of John the Baptist, 'Among those who have been born of women there is not a greater prophet.' John the Baptist said of Jesus: 'Behold the Lamb of God who takes away the sin of the world.' He compared himself with Jesus and insisted, 'He must increase, and I must decrease.'

Prosper of Reggio

Visitors to Reggio Nell'Emilia, Italy, will be surprised to discover that the city's most famous saint, Bishop Prosper, is commemorated not by the great cathedral but by the little church of San Prospero, tucked away behind it in the market square. None of this would have troubled the humble Saint Prosper, who died on 25 June in the year 466. He cared so little about his own glory that he built and consecrated a church outside the walls of Reggio, and directed that there he should be buried after his death. But, far from forgetting about him, the people of Reggio made Prosper their patron saint, and in the year 703 his remains were moved to their present resting place inside the city walls. The citizens of his own day also recognized Prosper's worth, and he ruled as their father-in-God for no fewer than twenty-two years.

When a rich young man asked Jesus, 'What have I to do to inherit eternal life?' Jesus replied, 'Sell all that you own and distribute the money to the poor, and you will have treasure in heaven: then come, follow me.' Prosper, a true follower of Jesus, took this command so seriously that he gave away all his possessions.

John and Paul

Two brothers named John and Paul served as army officers in the court of Constantia, daughter of the Emperor Constantine, about the middle of the fourth century. One became her steward, the other the master of her household.

The emperor next sent them to serve under his general Gallicanus, who was defending Thrace from the Scythians. The Scythians were such formidable enemies that some of Gallicanus's army surrendered. John and Paul told him that victory would be his if he would become a Christian. He did so, and the Scythians were routed.

The two brothers prospered until shortly after the year 360, when the Emperor Julian began a policy of systematically degrading Christianity and promoting paganism. The two saints declared that they would no longer serve him. Summoned to his court, they simply stayed away and reiterated their dislike of his pagan ways. He gave them ten days to reconsider their attitude, but they remained firm. Julian then sent a captain of his bodyguard, and the two Christian brothers were executed on the Cœlian Hill, Rome, in their own home.

About thirty-five years later a wealthy senator named Pammachius built a church on the site of their home. This church, Santi Giovanni e Paolo, has been excavated, and underneath twelfth-century alterations has been uncovered the original façade. One wall consists of a former pagan house, several stories high. Usually burials were allowed only outside the city walls, but here bodies of martyrs have been discovered – fitting in with the legend that the captain of Julian's bodyguard secretly buried the bodies of John and Paul in their own garden, announcing that they had gone into exile.

Cyril of Alexandria

Cyril became bishop of Alexandria about the year 380. He was a stern ruler, perhaps too stern. He took part in the deposing of Saint John Chrysostom, Patriarch of Constantinople, even though the charges were unjust, and he threw the Jews out of Alexandria. But his fame lies not in his hasty actions but in his work as a Christian theologian. Cyril was particularly keen to stamp out the teaching of a man named Nestorius, who disbelieved the divinity of Jesus and refused to call Mary the mother of God. Nestorius wanted to draw a line between the human Jesus and the divine word of God. Cyril of Alexandria held that this made it impossible to be certain that Jesus preached the truth about God the Father. Cyril's sharp mind undoubtedly helped to keep the Christian faith in its integrity at a time when men like Nestorius were watering it down. Against them Cyril insists on two essential facts about Jesus – however difficult Christians might find it to hold them together:

  i. that Jesus was begotten by God the Father before all ages; and
  ii. that Jesus was also begotten in the flesh of the Virgin Mary.

Irenaeus of Lyons

Irenaeus was born in Smyrna and he was proud of the fact that through his friendship with Bishop Polycarp of Smyrna, who was martyred in the year 155, he could trace his faith back to the time of the first apostles. Irenaeus once told a friend he could remember perfectly Polycarp's appearance, voice and very words as he spoke of what he had learned from St John. 'The things we learned in childhood are part of our soul,' he wrote, and he cherished Polycarp's teaching 'not on paper but in my heart'.

Irenaeus left Asia Minor and journeyed to Gaul. Several times he came to Rome, and was there in the year 177 when Bishop Pothinus of Lyons was martyred at the age of ninety. After peace was restored in Gaul, Irenaeus succeeded Pothinus as bishop. Saint Gregory of Tours speaks with pardonable exaggeration when he says that the saint's missionary endeavours had within a short space of time made the whole of Gaul Christian.

Because Irenaeus treasured his connections with the apostles, he was particularly keen to teach that the surest way to hold fast to the truth was to cleave to the doctrines handed down from them. 'Hold in suspicion those who depart from the primitive succession,' he counselled. Christians should especially shun 'those who put forward their own compositions, boasting that they possess more Gospels than there really are.' Saint Irenaeus was one of the first to insist that our four Gospels – Matthew, Mark, Luke and John – are the ones we may trust, and no others, and he became the most considerable theologian of his age.

St Irenaeus of Lyons

'Give perfection to beginners, O Father; give intelligence to the little ones; give aid to those who are running their course. Give sorrow to the negligent; give fervour of spirit to the lukewarm. Give to the perfect a good consummation; for the sake of Christ Jesus our Lord. Amen.'

Prayer of St Irenaeus

Peter and Paul

'Be sober, be vigilant; because your adversary the devil, as a roaring lion, walketh about, seeking whom he may devour.'

First Letter of St Peter

Peter was the most impetuous of Jesus's apostles and also in many ways their undoubted leader. Jesus, meeting him when he was a fisherman of Galilee, promised to make him a 'fisher of men'. He was a married man, with a brother named Andrew, who was also a fisherman and, like Peter, called to follow Jesus.

Peter's name originally was Simon. Jesus changed it to Kephas, an Aramaic word meaning 'rock' (from which we take our English translation Peter). When Jesus asked the disciples who they thought he was, Peter replied, 'You are the Christ, the Son of the Living God.' Jesus said to him, 'You are Peter, and on this rock I will build my church, and the powers of death will not prevail against it.' He added: 'I will give you the keys of the kingdom of heaven, and whatsoever you bind on earth shall be bound in heaven, and whatsoever you loose on earth shall be loosed in heaven.' Only later was this power extended to the rest of the apostles.

Peter sometimes let Jesus down, especially when he promised that he would die with his Lord and then three times told people he had never known Jesus. Yet he was the first of the apostles to be given sight of the Risen Lord, and Jesus told him that his responsibility was to feed the flock of Christ's followers. The saint in all probability wrote at least the first of the letters attributed him in the New Testament; and tradition is almost certainly right in saying that he was martyred in Rome under Nero – perhaps by being crucified upside-down. There is a spot below the altar in the Vatican which tradition honours as his grave.

Tradition also has it that St Paul was also martyred in Rome, though as a Roman citizen he had the right to be beheaded with a sword and not crucified. Paul was a tent-maker and a fanatical opponent of Christians, urging bystanders to stone St Stephen and trying to bring as many Christians as possible to their deaths. Thrown from his horse on the way to Damascus, he had a vision of Jesus and was converted. Tirelessly he preached his new faith, writing letter after letter to the churches he had founded. He led the mission to non-Jews. Flogged, imprisoned, starving, stoned, shipwrecked and on trial, he never lost his faith. The supreme gift, he preached, was love. 'If I speak in the tongue of men and of angels, but have not love, I am a noisy gong or a clanging cymbal,' he wrote. 'If I deliver my body to be burned but have not love, I gain nothing.'

Martial of Limoges

From a very early date Saint Martial of Limoges was venerated throughout much of Gaul as the most vigorous apostle of the whole region of Limousin and the founder of the bishopric of Limoges. The city grew up around the tomb of the saint. He was honoured as the equal of the earliest apostles, and today the north transept of Limoges cathedral has a great gothic door depicting side by side the exploits of Martial and Saint Stephen.

Shortly before the middle of the third century seven missionaries are said to have been sent from Rome to Gaul. All became saints. Gatian went to Tours, Paul to Narbonne, Denis to Paris, Saturninus to Toulouse, Trophemus to Arles, Austremonius to the Auvergne and Martial to Limoges. Each saint missionized his own district, setting up a bishopric in each region.

Martial is said to have brought the staff of St Peter to Aquitaine. Later legend recounts that he raised from death the son of a Roman proconsul with this staff, after the boy had been strangled by a demon. He also used Peter's staff to strike blind any pagan priest that dared oppose him. He converted Christians throughout Aquitaine, including in particular a girl named Valeria who then renounced her pagan fiancé. The fiancé in return struck off her head, whereupon Valeria picked it up and carried it in her own arms to Martial, before dropping dead at his feet. She can be seen today carrying her head in a carving on Limoges cathedral.

So famous became Saint Martial of Limoges that chroniclers decided he must have been one of the seventy-two disciples whom Jesus sent to the non-Jewish nations. Another legend has him as a young lad producing the five loaves and two fishes with which the Saviour fed the multitude, according to the Gospels. But these legends conflict with the true history of one of the most energetic missionaries of third-century France.

July

'We were created to praise, to reverence and to serve God. And everything else on the face of the earth was created for our sake, to help us to achieve the goal for which we were created.'

'In a time of desolation, never forsake the good resolutions you made in better times. Strive to remain patient – a virtue contrary to the troubles that harass you – and remember that you will be consoled.'

Ignatius of Loyola (July 31)

Simeon Salus

Processus and Martinian

'But God hath chosen the foolish things of the world to confound the wise; and God hath chosen the weak things of the world to confound the things which are mighty.'

1 Corinthians 1:27

After twenty-nine years of self-discipline in the Sinai Desert Simeon decided to go home to Emesa in Syria, to look after those generally considered outcasts. If we are really to learn humility, he argued, we must love humiliations. On this reasoning Simeon deliberately began to behave as a fool – hence his nickname, 'Salus' which in Syriac means 'crazy'. No-one could respect someone who cavorted so stupidly. But the pathetic creatures whom he desired to love welcomed him as one despised like themselves. And it is recorded that God blessed him with extraordinary happiness. Simeon Salus died when nearly seventy in about 590.

Shenute

All the hermit monks looked in awe on Shenute, whom the Coptic Christians describe as 'the father of the church of Egypt'. Saint Cyril of Alexandria greatly admired and trusted Shenute, and he appointed him superior of all the abbots of the desert monks. Saint Shenute was extraordinarily stern but his very sternness attracted over four thousand disciples. He died aged a hundred and eighteen years in the mid-fifth century.

In one of the Roman catacombs an ancient fresco depicts Saint Peter, striking a rock as Moses did to bring forth a spring and with it either baptizing or giving drink to two soldiers. Legend has it that these two men were his chief gaolers when he was imprisoned in Rome before his crucifixion. They were called Processus and Martinian.

The gaolers offered to let Peter escape, but instead he brought forth the spring and baptized them. For this, Paulinus, the officer in charge of the Roman prison, had the two soldiers killed by the sword. A woman called Lucina took their bodies and buried them on the Aurelian Way. In the ninth century Pope Paschal I placed their remains under an altar in the south transept of St Peter's, Rome.

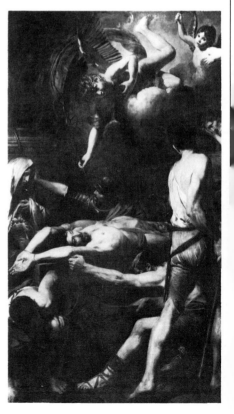

Thomas

Jesus's disciple Thomas is called in the New Testament 'Didymus', 'the twin'; but he is universally known in the Christian world as Doubting Thomas.

He was a disciple who searched for the truth, found it difficult to accept or understand at first, but in the end triumphantly believed. St John's Gospel tells us that Jesus told his disciples: 'I go to prepare a place for you. And I will come again and will take you to myself, that where I am you may be also. And you know the way where I'm going.' At this Thomas, puzzled, but bold enough to ask his Lord to explain, said 'Lord, we do not know where you are going; how can we know the way?' Jesus replied, 'I am the way, and the truth, and the life; no-one comes to the Father, but by me. If you had known me, you would have known my Father also. Henceforth you know him and have seen him.'

Thomas was not with the other ten apostles when Jesus first appeared to them after his death. He refused to take their word that Jesus was alive. 'Unless I see in his hands the print of the nails and place my finger in their mark and place my hand in his side, I will not believe,' Thomas declared.

Eight days later Jesus appeared again to the apostles. Thomas was there. He touched Jesus's hands and side, and cried, 'My Lord and my God.' Jesus observed, 'Blessed are those who have not seen and yet believed.'

It is certainly possible that Thomas reached India as a missionary. Indian Christians often call themselves 'Christians of St Thomas', and an ancient sixth-century cross which speaks of him in an inscription lies in the church of Mylapore near Madras, where he is said to have been buried.

Elizabeth of Portugal

Antony Zaccaria

'That which God commands seems difficult and a burden . . . The way is rough; you draw back; you have no desire to follow it. Yet do so and you will attain glory.'

St Antony Zaccaria

By an arranged marriage when she was only twelve Elizabeth became wife of Denis, King of Portugal. Denis was not a good man, but he did not interfere with her commitment to good works. She built lodging houses for travellers, a hospital, an orphanage, a home for women who wanted to leave a life of sin. She herself would look after the sick. When her husband fell ill and was dying, she forgave all his cruelties and nursed him in his last illness. He died in 1325. Elizabeth now was able to live as a Franciscan nun. She founded a great nunnery at Coimbra, and lived near it, often humbly serving the other nuns at their food.

Elizabeth died seeking peace and reconciliation amongst the fierce monarchs of her age. Her son was now King Alfonso IV, and in 1336 he set out to do battle with his son-in-law, the King of Castile. Elizabeth, though sick, set off to bring peace between them. She succeeded in her mission, but the exertions were too much for her ailing body and she died before she could return to her beloved nuns at Coimbra.

Born in Cremona in the year 1502, Antony Zaccaria studied medicine at the University of Padua. At the age of twenty-five he set up in practice at his home town. As a medical man he found himself ministering not only to the sick but also to the dying and the bereaved. He found men and women sick not only in body but also spiritually, and so he turned to the study of theology to learn more about the comfort and ways of God. By the year 1528 it seemed natural that the young doctor should also be ordained priest.

Soon he moved to work in Milan and in 1530 he and a few other priests formed a society 'to revive the love of divine worship and a true Christian way of life by continual preaching and faithfully administering the sacraments.' Pope Clement VII gave the society the title of the Clerks Regular of St Paul. He was only thirty-seven when he died. He had just bought for his Clerks of St Paul the church of St Barnabas in Milan, and the society he founded is today called the Barnabites.

Antony used to say, 'That which God commands seems difficult and a burden. But he would also add that all God's commands are made easy by love. 'The way is rough; you draw back; you have no desire to follow it. Yet do so and you will attain glory.'

Godelva

Ethelburga

When she was no more than eighteen Godelva married a Flemish nobleman named Bertulf of Ghistelles. Bertulf's mother was enraged by this, and she persuaded Bertulf to leave his poor wife even before the wedding feast was over.

There was little reason to persecute the poor girl, since she was given to good works, prayer and kindliness. But her mother-in-law confined her to a tiny room and fed her on scraps until she escaped and found her way home. The Bishop of Tournai and the Count of Flanders both insisted that Bertulf take her back and treat her gently and lovingly.

At first Bertulf pretended to love Godelva. Soon however, he became violent to her. On 6 July 1070, he went away to Bruges and that night two of his hired hands lured Godelva through the back door of the castle, tied a rope round her neck and drowned her in a pond. Although it was obvious that she had been killed on his orders, no-one was able to prove Bertulf guilty.

What seems to have persuaded many that she was a saint were the many miracles which soon began to be performed at the site of Godelva's murder.

The daughter of King Anna of the East Angles, Ethelburga longed to live the life of a nun. Her eldest sister, Saint Sexburga, married King Erconbert of Kent. Sexburga greatly influenced her husband. The Venerable Bede says that Erconbert was 'the first English king to order the complete abandonment and destruction of idols throughout his kingdom'. He also ordered everyone to observe the Lenten fasts. The daughter of Erconbert and Sexburga was called Ercongota, and she and her aunt Ethelburga entered nunneries in Gaul since (again according to Bede 'as yet there were few monasteries in England'.

Ethelburga became abbess of the monastery of Faremoutier in the forest of Brie. The French called her Aubierge, as she is known to this day. She began to build a church there dedicated to all twelve apostles, but she died before completing it and was buried in the half-finished building in the year 665.

Later the nuns decided they could not afford to complete the church and Ethelburga's bones were interred in the nearby church of St Stephen the Martyr.

St Ethelburga

Procopius

Procopius was a man of great self-discipline. The church historian Eusebius of Caesarea, who was his contemporary, tells us that 'he had reduced his body until it looked like a corpse, but his soul drew from the word of God such strength that the body was refreshed too'. Eusebius says that Procopius lived mostly on bread and water, and sometimes ate nothing for a whole week.

This man was gentle and humble too. Born in Jerusalem, he moved to Scythopolis where he worked for the church in various lowly but extremely useful ways. He read the Scriptures during services. He was cherished because of his gift of understanding languages, especially Syriac.

One day the church sent him on a mission with some companions to Caesarea. At this moment the persecutions of the age of Domitian were just starting. A Caesarean magistrate named Flavian condemned Procopius to be beheaded. 'He passed happily to eternal life by the shortest road,' wrote Eusebius, 'in the first year of our persecutions. This was the first martyrdom that took place at Caesarea.'

Veronica Giuliani

Ursula Giuliani, who was born in Urbino in 1660, distressed her father Francesco by deciding at an early age to become a nun, whereas he planned to find her a fine husband. She distressed others too by her apparent religious arrogance, expecting everyone to share her own attitude to the spiritual life.

One day in a vision she seemed to see her own heart. It was made of steel. From that moment Ursula became a more gentle woman, without for one instant weakening in her determination to devote herself to Christ. Later her heart, hands, feet and head were to show the most remarkable imprints of her Saviour's love for mankind.

In 1677 she joined the Capuchin convent at Città di Castello, Umbria, and took the name Veronica. She was to stay there for the rest of her life. For thirty-six years she was novice-mistress at the convent, and then abbess until her death in 1727.

In all but one respect she was a straightforward, though model sister. She cared for her novices and busied herself both with her devotions and with the practical affairs of the convent. But she experienced curious, disturbing pains in her heart at times, supremely when she meditated on the sufferings of Jesus. In the year 1694 Saint Veronica Giuliani showed marks on her head as if a crown of thorns had been placed there. And on Good Friday 1697 five wounds appeared on her body – as if nails had pierced her hands and feet and a sword her side. The Bishop of Città di Castello feared some trickery and for a long time would not let Veronica Giuliani appear in public. But at last he was convinced that these stigmata were genuine and the saint was allowed to resume her normal busy life in the convent. After her death an autopsy was performed and marks – some said like those of Christ's passion – were found there.

Rufina and Secunda

Benedict

Benedict was born at Nursia in Umbria about the year 480 and went to Rome to be educated. At about twenty he went to live as a hermit in a cave in the mountains of Subiaco. So many men came to imitate his austere life that Benedict was able to set up twelve monastic communities, each consisting of twelve monks.

In the year 529 the saint left Subiaco with a handful of faithful monks and moved to Monte Cassino, half way between Rome and Naples.

On the summit of Monte Cassino was a pagan temple dedicated to Apollo. Benedict replaced it with the most famous monastery in Western Christendom. For the many monks that were attracted to Monte Cassino by Saint Benedict's holiness he wrote his famous monastic rule, which was to become the basis of all subsequent western monasteries because of its supreme common sense.

'If you are really a servant of Jesus Christ, let the chain of love hold you firm in your resolve, not a chain of iron.'

St Benedict

'Idleness is the enemy of the soul.'

St Benedict

'The first degree of humility is obedience without delay.'

St Benedict

Asterius, a Roman senator, had two daughters, Rufina and Secunda. He found for them fiancés, Armentarius and Verinus, and since all four betrothed were Christians, the matches seemed perfect.

Soon, however, the Emperor Valerian began to persecute the church and Armentarius and Verinus renounced Christianity. Neither girl would do this. Both decided to escape to Etruria, but on their way they were captured and brought before a prefect named Junius Donatus.

Junius Donatus decided on a cruel torment: he would scourge Rufina while her sister watched. As the scourging began, Secunda shouted, 'Why are you honouring my sister in this way and dishonouring me? Please scourge us both at the same time. We both declare that Jesus Christ is God.' Realizing that neither girl would recant, Junius Donatus had them beheaded.

A pagan lady named Plautilla buried their bodies outside Rome on the Via Aurelia in a spot known as the Black Forest. It was later renamed the White Forest because of their sacred bones, and the church of Sante Rufina e Secunda was built in their honour in Rome.

Veronica

Veronica's story first appears fairly late in the history of the early church, though it relates to the very heart of the Gospel – Jesus's way to Golgotha. As he fell, carrying his cross on the way to be crucified, she wiped his face with her cloth. On the cloth was left an image of his divine face. Scholars have been quick to point out that Veronica's name may well derive from the story itself and not be historical, since Vera means 'true' and icon means 'image'. Thus she obtained the true image of Jesus. A 'veil of Veronica is preserved at St Peter's, Rome.

Henry II

Henry, Holy Roman Emperor, longed to become a monk of Saint-Vanne at Verdun. He came to the abbot and pledged total obedience. The abbot accepted his vow, and commanded Henry to continue serving God as Holy Roman Emperor. He had been born to Gisella of Burgundy, wife of Duke Henry of Bavaria in 972, and educated by St Wolfgang, Bishop of Ratisbon, who taught him humility.

As Holy Roman Emperor, Henry II believed it was his duty to keep the clergy up to scratch. He called synods throughout his territories to enforce canon law and inspire a greater devotion to the pastoral duties the priests often seemed ready to neglect. And above all he restored many bishoprics: Strasbourg, Hildesheim, Magdeburg, Meersburg among them. The diocese of Meersburg had been grievously ravaged by the Slav invaders, but Henry waged a holy war against them. He asked every soldier to receive holy communion before engaging battle, and afterwards thanked God for the victory by munificently restoring the see. His greatest foundation was the new diocese of Bamberg, where he built a magnificent cathedral. Henry died near Göttingen in Germany in the year 1024.

JULY 14

Camillus de Lellis

Camillus de Lellis, born in the kingdom of Naples in 1550, was a hot-tempered man. He once took a job as a hospital servant in Rome and was soon dismissed for bad behaviour. He became a soldier, fighting for anyone that would hire him. He fought for Venice against the Turks. He was unable to resist gambling, lost everything he possessed, and found himself penniless. The Capuchin monks of Manfredonia were putting up some new buildings and Camillus became a labourer for them. One day he heard a friar preaching. Camillus fell to his knees and asked God's mercy on his former turbulent life.

By now, though only twenty-five, he suffered a diseased leg. Twice he was refused permission to join the Franciscans. He decided to return to the hospital of San Giacomo in Rome, from which he had previously been dismissed. The former turbulent servant now wore a hair shirt and day-in-day-out watched by the beds of the sick and dying. Soon he became bursar of the hospital.

But Camillus had more sympathetic eyes than before. He now perceived how inadequate the hospital was. St Philip Neri, his confessor, encouraged him to become a priest. With two companions at first, he set up a society of Servants of the Sick, caring for those who were suffering, either in hospitals or at home. Soon Camillus's new pattern of life was attracting gifts from rich patrons. He was able to open hospitals of his own, in Naples and elsewhere. His followers in times of plague went where no-one else would, to ease the pains of the dying. They even braved the dangers of Naples harbour, clambering aboard ships to offer succour.

As a former soldier he knew the hardships of the field; and in 1595 and 1601 he sent some of his followers to serve the wounded and dying in wars in Hungary and Croatia. Camillus would say, 'A good soldier is willing to die in battle and a good servant of the sick in hospital.' His Servants of the Sick were fearless for their own health, and Camillus de Lellis himself died after a long illness on 14 July 1614.

Camillus de Lellis

S. CAMILLO DE LELLIS
PATRONO DEI MALATI, DEGLI OSPEDALI
E DEGLI INFERMIERI

Nicodemus of the Holy Mountain

In 1775 Nicodemus, a twenty-six year old student, was forced by Turkish persecutors to flee from Smyrna. He joined a monastery on Mount Athos, which Greeks call the 'Holy Mountain' and stayed there for the rest of his life. Nicodemus found inspiration in the writings of western Catholic Christians as well as in those of his own Orthodox church. He translated into Greek the *Spiritual Exercises* of St Ignatius of Loyola and the *Spiritual Combat* of Lorenzo Scupoli. He saw the rules of the church as a means of guiding men and women in the right direction, the way a rudder guides a ship, so he made a collection of Greek church laws which he called the *Pidalion*, which in Greek means 'Rudder'.

His greatest work was to edit and publish a book on mysticism and prayer, the *Philocalia* (which means 'Love of what is beautiful'). The book concerns itself above all with a prayer renowned in Greek Christendom, the so-called 'Jesus-prayer':

'Lord Jesus Christ, Son of God,
have mercy upon me.'

Nicodemus of the Holy Mountain died on 14 July 1809, and in 1955 the Greek Orthodox church declared him a saint.

Bonaventure

Mary Magdalen Postel

*Thorns and cross and
 nails and lance,
Wounds, our rich
 inheritance . . .
May these all our
 spirits fill,
And with love's
 devotion thrill . . .
Christ, by coward
 hands betrayed,
Christ, for us a captive
 made,
Christ, upon the bitter
 tree,
Slain for man – all
 praise to thee.'*

St Bonaventure
(*Hymn on Our Lord's Passion*)

Bonaventure rose to the highest offices in the church. He was a brilliant philosopher, and taught philosophy at Paris, combining this with courses on the Holy Bible. He had been made head of the Franciscans, and though hostility to the Franciscans held back his degree of doctor of theology for many years this did not sour him. Later he became Bishop of Albano, and a cardinal.

Bonaventure believed that the created world gave us a sign of God. But faith was needed, honed by reason, to lead to contemplation of the divine. When his friend Saint Thomas Aquinas asked him where he gained his own great knowledge, Bonaventure pointed to a crucifix. 'I study only the crucified one, Jesus Christ,' he replied.

The saint died in 1274.

Julie Postel was a young woman running a girls' school at Barfleur in France when the French Revolution broke out. Under the stairs of her home she created a secret chapel where 'underground' priests could say Mass.

Only when the pope made a concordat with Napoleon in 1801 could Julie take up teaching again as her life's work. Then, at the age of fifty-one, she decided to set up a group of religious women to teach the young, inspire them to love God, and help the poor in their misery.

In 1807 Julie took her religious vows and a new name, Mary Magdalen Postel. Within three years two hundred girls were being educated. For some time Mary Magdalen Postel and her nine fellow-teachers lived in great poverty in a barn next to their schoolroom. Whatever work they could find – as farm-labourers, sempstresses, and so on – was eagerly seized so that they could carry on with their teaching. But their tenacity triumphed. In 1830 they moved into an abandoned abbey at Saint-Sauveur-le-Vicomte.

She died aged ninety in 1846, having seen the ruined abbey rebuilt and her community spreading the Christian gospel ever wider afield.

Alexis

Pambo

Alexis was born to a rich Roman senator named Euphremian and his wife Agloë late in the fourth century. His parents arranged for him to marry an heiress, but Alexis was determined to devote himself to God. Obliged to leave Rome, Alexis escaped to Edessa in Mesopotamia, and there – revealing his name to no-one – lived on whatever people would give him. His home was a tiny hut beside a church. Though extremely poor, Alexis still shared whatever he gained with those poorer than himself.

After seventeen years he went back to his parents' home as a beggar. They gave him work as a servant, and for the next seventeen years Alexis worked humbly, still unrecognized, sharing crumbs of what was rightly his, and sleeping in a corner under the staircase of his own sumptuous home.

He died in the year 417. Only then, hidden among his scanty garments, was found a parchment giving the truth about him and his life. Alexis was given a dignified Christian burial. In the year 1216 Pope Honorius III discovered his body and reverently placed it under the high altar of the church of St Boniface, Rome, whose name now bears the names of both saints: Sant'Alessio e Bonifatio.

Though one of the greatest teachers of the desert fathers of the fourth century, Pambo could not read. When he first set out to be a hermit and monk, his brethren began to teach him the psalms by heart. They began with the first verse of Psalm 39: 'I said, "I will guard my ways, that I may not sin with my tongue".' This became one of Pambo's greatest virtues and he taught his followers the gift of silence. Once a patriarch asked Pambo to say something edifying. Pambo turned to his followers and said, 'If he is not edified by my silence, he will not be edified by my speech.'

Pambo never forgot the advice he had learned from another desert father: 'Do not be confident of your own righteousness; do not grieve over a thing that is past; and be continent both of your tongue and your belly.' On the rare occasions when he gave way to speech, he would repeat his favourite sayings: 'Show mercy to all, for the merciful have the favour of God'; 'If you have a mind to it, you may be saved.'

A lady who afterwards achieved sainthood, Melania of Rome, came to Pambo for counsel. She also brought him a gift of three hundred pounds weight of silver. Pambo instantly gave it to a follower, telling him to sell the silver and give what he earned to the poor of Libya. Melania waited for a word of thanks from Pambo. When none came, she said, 'Sir, do you not know how great a gift is three hundred pounds weight of silver?' Pambo turned to her and said, 'God for whom you brought this gift does not need to know its value. He who weighs the mountains in his hands surely knows already the quantity of your silver. Had you brought it for me, well might you have told me its weight. But if you brought it for God, then be silent.'

Arsenius

Margaret

'I know a great deal of Greek and Latin learning. I have still to learn even the alphabet of how to be a saint.'

St Arsenius

Arsenius was one of the most renowned teachers in the world; as a deacon in Rome, Pope Damasus recommended him as a tutor for the emperor's own children. He had been rewarded with money and servants, with honour and possessions. But after ten years of luxury in high places, he kept hearing the voice of God telling him that only by abandoning it all could he be saved, and he went to the desert monks near the Wadi Natrun, Egypt.

Arsenius craved silence. He had, he said, frequently been sorry for what he had said, but never for saying nothing. When barbarian invasions forced him to leave the Wadi Natrun he found it no burden to live for some years on a rock called Petra near Memphis. What he despised now were his former riches. He felt he was dead to that world. A relative left Arsenius in his will most of his wealth. 'I died before he did,' responded the desert saint and tore the will in two. Arsenius feared damnation because of his former self-centered ways; but in the year 449 he had found peace when he died in the desert.

To a fellow-monk he left all his earthly possessions: a skin coat, palm leaves woven into sandals, and a goat-skin shirt.

At Antioch in Pisidia lived a pagan priest whose daughter Margaret embraced Christianity. Her father threw her out of his home but Margaret's nurse was still alive and she sheltered the girl. Unfortunately the pagan prefect Olybrius saw her and was entranced by what he saw. He asked if she were free or a slave. If she were free he promised to marry her. If she were a slave, he would take her as his slave. Margaret had no desire to marry an unbeliever, having escaped from one already. She knew she was in danger, but she refused Olybrius, both as a husband and a master.

Enraged at her refusal, Olybrius decided that if he could not have Margaret, no-one should. Knowing that Margaret was a Christian, he brought her before the pagan authorities, who insisted that she give up her faith. The saint refused, and was therefore tortured grievously and then thrown into prison. In prison, according to the old legends, she fought against a dragon, which almost swallowed her, till the cross she carried scratched its throat and she was disgorged. This fabulous tale can readily be seen as an image of her spiritual torment – the dragon representing the terrible temptation to save her life by denying Christ; the cross representing Margaret's saving faith.

She did not give in. After more tortures with both fire and water, the saintly martyr was beheaded, and a widow of Antioch kindly buried her body. In Italy she is known as Saint Marina, and in sacred art she is often depicted with a dragon.

Lawrence of Brindisi

Mary Magdalen

One of the three women, the first three persons ever to learn about the empty tomb of Jesus, was Mary Magdalen. Later Mary Magdalen was granted the first sight of the Risen Jesus. On Easter day she was weeping outside the tomb. She turned round and, through her tears saw someone she supposed to be the gardener, who asked why she was weeping. Mary Magdalen replied 'Sir, if you have carried him away, tell me where you have laid him and I will come and take him.'

This man was Jesus. He spoke to Mary in their own tongue, saying her name, 'Mary'. She replied 'Rabboni', which means 'Teacher'. Jesus would not let Mary Magdalen cling to him, saying he must ascend to his Father and her Father, his God and her God. He told her to go and tell these things to the disciples, and Mary Magdalen obeyed him.

The accounts of Jesus's crucifixion show Mary Magdalen watching. She saw him die, and then alive again. Her emotions on seeing the Risen Lord – described by St Matthew as 'fear and great joy' – are intensely human, intensely moving.

During Lawrence's lifetime the Turks almost overran Hungary. The Emperor Rudolf II begged Lawrence to persuade the German princes to repel the Turks. He possessed instinctive tactical skills and would clearly have made a good general had he not been a clergyman. Consulted by the leaders of the Christian army – who were hesitating before the might of the Turks – Lawrence said they had no option but to attack, and that he would lead the attack, a crucifix in his hand. He did so, and the Turks were routed.

As a peacemaker Lawrence was equally successful. In the year 1619, the citizens of Naples begged him to seek out the Spanish king and beg him to stop his allies from terrorizing the Neapolitans. Lawrence trailed through Italy and across Spain and Portugal until he found the king and persuaded him to grant the Neapolitans peace. The journey wore out Lawrence, and he died on his fiftieth birthday that same year.

Brigit of Sweden

Brigit became a lady-in-waiting to Queen Blanche of Namur, wife of King Magnus II of Sweden. Few courtiers can have been more outspoken than Brigit about the royal family's frivolousness and shortcomings. Under her influence Magnus II improved his manner of life. After Brigit left the royal circle and her husband had died, she was inspired by four years of self-discipline in a Cistercian monastery to found her own religious house at Vadstena in Sweden. Magnus generously endowed it on her behalf.

Brigit went to live in Rome in the year 1349. There her great spiritual insight, her love for those who had fallen into misfortune and her complete unselfishness won over many of the saint's critics. She still needed the pope's support for her religious house at Vadstena, and in 1370 Urban V gave it – even though Brigit had frequently told him off for what she considered his shortcomings. She died in 1373 and was declared a saint in 1391.

Christina

'Christina the Astonishing' was born in Belgium, at Brustheim near Liège, in the year 1150. By the time she was fifteen she and her two elder sisters were orphans. Her first extraordinary piece of behaviour happened after she had suffered some sort of fit, so that she fell deeply unconscious and seemed quite dead. A requiem Mass was being said for the saint's soul when she suddenly rose from her open coffin and sped up into the rafters of the church. Only her elder sister had the presence of mind not to run away in fright.

Thenceforth the saint continued to behave as one of the great eccentrics of Christendom. She dressed in rags bound together with saplings. She liked being swung round and round mill wheels, and seemed never to get hurt doing so. To escape the smell of humans she would frequently hide inside ovens. At a church in a place called Wellen she climbed into the large font and sat in the water.

Yet many people came to her for good advice. In her later years she settled in a convent at Saint-Trond, and there many came to seek her counsel.

'True wisdom, then, consists in works, not in great talents which the world admires; for the wise in the world's estimation . . . are the foolish who set at naught the will of God, and know not how to control their passions.'

St Brigit of Sweden

Christopher

St Christopher

Many legends account for the name of Christopher being attached to the third-century martyr who was in all probability first called Reprobus. One recounts that he was an enormous giant who first served the Canaanites. At length he decided he would try to serve the greatest king in the universe.

He knew this would not be the devil, since the devil feared God. Christopher, despairing of meeting this great king, decided to earn his livelihood carrying wayfarers across a deep river.

One day as he slept in his hut by the river he heard the voice of a child calling 'Christopher, come and carry me over.' Christopher lifted the child onto his shoulders, took his staff in his hand and stepped into the water. The swollen stream rose higher and higher, and as it did so the child seemed to grow ever more heavy. Almost stumbling, Christopher cried, 'Child, I am in great danger. You weigh almost as if the whole world were on my shoulders. I can carry no greater load.' The child answered, 'Christopher, do not wonder that this is so. I am Jesus Christ – the king whom you serve in this work. And on my shoulders I bear the burdens of the world.' So Reprobus took the name Christopher, which in Greek means 'Christ-bearer'.

Later the saint was martyred for his faith – traditionally at a place called Lycia – even though he was strong enough to overcome his murderers, had he wished to fight them.

In the middle ages it was commonly believed that anyone who looked on an image of Saint Christopher would be kept safe that day. The custom therefore arose of painting the saint, the child on his shoulders, on the walls of churches. He became the patron saint of wayfarers and (in the twentieth century) of motorists.

Joachim and Ann

Although the Bible tells us nothing about the parents of the Blessed Virgin Mary, Christian tradition has attributed to them the names of Joachim and Ann and has filled up the story of their lives.

Joachim is said to have been born at Nazareth and married Ann when he was still a young man. For many years they gave birth to no child, and sometimes he was publicly mocked for this. In a last prayer for a child he withdrew to the wilderness and there he fasted for forty days.

Ann's father is said to have been a nomadic Jew named Akar, who brought his wife to Nazareth for their daughter's birth. Ann too, after her marriage to Joachim, was saddened by their lack of a child. She would weep and pray for at least one infant. One day as she was praying beneath a laurel tree, an angel is said to have appeared to her, declaring that God had heard her prayers. She would indeed have a child who should be praised the world over. Ann replied, 'As my God lives, if I conceive either a boy or a girl, the child shall be a gift to my God, serving him in holiness throughout the whole of its life.'

Saint Ann gave birth to the Blessed Virgin Mary when she was about the age of forty. She and Joachim, according to the tradition, lived to see the birth of Mary's child Jesus, and Joachim died just after seeing his divine grandchild presented to God in the Jerusalem Temple.

Because the stories of Joachim and Ann are not found in the Gospels, he especially is often given other names in early apocryphal writings, appearing, for example, as Heli, Sadoch, Jonachir, Eliacim and Cleopas.

Pantaleon

Nazarius and Celsus

St Nazarius and St Celsus

Pantaleon was a doctor of such repute that the Emperor Maximian made him court physician. He had been raised a Christian, but in that fanatically anti-Christian and dissolute court, Pantaleon lost his faith. In time, however, a fellow-Christian named Hermolaos reminded the doctor of the faith he had abandoned. From that moment Pantaleon's skills were at the disposal of the poor, at no cost to themselves. His wealth, gained from his successful practice, was given away. Other members of his profession, jealous of Pantaleon's position, perceived the saint's recovered faith as a way of discrediting him with the imperial authorities. This time Pantaleon refused to recant and chose death.

Along with Cosmas and Damian, Pantaleon is a patron saint of the medical profession – a patronage doubly fitting since his name means 'the all-compassionate'.

When the Emperor Nero was persecuting Christians in Rome Saint Nazarius, the son of a Roman officer and his Christian wife Perpetua, began to preach the Christian faith so powerfully that his friends begged him to leave the city to avoid punishment. He went to Milan. There he found already in prison two other Christians named Gervase and Protase. In spite of the danger, Nazarius rushed to comfort them, for which the city rulers beat him and threw him outside their walls.

Undeterred, Nazarius went on into Gaul. He was asked to look after a child called Celsus, baptized him, and travelled further, reaching Trier in Germany, always preaching the Gospel. Celsus went with him, supporting Nazarius in every way he could.

At Trier they were tried by Nero who found them guilty of being Christians, and ordered that they should be drowned in the sea. Both Christians were taken in a ship and thrown overboard, but a storm which suddenly arose frightened the sailors. Imagining that the storm was a punishment for their treatment of the two Christians, the sailors pulled Nazarius and Celsus back on board.

They landed at Genoa, and Nazarius decided that they ought to try once more to convert the people of Milan. But the Milan city rulers again caught Nazarius and Celsus with him. This time they were beheaded.

The two saints were buried outside the walls of the city, close by the graves of Gervase and Protase. So it happened that towards the end of the fourth century Saint Ambrose, Bishop of Milan, discovered the four bodies and placed them reverently inside his great new church of the Apostles.

Martha

In the little village of Bethany not far from Jerusalem Jesus had three close friends, Martha and her sister Mary and their brother Lazarus, with whom he often stayed and talked. Jesus raised Lazarus from death. But before that happened Martha had met him when he was still a couple of miles outside their village. She said to him, 'Lord, if you had not been here, my brother would not have died.' She added that she still believed God would grant whatever Jesus asked.

In response to this act of faith she was the first to hear one of Jesus's deepest revelations. As Jesus continued to question her, Martha said she believed her brother would rise again at the end of time. Then Jesus said to Martha: 'I am the resurrection and the life.' He added that no-one really died who believed in him. 'Do you believe this?' he asked Martha. She replied, 'Yes, Lord, I believe you are the Christ, the Son of God.'

Abdon and Sennen

In a fresco in the Roman cemetery of Pontianus are painted two martyrs, inscribed with the names Abdon and Sennen.

They are said to have been Persians who had become Christians and were captured during one of Diocletian's persecutions – possibly having already been taken prisoner during a Roman campaign in Persia. Following the glorious tradition of those Christians who preferred death to renouncing Jesus, when the Romans brought idols to be worshipped by the two saints, Abdon and Sennen spat on them.

Their story has one strange twist. The two men were taken to the Roman Coliseum, to be torn apart by wild beasts. But, we are told, the bears and lions simply refused to touch or harm them. They had to be cut in pieces by gladiators, who thus showed themselves more savage than untamed animals.

A brave Roman Christian named Quirinus gathered together their dismembered corpses and buried them. And when the Emperor Constantine the Great became a supporter of Christianity, they were reburied with honour in the cemetery of Pontianus.

Ignatius of Loyola

*'Prefer neither health
  nor sickness,
neither riches nor
  poverty,
neither honour nor
  ignominy,
neither a long life nor a
  short one.'*

Ignatius of Loyola

Born a nobleman's son in the castle of Loyola in the country of the Basques, Saint Ignatius began his career as a soldier in the army of the Duke of Nagara. At the siege of Pamplona in 1521 he was so seriously wounded that he needed to convalesce for months. During this time he read a life of Jesus and other lives of saints. 'Since these men were as human as I am,' he noted, 'I could be as saintly as they were.' After his recovery, instead of re-enlisting as a soldier, he exchanged his military dress for the clothing of a beggar, and at Montserrat in Barcelona visited the famous portrait of the Virgin in the Benedictine monastery, there to hang before her his sword.

Ignatius then retired to a place called Manresa, and in deep prayer and discipline wrote the first draft of his famous *Spiritual Exercises*, a manual for training the soul to grow daily nearer God.

The saint now went on a pilgrimage to Rome and to Jerusalem, riding from Jaffa to the Holy City on a donkey. He returned to Europe, and for the next seven years – at Spanish universities and in Paris – devoted himself to study. In Paris was laid the foundation of the great society of Jesus which Ignatius was to found. Six students joined him in vowing poverty, chastity and obedience, in joining themselves together by means of the *Spiritual Exercises* and in determining once their studies were over to preach Christianity in Palestine.

War in the middle east made this last plan impossible. Instead Ignatius and his followers offered their services to Pope Paul III. In 1540 the pope formally approved the Society of Jesus. Ignatius had sixteen more years to live. During that time he tirelessly watched over the development of the Society which soon had a thousand adherents throughout Europe, working as missionaries and in universities and schools.

August

'The character of God's eternal and just law is this: that those refusing to be ruled by God's gentleness will have the misfortune of being ruled by their own selves; that whoever voluntarily throws off the gentle yoke and light burden of charity will be obliged to carry the unbearable burden of their own will.'

Bernard of Clairvaux (August 20)

Alphonsus Liguori

Eusebius of Vercelli

'A soul can do nothing that is more pleasing to God than to communicate in a state of grace.'

St Alphonsus Liguori

'He who trusts in himself is lost. He who trusts in God can do all things.'

St Alphonsus Liguori

Born near Naples in 1696, Alphonsus Liguori at first turned his brilliant skills as an orator to his own worldly advantage. He had become a doctor of both canon and civil law when he was only sixteen, undoubtedly the best scholar of his year, and for eight years was a successful barrister.

One day his rhetoric carried him away. The case was over an estate worth £100,000. Alphonsus spoke with his customary eloquence. But he had failed to read his papers properly. One crucial point he had not even spotted. His opposing lawyer told him he had wasted his breath. Alphonsus lost the case, and vowed never to enter a courtroom again.

Alphonsus began to study theology and was ordained priest. Now his skills as a speaker were devoted to the field of mission. He preached persuasively in and around Naples, making such a name for himself that he was able to bring together a group of followers (known as Redemptorists) to develop this work. Yet this did not bring him peace of mind. The Redemptorists quarrelled. They unscrupulously excluded Alphonsus from their councils. He was deeply depressed for many years, a sadness exacerbated by continual physical illness.

Two achievements shone through all these troubles. First, Alphonsus turned his legal brain to writing a massive work of moral theology, in which he tried to analyse what exactly was sinful in the actions of human beings and what can be regarded as merely error. Secondly, he wrote and preached beautifully. Subtle as he was in his theology, in his preaching and devotional writing he said that the simplest person in a congregation should understand him.

Alphonsus Liguori died in 1787, but his writings have continued to inspire and to draw men and women nearer their Saviour ever since.

Eusebius was born on Sardinia, educated in Rome, and elected Bishop of Vercelli in 340. He decided that his best way of fostering the life of prayer was to live with some of his fellow-clergy as a community of monks, supporting each other and cherishing him as he cared for his whole flock. Eusebius was the first western bishop to seek this pattern of spiritual life.

His sufferings came because of his refusal to condemn the great theologian St Athanasius. Athanasius almost alone stood up against those who could not admit that Jesus was both God and man. The emperor turned against him, and Eusebius was one of the bishops ordered to condemn the great saint. He refused, even under the threat of death, and was banished to Palestine. There the emperor put him in the hands of his opponents, the enemies of Athanasius, who humiliated him. The death of the emperor made his life easier, and he gained the friendship of Hilary of Poitiers, who supported him in the trials. Many scholars think Eusebius helped to write the famous 'Athanasian Creed', which has had an enormous influence in bringing both Catholics and Protestants to a proper understanding of their faith and their Saviour.

Nicodemus

John Baptist Vianney (the Curé d'Ars)

The supreme Council of the Jews in Jerusalem, and their highest court of Justice, was known as the Sanhedrin. This was the Council that wished to condemn Jesus. Any member of the Sanhedrin who showed sympathy towards Jesus would have been considered by many of his colleagues as a traitor and an outcast.

Yet we know that at least one member did. His name was Nicodemus. Even before Jesus was put on trial, St John tells us that Nicodemus came to see him – secretly, and at night – to talk about what it means to see the kingdom of God. On this occasion Nicodemus partly confessed his belief in Jesus, saying, 'We know that you are a teacher come from God, for no-one can do these signs that you do unless God is with him.' Jesus tried to teach him about being born again by the Holy Spirit and by baptism. St John even says that it was to Nicodemus that Our Lord said the words, 'God so loved the world that he gave his only Son, that whoever believes in him should not perish but have eternal life.'

John Baptist Vianney was ordained in 1814 and by 1818 had become parish priest of the woebegone village of Ars-en-Dombes. He stayed there until he died forty-one years later. His effect was extraordinary. Ten years of patience and good example transformed Ars into a village thriving with Christian spirit. And soon the humble Curé d'Ars (as John Vianney came to be known) was attracting penitents from all parts of France and beyond. So great was his insight into people's problems that by 1855 the number of his visitors was said to be twenty thousand a year.

The French government once made him a knight of the Legion of Honour. John Vianney was amazed. 'Suppose I die,' he mused, 'and God says, "Away you go. You have already been rewarded".' So he refused to have the medal even pinned on his old cassock.

John Baptist Vianney died in 1859.

Afra

Justus and Pastor

St Justus

Afra, a prostitute, had been converted when the Bishop of Gerona, driven from his diocese by persecution, reached Augsburg and took refuge in her mother's house.

The transformation of her life was complete, though Afra never ceased to live as if she were doing penance for her former sins. When her time came to suffer she saw this too as a form of atonement. The pagan judge before whom she was brought, accused of being a Christian, told her that her own Lord would have nothing to do with such a sinner as she had been. But Afra replied that although she was without doubt unworthy to be called a Christian, Jesus Christ had indeed admitted her as one.

'My body has sinned,' confessed the saint at her trial. 'Let it suffer. I will not ruin my soul by idolatry.' Her executioners tied her to a stake on an island in the River Lech. Dried vine branches were piled up around her and set alight.

That night Afra's mother and three other women sailed to the island, gathered up Afra's body and took it to a large tomb at Augsburg. The pagan authorities saw them performing this last act of mercy. The four women were shut up in the family tomb, which was then set alight. They, like Saint Afra, were burned to death.

One of the emperors' chief persecutors of Christians in the early years of the fourth century was a man named Dacian, who journeyed through Spain in a frenzy of violence and terror.

In the year 304 he reached the town of Alcala. Proclamations demanded that all Christians, on pain of death, renounce their faith. Two schoolboys, Justus and Pastor, heard of this and determined to show that their own Christian faith was as strong as that of any of their elders. At this time Justus was thirteen years old and Pastor no more than nine.

Dacian thought it simple to cow schoolboys. He ordered that both young Christians be savagely flogged. But although the sentence was viciously carried out, neither flinched. Instead the two boys shouted words of encouragement to each other, which only whipped their tormentors to further fury.

Dacian was put to shame by their bravery. He still wished to have them killed, but the sentence was carried out secretly. They were beheaded outside Alcala, when no-one was about, but some fellow-Christians found their bodies and buried them where they had died.

Today Saints Justus and Pastor are considered among the patron saints of Alcala and Madrid. Their alleged bodies were discovered in the eighth century and taken to Huesca. In 1568 they were brought back to Alcala, where they lie under the high altar of the collegiate church.

Sixtus II

Pope Sixtus II was (perhaps) a Greek philosopher who embraced the Christian faith, reached this pinnacle of the church's offices and lasted in it no more than a year, suffering a brave martyr's death in the year 258.

Although Sixtus II was convinced that anyone baptized by a heretic was not truly baptized, he nevertheless refused to excommunicate or otherwise punish those theologians who disagreed with him. In later centuries, the church decreed that provided a heretic had properly used the formulas of baptism, any person so baptized could not be held to be outside the Christian faith. Why should a man or woman who had embraced Christianity be considered a pagan simply because the one who performed the rite of baptism was in error in his own beliefs?

The Emperor Valerian had set forth his first decree condemning Christianity in 257. He ordered that the farms and estates, the honours and the goods, the freedom and even the lives of those who refused to renounce their faith should be sacrificed. The pope took refuge in the catacombs on the Appian Way. He was discovered, preaching to his flock, seated in his chair; still seated, he was beheaded; and with him were martyred four deacons. Their bodies were carried across the Appian Way by their mourners, and placed in the cemetery of St Callistus. He was one of the most highly esteemed martyrs of the early Roman church.

Dominic

The rise of the heretics known as the Cathars or Albigensians raised a perennial problem for the orthodox: should false teaching be fought by all the apparatus of the state, including force; or can it be opposed only by love and argument?

Dominic, who was born in the year 1170 in Castile, sought to counteract error by reason rather than force. He became a cathedral canon at the age of twenty-six, and his bishop became leader of a papal mission to convert the Albigensians to the faith of orthodox Christians. Many of these heretics led fine lives. They exalted the soul rather than the body. But others were led to believe that whatever their bodies did had no relevance to the state of their souls. In consequence, they felt that they could sin freely without any mortal peril to their souls.

Dominic's bishop chose the young canon as his special companion in the quest to bring these heterodox Christians back into the fold. While they were attempting to persuade the heretics by reason and by love, an army led by the fearsome Simon de Montfort set about bringing them back to orthodoxy by brute force. Simon de Montfort's armies sacked fine cities in the south of France, burning them to the ground and slaughtering the inhabitants simply because of their unorthodox faith. Dominic, by contrast, used only patience and gentle argument to bring men and women back into the Catholic fold.

He hated to see heretics burnt at the stake. Once he managed to persuade the judges that a young man would surely return to Catholicism one day. The man was spared, and later, happily, became one of Dominic's own companions.

This humble saint – who three times refused to be made a bishop – founded a great teaching order known as the Dominicans. He died in 1221.

Oswald of Northumbria

In the year 617 the King of Northumbria was killed by King Redwald of the East Angles. His three sons, including Oswald, fled to Scotland, and there they became Christians. They were baptized at Iona.

Two brothers soon lost their faith. Oswald's persisted. And when his brothers were killed by the British King Cadwalla, Oswald gathered an army and marched against him. The day before the battle he made his soldiers construct a wooden cross. Oswald himself knelt down, holding the cross in position until enough earth had been thrown in the hole to make it stand firm. Then he prayed, summoning his army to join him with the words, 'Let us all kneel together and ask the true, living and almighty God in his mercy to protect us from the arrogant savagery of our enemies, for He knows that we fight in a just cause to save our nation.'

Oswald defeated Cadwalla, recovered his father's throne, and asked the monks of Iona to send missionaries to his kingdom. St Aidan was sent, and King Oswald gave him the island of Lindisfarne as his episcopal see. 'The king always listened humbly and readily to Aidan's advice,' says the Venerable Bede, 'And while the bishop, who was not yet fluent in English, preached the gospel, it was delightful to hear the king himself interpreting the word of God to his nobles and leaders.' Oswald invited other Scots to missionize his kingdom. He gave money and lands to establish monasteries and churches.

The pagan king of Mercia killed him at the battle of Maserfeld, when he had reigned no more than seven years. His last prayer, as his enemies pressed round him, was 'O God, be merciful to their souls.' His head was placed in St Cuthbert's coffin, and found there centuries later in 1827.

Lawrence

Lawrence was a Spaniard who came to Rome to serve Pope Sixtus II as a deacon. The pope himself was put to death in the year 258 during the persecution of the Emperor Valerian. Lawrence was heartbroken. He followed the pope and his captors to the place of execution, asking why Sixtus II should be murdered and not his deacon. Sixtus replied, 'My son, I am not leaving you. In three days you will follow me.'

Lawrence, overjoyed that he was to follow his master to martyrdom, had one task left. He gathered together all the poor persons, the orphans and the widows he could find and gave them all he possessed. Lawrence even sold some of the church's gold and silver, handing over this money too to the needy.

The prefect of Rome summoned the deacon and said he wished Lawrence to turn over to the authorities all the wealth of the church. Lawrence said he would need three days to gather it together. In those three days he brought together thousands of lepers, blind and sick persons, the poor, widows, orphans, the aged. He brought these to the prefect, observing, 'The church is truly rich, far richer than your emperor.'

In his rage the prefect threatened to kill Lawrence slowly. He took a huge gridiron, heated it until it glowed, and binding Lawrence to the metal, roasted him to death. Before he died, he prayed for the conversion of the city of Rome.

Clare

The life and work of Saint Francis of Assisi so impressed Clare Offreduccio, the daughter of rich parents, that she gave up all she possessed and joined him in the village of Portiuncula, two miles out of Assisi. Since Francis had founded no women's convent, he sent Clare to stay with Benedictine nuns near Bastia, but in 1215 Francis set up a women's community, appointing Clare as abbess – a position she held till her death in 1253.

The saint was delighted when she obtained from the pope the privilege of total poverty. Her sisters, Poor Clares as they came to be called, possessed not even property in common, belonging to the community. They never ate meat. They did without shoes and stockings. Clare went further than most of her nuns. She wore a hair shirt, and lived on bread and water throughout Lent.

When later popes tried to persuade the Poor Clares to accept at least common property, so as to mitigate the rule of absolute poverty, Clare herself would have none of it. Later in life she grew less harsh with her followers, writing to Sister Agnes of Prague not to be quite so rigorous in her pattern of life, 'since our bodies are not of brass'. Yet she herself remained austere and gentle at the same time, kissing the feet of those who brought the goods they had begged in the streets and yet walking round her nunnery at night to make sure the Poor Clares were warmly covered up in bed.

St Clare

'They say we are too poor. Can a heart which possesses God really be called poor?'

St Clare

Euplius

During the persecutions of the Emperor Diocletian in the year 304 a deacon named Euplius was found in Catania, Sicily, reading the Gospels to some poor persons. He was brought before the local governor, Calvisian. Evidently Euplius had already decided that he was going to die for the faith and called out that he was a Christian ready to suffer martyrdom even before he was brought into Calvisian's presence.

Euplius was carrying a copy of the four Gospels in his hand. The governor told him that to possess such books was now illegal. Euplius simply read to him passages about suffering for the sake of Christ:

> 'Blessed are those who are persecuted for righteousness' sake; theirs is the kingdom of heaven';
> 'If anyone would come after me, let him deny himself, take up his cross, and follow me.'

Calvisian presumed that Euplius was confessing to breaking the laws and ordered the saint to be stretched on a rack. The tortures clearly distressed the saint, though he still cried out prayers to Jesus. Calvisian therefore hoped he might be able to break Euplius's will and ordered him to worship three pagan gods, Apollo, Mars and Aesculapius. At this point Euplius repeated his profound belief in the blessed Trinity: 'I revere only the Father, the Son and the Holy Spirit. There is no other God.'

The men who were torturing Euplius resumed their work. He continued to pray, though the pain stifled his words and the onlookers could in the end see only his lips moving. Calvisian wrote out his sentence: Euplius was to be beheaded.

The executioner took the saint's book of the Gospels and hung it around his neck. In fact this only increased the saint's joy, as he was borne away, described (in the words of the governor) as 'an enemy of the gods and of the emperor'.

AUGUST 13	AUGUST 14

Hippolytus

Maximilian Kolbe

Hippolytus – by far the most important Roman theologian of the third century – is at first sight an odd person to have been made a saint since he was in effect also the first 'anti-pope'. He disagreed with the teachings of Pope Zephyrinus, and under Zephyrinus's successor (Pope Callistus) set himself up as a rival pope. What reconciled him to the church was persecution. Both he and Pope Pontianus were exiled to Sardinia during the persecutions under the Emperor Maximinus. They became friends, and after both had died as martyrs around the year 236, their bodies were brought back in honour to Rome.

Later, many stories circulated purporting to describe Hippolytus's actual martyrdom. He is said to have attended St Lawrence's funeral, and as a punishment for this been tied to a pair of untamed horses and dragged along the ground till he died. His last words were, 'Lord, they break my body; receive my soul.'

In 1551 a headless statue of Hippolytus was found just outside Rome during excavations of part of the Via Tiburtina. Inscribed on either side of the chair are tables for working out the date of Easter. This statue, showing the saint as teacher, was carved during his own lifetime.

Hippolytus wrote the first Christian commentary on any book of the Bible: a commentary on Daniel. He wrote a second commentary on the Song of Songs, as well as another on the Psalms (though so far scholars have found only fragments of this). But his most fascinating work is called *The Apostolic Tradition*. It tells us far more about the life and worship of the early third-century Roman church than scholars once dreamed possible. Hippolytus longed to strengthen the traditional patterns of Christianity. He strongly opposed those who introduced what he called 'novelties' which included, in his view 'new fasts and feasts, abstinences and diets of radishes'.

If (as even scholars admit) his style can be boring, he clearly was a passionate and an extremely learned Christian.

Hippolytus is shown in the picture opposite.

'Pray that my love will be without limits.'

St Maximilian Kolbe's last letter to his mother.

At Oswiecim in southern Poland the Nazis in 1940 established a concentration camp which they called Auschwitz. Prisoner no. 16670, a Catholic priest named Maximilian Kolbe, was brought there on 17 February 1941. Priests in Auschwitz were especially vilified. One of the savage guards once horsewhipped Kolbe fifty times and left him for dead in a wood. The saint recovered some of his strength, and continued to comfort his fellow prisoners, insisting that everything, even sufferings, came to an end, and the way to glory was through the cross.

One day a prisoner escaped. In reprisal the prison guards chose ten men, whom they planned to starve to death. One was a married Polish sergeant named Francis Gajowniczek. Maximilian Kolbe begged the camp commandant to let him take Gajowniczek's place, and the request was granted. 'I am,' argued the forty-seven year old priest, 'old and useless.' Maximilian Kolbe comforted each one as they died. He was the last to die. His guards could scarcely bear the saint's composure, and they speeded his end by injecting Maximilian Kolbe with carbolic acid.

Maximilian Kolbe had been a brilliant scientist, mathematician and religious journalist.

Mary

'My soul magnifies the Lord,
and my spirit rejoices in God my Saviour,
for he has regarded the lowliness of his handmaiden . . .'

St Mary

When the mother of Jesus had been betrothed to Joseph, wrote St Matthew, 'before they came together she was found to be with child of the Holy Spirit.' St Luke's Gospel adds that this was told to Mary herself by the angel Gabriel, who said, 'Hail, favoured one, the Lord is with you.' Mary simply replied, 'Behold, I am the handmaid of the Lord. Let it be to me according to your word.'

While Mary carried Jesus in her womb, she visited her cousin Elizabeth, the mother of John the Baptist. Elizabeth cried, 'Blessed are you among women, and blessed is the fruit of your womb.' It was on this occasion that Mary sang her beautiful Magnificat.

Little is told us in the New Testament about the boyhood of Jesus. St Luke recounts his journey with his parents to Jerusalem when he was twelve. Mary, he says, kept in her heart everything she saw and learned of her son. From time to time we read of her appearances in the events of Jesus's public ministry. But at the crucifixion, according to St John, came one of the tenderest moments between the mother and her son, as she watched him dying on the cross. Mary was standing by the disciple whom Jesus loved. He said to her, 'Behold your son', and to him, 'Behold your mother.' From that hour the disciple took Mary to his own home.

The last mention of Mary in the New Testament occurs in the Acts of the Apostles, where we learn that she was with Jesus's disciples at Jerusalem when the Holy Spirit came upon them all. But many ancient traditions of the church glorify her – in particular by speaking of her lifelong virginity and of her bodily assumption into heaven. Other legends claim that Mary spent her childhood in the Temple.

Rock

Hyacinth

St Rock

Among the many saints called on for defence against the plague in the middle ages, none was more popular than Saint Rock. The son of the governor of Montpellier, Rock was left as an orphan by the time he was twenty years old. He therefore decided to give his money to the poor and make a pilgrimage to Rome.

By the time he reached Italy the plague was devastating most of that land. Almost certainly the year was 1348 – the year of the Black Death. Since there was at that time no known cure for the plague, any person who even cared for those who had contracted it was hailed as a saint. Rock also seemed capable of healing people as well. He had since birth been curiously marked on his chest with a cross-like spot. He made the sign of the cross over those sick of the plague and many miraculously recovered.

Inevitably he caught the infection himself. Saint Rock crawled into the woods near Piacenza to die alone; but a dog came, licked his sores and brought him food, and the saint recovered.

Eventually Saint Rock returned to his native Montpellier. No-one recognized him; and since that part of France was divided by war, the citizens decided that the saint was a spy. Rock was thrown into jail. Only on his death in 1378 was the cross-shaped birth-mark discovered. The unjustly imprisoned saint was given an honourable funeral after his death.

His canonization was undoubtedly hastened by the fact that a local plague broke out when the Council of Constance was assembled between 1414 and 1418. The delegates hastily begged Saint Rock's intercessions; the plague was lifted; and Rock's cult was speedily approved.

In art, Rock is frequently depicted with a dog – a reference to the legendary dog that succoured him in his illness.

Saint Hyacinth's name derives from a corruption of Jacek – the Polish name by which he was baptized in 1185. He joined the Dominicans in Rome in the year 1218 and three years later was sent as a missionary preacher to Cracow.

In those days Cracow was a city of much immorality. Saint Hyacinth's preaching changed the hearts and lives of many. Even the nobility became humble. Long-standing quarrels were patched up. Hyacinth wished to convert men and women by the power of the word rather than by signs and wonders; and although the traditions about him claim that he worked miracles, we are also told that he did his best to keep them quiet.

He was determined to ensure the long-term success of his preaching by founding Dominican convents – at Sandomir, at Plock, and in Cracow itself. The saint then journeyed into the remote and (in those days) wild north. He reached the Baltic Sea, and he crossed over into Denmark, Norway and Sweden, always leaving behind newly founded convents from which a steady flow of preachers consolidated the saint's work. Tireless in his labours, Hyacinth reached the Ukraine, Ruthenia and Russia, earning himself the title 'apostle of the north'.

Among the many miracles attributed to the saint, one stands out as extraordinary. Towards the end of his life a noblewoman sent her son to invite the saint to come and convert her servants and tenants. The young man was drowned as he crossed a river on his way to Hyacinth. The corpse was brought to the saint. Hyacinth took his hand, prayed, and then raised the man from death. This was in the year 1257. In that year – on 8 August, the feast of Saint Dominic himself – Hyacinth, aged seventy-two, received his last Sacrament and died.

AUGUST 18

Helena

Saint Helena suffered great exaltation and great humiliation during her lifetime, and yet remained constantly noble during all her trials. She was the daughter of an innkeeper, and married the Roman general Constantius Chlorus. She bore him a son, Constantine. And in 293 Constantius was proclaimed Caesar.

For nakedly political reasons, he renounced Helena, and in her stead married the stepdaughter of the Emperor Maximian. For fourteen years her former husband ruled the Roman empire. He died in 306 and Constantine's troops proclaimed him Caesar. Defeating his enemies at the battle of Milvian Bridge in the year 312, he entered Rome and declared Christianity a tolerated religion. And he conferred on his mother the title Augusta. Coins were now struck bearing her image. But at the age of sixty-three Helena was baptized a Christian. She built churches. She loved the poor, and went about dressed humbly and modestly.

In the year 324, when she was in her seventies, Helena decided to make a pilgrimage to the Holy Land. The Emperor Hadrian had built a Temple to Venus over the place where Jesus was crucified and over his tomb. Helena ordered its removal, and there she supervised the building of a great new church at her son's expense.

In 395, sixty-five years after Helena had died, Saint Ambrose of Milan declared that she had actually found the holy cross on which Jesus hung. She worshipped, said Ambrose, 'not the wood, but the king who hung on that wood.' Part of this cross was kept at Jerusalem. Another part was sent to Rome.

Helena spent her last years in Palestine. When she died her body was solemnly borne back to Rome.

Eusebius, the church historian, wrote that she 'continually worshipped in church in the sight of all, humbly dressed among the women praying there. In addition, she beautified the churches with rich ornaments and decorations, not forgetting the chapels of the least significant towns and villages.'

John Eudes

Bernard of Clairvaux

'Take away free will, and there is nothing left to be saved. Take away grace, and there is no way of saving. Salvation can only be accomplished when both co-operate.'

St Bernard of Clairvaux

'Just as a tiny drop of water falls into a great quantity of wine and becomes diluted so that it seems to disappear, so should all human affection in believers finally dissolve and become liquefied, so as to flow completely into the will of God.'

St Bernard of Clairvaux

John Eudes, a farmer's son from Normandy, became a Jesuit and he conceived the desire to care for fallen, wayward women.

In 1641, inspired by one of his friends, a woman named Madeleine Lamy, John Eudes founded a home for them at Caen. Eventually the women who ran it for him took the name of Sisters of our Lady of Charity. This work, which seems clearly of immense value, was looked on askance by many at the time. Eventually he decided to resign as a Jesuit and found another order of priests, dedicated to improving the standards of the clergy themselves. His new foundation – which he called the Congregation of Jesus and Mary – was attacked on all sides. John Eudes sent a trusted friend to Rome to try to obtain papal approval for his new plans. Twice opposition there led to a refusal. But John Eudes was used to taking blows, whether spiritual or physical, and he tried again. This time he was successful.

Throughout all this time John Eudes never ceased to preach powerfully, seeking especially those outside the churches. In his seventy-ninth year he preached in the open air every day for nine weeks. This in truth wore out the old saint, and he died of the exertions that same year.

Born in 1090 in the château of his family near Dijon in Burgundy, Bernard led a careless life until the year 1113, when he persuaded four of his brothers and another twenty-seven friends to enter the new and strict monastery at Cîteaux. So impressive was the young Bernard's commitment to the reformed monastic ideals that after two years the Abbot of Cîteaux sent him to found a daughter house at Clairvaux in Champagne. From Bernard's new foundation no fewer than sixty-eight daughter houses sprang – including Fountains and Rievaulx in Britain. And Bernard's pupils were as famous and important as his monastic foundations. In 1145 one of them was elected pope, and never forgot to whom he owed his deep spirituality.

Bernard had the authority to decide between rival popes and persuade the wayward rulers of Europe to support his choice. He was ready to preach powerfully against the Albigensian heretics of Languedoc. He inspired countless Europeans to follow Emperor Konrad III and King Louis VII on the second crusade. He attacked the teaching of Peter Abelard, which held that reason was man's supreme faculty, and he managed to bring to an end the Jewish pogroms in the Rhineland.

Bernard died at Clairvaux in 1153.

AUGUST 21

Pius X

I was born poor, I have lived poor, and I want to die poor,' said Pope Pius X. He was in fact the second son of a shoemaker and postman who lived near Treviso in Italy. His education began at the local village school, before he entered a seminary for priests at Padua in the year 1850.

Ordained in 1858, the saint spent the next seventeen years in patient, faithful parish work before being appointed chancellor of the diocese of Treviso in 1875. Nine years later he was offered the dilapidated diocese of Mantua. His devotion revived its spiritual and pastoral life.

Elected pope in 1903, he was ready to take on the French state two years later when it proposed the separation of church and state, with 'cultural associations' in charge of church property. Pius X, ever content with poverty, chose financial ruin for the French church in order to secure its independence from the state.

Pius X opposed both those who thought Catholics must be old-fashioned royalists and those who insisted they should be modern revolutionaries. Saint Pius X was very much criticized for putting a stop to tendencies which cast doubt on traditional interpretations of the Bible. He was totally opposed to what was called 'Modernism' in theology. Pius X loved the liturgy, particularly Gregorian chant, and he encouraged the faithful to make frequent communions – every day if possible.

St Pius X

'Holy Communion is the shortest and safest way to heaven.'

St Pius X

Symphorianus

Symphorianus lived in Gaul, in the Roman city of Autun, where the pagan goddess Cybele was particularly revered. On her feast day the image of this goddess was wheeled through the streets of Autun on a chariot, while the mob bowed and worshipped.

Taking part in the ceremonies was the provincial governor, Heraclius. Heraclius commanded Symphorianus to worship Cybele as the mother of all the gods. Declaring that he worshipped the one true God, Symphorianus asked for a hammer to smash the pagan idol.

Learning that Symphorianus came from a noble family, the governor decided to give him another chance. When the saint persisted in his faith, he was flogged. The governor then tried to bribe him, offering him an army commission if he would recant. But all this was in vain, and he eventually condemned the saint to be killed by the sword. Soldiers led him to the place of execution outside the city walls. As they went he saw his mother standing on the walls. She shouted to her son, 'Do not be afraid, Symphorianus. Your death will lead straight to eternal life.' The swordsman cut off his head and he was buried in a tomb.

Philip Benizi

Around the time Philip Benizi was born in Florence, seven men of that city came together to found the Order of the Servants of Mary. Philip took a degree in medicine at the University of Paris, but on his return to practise in Florence, he became more and more interested in studying the Bible and the writings of the Church Fathers. By 1254 he was convinced that it was God's will for him to join the Servants of Mary. For several years this brilliant man worked as gardener and general labourer to the new order, living in a cave behind their church, revealing his learning to no-one.

On day in 1258 he was sent on an errand to Siena. On the way he fell into conversation with some Dominicans and unwittingly revealed his fine mind to them. The rumour that a man of such gifts had hidden himself away reached the head of the Servants of Mary. Completely against his own wishes he was made Prior General of the order. He sent out missionaries to the orient. He established a group of Servants of Mary consisting entirely of women. He codified the rules of the order. But when he learned in 1268 that Cardinal Ottobuoni planned to put his name forward for election as the next pope, he hid himself until the danger that he might be elected was past.

Philip Benizi longed to bring to an end the wars between the Guelfs and the Ghibellines in northern Italy. Towards this end he put his talents as a preacher. He died, still urging peace, in 1285.

August 23 is also the feast day of Saint Rose of Lima, a young girl of extraordnary beauty as well as holiness. She died in 1617 and was canonized in 1671, the first ever canonized saint of the New World.

St Philip Benizi

'My God, the closer I come to you, the more I need to humble myself in the dust.'

St Philip Benizi

Bartholomew

Louis IX

St John's Gospel records an extraordinary conversation between Jesus and Bartholomew, one of Jesus's first twelve disciples. Jesus said that Bartholomew was a man without deceit. The surprised future disciple asked, 'How do you know me?' and Jesus answered, 'Before Philip called you, when you were sitting under a fig tree, I saw you.'

Bartholomew's earlier scepticism disappeared. He said to Jesus, 'Teacher you are the Son of God. You are the King of Israel.' Jesus said more: 'Because I said to you that I saw you under the fig tree, do you believe? You shall see greater things than these.'

He then added: 'Truly, truly, I tell you, you will see the heavens opened, and the angels of God ascending and descending upon the Son of man.' According to John's Gospel, Bartholomew persevered as an apostle, and was granted a vision of the Risen Lord. Later traditions record that he preached in India and Armenia after the resurrection. The saint is said to have met his death in Armenia, where King Astyages commanded that he be flayed alive. He was killed after this torture by beheading – and his emblem in art is a butcher's knife. Eventually his relics are said to have been transported to Benevento in Italy.

King Louis IX of France ascended the throne at the age of twelve, and after the regency of his mother (Blanche of Castile) took power in 1235 and for thirty-five years ruled with deep piety, charity and wisdom. In a savage era, he was an amazingly merciful man. Once, for instance, Hugh de la Marche led a revolt against the king. Louis IX could have put to death Hugh's son, who had taken the side of the rebels. Louis spared him, saying that no loyal son could go against his father.

Sometimes the king's courtiers complained at the long time he spent in prayer. Louis retorted that they wasted far more time gambling. No-one ever heard an oath pass the king's lips. But he used to say, 'Make sure you never willingly do or say anything at all which – should it come to light – you could not gladly admit to, and say, "Yes, I did that," or "Yes, I said that".'

Louis IX was not too haughty to visit the sick and poor in their own wretched homes. He washed the feet of beggars. When one of his nobles had hanged three children for the petty crime of poaching rabbits, Louis jailed him and refused him the right to trial by his peers, since they would probably have supported the hangings.

Clearly Louis was a strong and pious king. He brought prosperity to France partly by subduing unruly subjects such as Raymond of Toulouse. He took control of Guyenne by defeating King Henry III of England at Taillebourg. He settled disputes between barons, and even arbitrated between Henry III and the English barons in 1263. Far less successful were his crusading forays into the east. On the first, Louis himself was taken prisoner in 1250 and had to be ransomed. On the second, in 1270, he landed at Tunis and died.

Louis the Pious presided over an age of stupendous Gothic architecture, and when in 1239 the Latin King of Constantinople gave him what was commonly held to be Jesus's crown of thorns, Louis had built to house it the soaring Sainte-Chapelle on the Ile de la Cité, Paris.

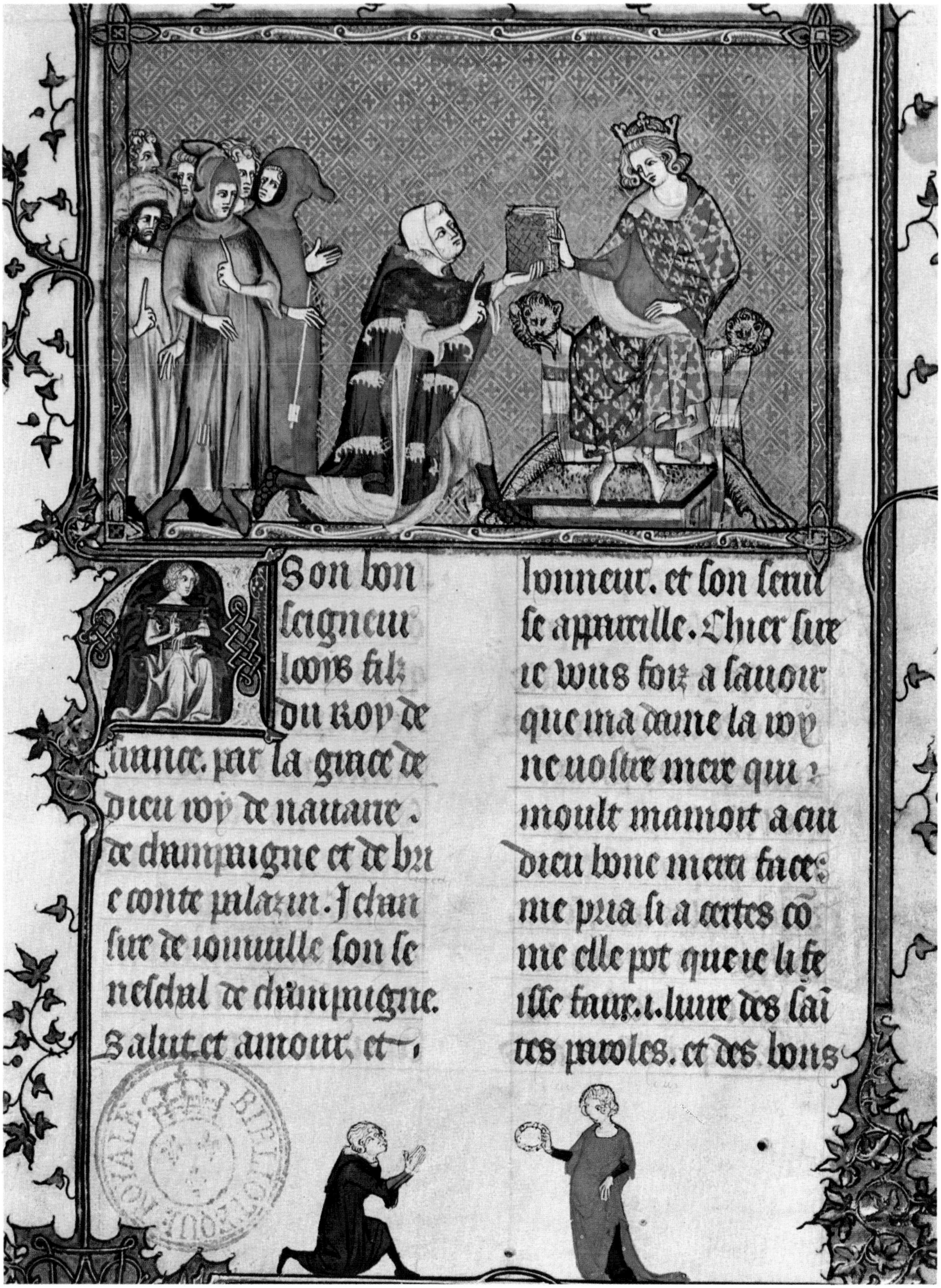

A son bon
seigneur
loois filz
du roy de
france. par la grace de
dieu roy de nauaire.
de champaigne et de bri
e conte palazin. Jehan
sire de ioinuille son se
neschal de champaigne.
Salut et amour. et

lonneur. et son serui
se appareille. Chier sire
ie uous fois a sauoir
que ma dame la roy
ne nostre mere qui
moult mamoit a cui
dieu bone merci face:
me pria si a certes co
me elle pot que ie li fe
isse faire .i. liure des sai
tes paroles. et des bons

AUGUST 26	AUGUST 27

Zephyrinus

Monica

St Monica

'We make ourselves a ladder out of our vices if we trample the vices themselves underfoot.'

St Augustine

'Love, and do what you will.'

St Augustine

Zephyrinus, pope from 198 to 217, is often counted as a martyr, though he died peacefully and his body now lies intact in the church of San Sisto Vecchio in Rome.

Those who count him a martyr mean that he was so taxed and troubled by the great quarrels amongst the Christian theologians of his time that it virtually broke his heart. Nevertheless, with the aid of his deacon (and successor as pope) Callistus, Zephyrinus strove hard to combine firmness and charity, ever ready to welcome back those who had seen the errors of their speculations while at the same time conscious that the truth about Jesus was far too precious to be perverted by false teachers.

His charity annoyed some people. One critic was the learned Saint Hippolytus, who said that Zephyrinus was far too lax when it came to keeping in order those leading Christians astray with their teaching. Whatever the justice of Hippolytus's criticism, Saint Zephyrinus was certainly capable of firmness when he judged it necessary but he was perpetually ready to restore those who came to believe that they had been wrong.

Monica was the mother of Saint Augustine, the eldest of three children she bore to her dissolute husband Patricius. In the year 371, at the age of forty, she was widowed. Augustine was then eighteen years old.

What distressed her most of all was the life of her elder son. He had taken a mistress, chosen (as he himself wrote) 'for no special reason save that my restless passions had alighted on her' – though he remained faithful to her and came to love the child she bore him. Monica was also saddened that Augustine dabbled in other philosophies and for many years was not a Christian. She wept for him (again Augustine wrote) 'shedding more tears for my spiritual death than other mothers shed for the bodily death of a son.' Around this time she was comforted by an unnamed bishop with the words, 'The son of so many tears cannot possibly be lost.'

In 383 Augustine set out for Italy. Boldly Monica left her native Africa and followed her son. In Milan she became a faithful disciple of Saint Ambrose, the bishop. Augustine too sat at Ambrose's feet and was gradually won over to Christianity. She was greatly devoted to Ambrose above all because he showed her son the way of salvation. Augustine adds that 'his heart too warmed to Monica because of her truly pious way of life, her zeal in good works and her faithfulness in worship. Often when he saw me he would break out in praise of her, congratulating me on having such a mother.' ('He little knew what sort of a son she had,' Augustine wryly notes.)

Four years later she and Augustine sat looking out of a window at Ostia, talking of heaven. Monica said: 'What I am still to do, or why I still linger in this world, I do not know. There was one reason, one alone, for which I wished to tarry a little longer: that I might see you a Catholic Christian before I died. God has granted this boon, and more, for I see you his servant, spurning all earthly happiness. What is left for me to do in this life?' About five days later she fell ill, and in nine days she had died.

AUGUST 28

Augustine of Hippo

'You have created us for yourself,' wrote Saint Augustine of God the Father, 'and our hearts cannot rest until they find repose in you.' Augustine's intellectual quest for God took him through the heresy of Manichæism, through Neo-Platonism to Christianity. His quest was moral and spiritual as well as philosophical. He had taken a mistress and she bore him a son, Adeodatus, whom he loved, though he knew himself to be driven by lust. Torn between honours and riches or a life devoted entirely to God, he was sitting tormented in a garden when he heard what seemed to be the voice of a child, repeating the words, 'Take it and read, take it and read.' He seized a copy of Paul's letter to the Romans, and read from chapter twelve the verses: 'Not in revelling and drunkenness, not in lust and wantonness, not in quarrels and rivalries. Rather arm yourselves with the Lord Jesus Christ; spend no more thought on nature and nature's appetites.' The moment was decisive. He, his son and a friend named Alypius were baptized on Easter Eve, 387, to the joy of Augustine's mother Monica.

The saint had been born in Algeria. He now went to Africa to form a monastic community. He was ordained priest and in 396 consecrated Bishop of Hippo.

For thirty-five years Augustine dominated the Christian world, writing against heretics, publishing sermons and tracts, and leaving behind two great works which have continued to entrance and inspire Christians ever since. One was his *Confessions*, an autobiography of amazing honesty and self-knowledge. The second was his treatise on *The City of God*. Although Augustine took thirteen years to write this work, it was occasioned by the sack of Rome by the Goths in 410 (a moment, wrote Saint Jerome, when it seemed 'that the whole universe had perished in one city'). *The City of God* advances a total philosophy of history, setting out the fundamental contrast between Christianity and the world, yet giving to the earthly city its own role in working for good.

Augustine died in 430 as the invading Vandals were at the gates of Hippo.

Beheading of John the Baptist

Shortly after he had baptized Jesus, John the Baptist began to denounce Herod Antipas, the tetrarch of Galilee. Herod had divorced his own wife and taken Herodias, who was not only his niece but also the wife of his half-brother Philip. John the Baptist declared, 'It is not lawful for you to have her,' so Herod flung him into prison.

Not only did Herod fear John and John's disciples. He also knew him to be a righteous man, so he did not kill him. Herodias determined to bring about the Baptist's death. One day Herod gave a banquet to celebrate his own birthday. His courtiers and officers were present, as well as the leading men of Galilee. Herodias's daughter Salome so pleased Herod when she danced before the company that he vowed, 'Whatever you ask me, I shall give you – even if you ask for half my kingdom.' Salome asked her mother what request she should make. Herodias replied, 'The head of John the Baptist.'

Herod was deeply sorry when she came to him with the request; but because he had made a vow in the presence of all his guests, he gave way. A soldier of the guard was sent to behead John in the prison. The soldier than placed his head on a platter, brought it to Salome, and Salome gave it to her mother. When John's disciples heard what had happened, they took away his body and laid it in a tomb.

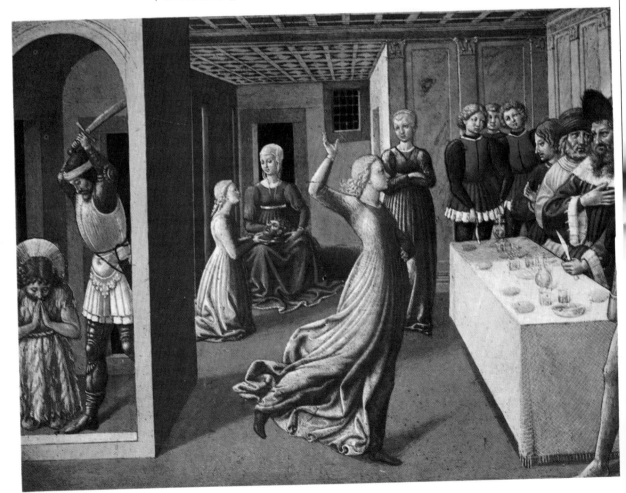

Felix and Adauctus

In the year 304 Felix was living piously and happily, doing the work of a Christian priest in Rome, when he was captured, along with many other Christians at the start of the persecutions under the Emperor Diocletian. First he was savagely tortured. Then he was sentenced to be beheaded, for no torture sufficed to make him give up his Christian beliefs.

Felix was led to the place of execution. So noble and apparently unconcerned did he seem at the prospect of imminent death that one of the crowd who had so far kept secret his own Christianity, shouted out: 'I too follow and believe the same commandments that this man confesses. I too follow and believe in the same Jesus Christ. And I too will give away my life to further his cause.'

The Roman soldiers rushed to seize the man, and he too was beheaded alongside Saint Felix. Unfortunately no-one even gathered his name. He was therefore dubbed 'Adauctus', which simply means 'the additional one'.

Both martyrs were reverently buried in the cemetery of Commodilla on the Ostian Way. By the time the list of martyrs known as the *Depositio Martyrum* was compiled in the year 354, they were simply known as 'Felix and Adauctus'.

About thirty years later Pope Damasus ordered that their tomb be restored and he put an inscription over it.

'Felix, truly and rightly named, for you were happy to have confessed Christ and looked for the kingdom of heaven, despising the prince of this world and departing with your faith unimpaired. Adauctus too, another conqueror, reveals, my brothers, the most precious faith which hastened his journey to heaven.'

Inscription on the tomb of St Felix and St Adauctus

169

Raymond Nonnatus

Peter Nolasco, a native of Languedoc, founded in the early thirteenth century a society known as the Mercaderians, devoted to ransoming Christians captured by the Moors.

Amongst those he received into the society was a Catalonian named Raymond. This Raymond's mother had died giving birth to her son, and he was delivered by a caesarian section – hence his nickname Nonnatus, which is Latin for 'not born'. So determined was Saint Raymond Nonnatus that when Peter Nolasco retired as chief ransomer, the saint succeeded him in this office. He set off for Algiers with a great sum of money, and there ransomed many.

When his money ran out, Saint Raymond Nonnatus could have made his own escape. But this would have involved leaving several slaves behind. He gave himself up in exchange for their liberty.

His own life was now in great danger. The Moors of Algiers were enraged that he had managed to convert some of their number. The governor would have put him to death by impaling the saint on a stake. What saved him were others who realized that a rich ransom would be paid for this particular Christian. Even so, he was still whipped publicly in the streets – partly to discourage those who might be tempted to learn from him the Christian faith. Reports of his tortures probably exaggerated the cruelty of his Moorish captors but after eight months of torture, Peter Nolasco arrived with Raymond Nonnatus's ransom. Even then he wanted to stay behind, hoping to convert still more men and women to Christianity; but Peter Nolasco forbade it.

On his return, Pope Gregory IX made him a cardinal. The pope wished to see Raymond Nonnatus in Rome, but on his way there in the year 1240 he reached only Cardona near Barcelona, where he died at the age of thirty-six.

September

'The Holy Bible is like a mirror
before our mind's eye. In it we see
our inner face. From the
Scriptures we can learn our
spiritual deformities and
beauties. And there too we
discover the progress we are
making and how far we are from
perfection.'

Gregory the Great (September 3)

Giles

William of Roskilde

*'Gracious Giles, of
poor folk chief patron,
Medicine to sick in
their distress,
To all needy shield and
protection,
Refuge to wretches,
their damage to
redress.'*

Poem on St Giles by John Lydgate

Giles was born in Athens in the late eighth century, but finding himself growing increasingly famous in his own land sought solitude in France and settled as a hermit near what is now called Saint-Gilles, close by Arles. He lived on roots, water and the milk of a friendly deer. For three years no-one troubled him till one day the Gothic King Flavius went hunting. His hounds pursued the very deer that served Giles with milk. The terrified animal fled to the saint; and when the huntsmen shot at it, they came upon the saint in his cave.

Flavius brought the Bishop of Nîmes to meet Giles. Eventually bishop and king built a monastery close by the hermit's cave and persuaded him to become its first abbot. Amongst Giles's many disciples was Charlemagne. He begged Giles to visit him, since he had much on his conscience. One sin was too shameful for him to confess, but in a vision Giles learned what it was, told the king and thenceforth had his special protection.

An Anglo-Saxon priest named William became court chaplain to King Cnut. Journeying to Denmark with the king, he decided that the missionary needs of that land were enormous, and stayed there for the rest of his life, eventually becoming Bishop of Roskilde, Zeeland.

To live on terms of great friendship with the royal family was no easy task for a bishop who wished also to witness to the demands of the Christian gospel, for Cnut's successor, King Sweyn Estridsen, in spite of many good qualities, was a headstrong, wilful man who several times greatly offended against Christian standards.

William managed both to rebuke the king – once risking his own life in doing so – and to remain in the end the king's good friend. Sweyn Estridsen put to death a number of men who, whether guilty or not, should have been granted first a fair trial. Saint William of Roskilde decreed that a person who had shed blood unjustly could receive no sacrament of the church until he had done public penance. King Sweyn Estridsen came to the saint's cathedral with armed men. William stood at the door, armed only with his crozier, and refused the king entry. The armed men drew their swords, at which the saint offered them his neck, ready to sacrifice himself for the Christian faith. Sweyn Estridsen was filled with remorse and publicly asked forgiveness, offering property to the church as a token of his great shame.

In his private life the king infringed the moral laws of the church by marrying his own stepdaughter. Repeatedly Bishop William remonstrated. He sought and received the public support of the Archbishop of Hamburg. But only after both pope and Holy Roman Emperor had also censured the king did Sweyn Estridsen put aside his unlawful wife.

Yet the two men clearly loved each other, in spite of their differences. Sweyn Estridsen died first, in the year 1070. As his body was being carried to Roskilde cathedral, the saint, clearly heartbroken, met the cortege and himself fell dead.

SEPTEMBER 3

Gregory the Great

Gregory the Great, pope for fourteen years from 590 till his death in 604, was for the first two decades of his working life a distinguished civilian administrator, rising to be prefect of Rome when the Lombards were threatening the city. About the year 574 he transformed his own home into a monastery and became a monk. He lived apart from the bustle of civic life for several years, until Pope Pelagius II ordained him and appointed the former administrator as one of his seven papal deacons.

Between 579 and 585 he was the pope's agent at Constantinople. The experience stood him in good stead later, for Gregory evidently decided that the Byzantine court had little interest in protecting the Italians and that even the Patriarch of Constantinople looked mostly after his own interests.

On his return he became abbot of his monastery, and then conceived a desire to go to convert the English. He had seen some Saxon slaves for sale in Rome, and learning they were Angles thought they ought to become 'angels'. On his way to Britain, he was recalled to Rome to help counteract the plague, which in fact killed the pope. Gregory was elected in his stead, and was obliged to entrust the conversion of the English to St Augustine of Canterbury and forty other monks from his own monastery.

Gregory was a tirelessly energetic pope, and a charitable one. He abolished fees for burials. He looked after those suffering from famine. He would not allow injustice to Jews. He wrote hymns. He also reformed the church's worship and introduced what today we call Gregorian chant. Disregarding the rights of the Byzantine emperor, he made his own peace with the marauding Lombards and ransomed their prisoners. He wrote prodigiously – over 800 of his letters survive, as well as rules for the life of a bishop, a commentary on the Book of Job, and the lives of many Italian saints.

He it was who described the office of a pope as to be 'the servant of the servants of God'.

Rosalia

'I Rosalia, daughter of Sinibald, the lord of Quisquina and Rosae, for the love of my Lord Jesus Christ left the world to live in this cave.'

Inscription of St Rosalia on the wall of her cave

Saint Rosalia is celebrated in the church and especially at Palermo for two reasons: first for her reclusive life and secondly for a miracle five centuries after she had died in which her bones rescued Palermo from the plague.

The daughter of a royal house, the young saint had no desire for the trappings of the world, nor for any company save that of the Lord she worshipped and his holy family. She gathered together a few possessions: a wooden crucifix; a Greek cross made of silver; another crucifix made of terracotta; and a string of twelve small beads and one large one, which was an early form of the rosary. With these she retired to a cave in Sicily. Probably because people still sought her out here, she transferred herself and her few possessions to a cave filled with stalagmites and stalactites on Monte Pellegrino near Palermo.

Lawrence Justinian, a Venetian brought up by his widowed mother, had an Uncle Marino who was canon of the chapter of St George, a religious community on the island of Alga. When he was nineteen the saint went to join this community, learning from his uncle all sorts of self-disciplines.

Eventually he was made Bishop of Castello. He got rid of the rich gold and silver plate of the bishopric, and used ordinary earthenware. He built churches and founded monasteries. He employed women to find out the names of those who were too ashamed to confess their poverty, so that the diocesan coffers could secretly help them.

In 1451, to his intense annoyance, the pope abolished the Bishopric of Castello and insisted that Lawrence Justinian accept the office of Patriarch of Venice. In vain Lawrence tried to persuade the Doge of Venice himself to object to the appointment. Lawrence remained Patriarch until his death in 1455, and carried out many necessary reforms.

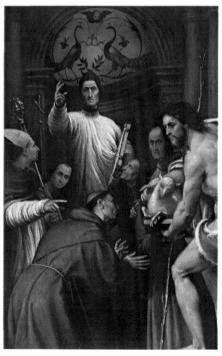

Cagnoald

Saint Columban's monastery at Luxueil was such a source of holiness that by the mid-seventh century it was the most important in France, producing a stream of saints who led the clergy and people to new heights of spiritual awareness. Two of these men were brothers, Saints Faro and Cagnoald. Faro became Bishop of Meaux, Cagnoald Bishop of Laon.

When King Theodoric II, angered because Saint Columban criticized his immoral life, banished the saint from his realms in the year 610, Saint Cagnoald threw in his lot with Columban and also left France. He and Columban worked as missionaries near Lake Constance; but Theodoric extended his sway into that region and implacably banished them again.

Yet the saints remained charitable, even to such a determined enemy. King Theodebert II of Neustria had given him and Columban refuge during their time as missionaries around Lake Constance. Columban's anxieties caused him once to dream that he saw Theodebert and Theodoric fighting. He woke up and told Cagnoald of his dream. 'Let us pray, then, that Theodebert may defeat our enemy Theodoric,' said Cagnoald. 'Certainly not,' responded Saint Columban. 'In no way would such a prayer please God. He has ordered us to pray for our enemies.'

So the two men travelled on into Italy, where Saint Columban founded the famous monastery at Bobbio. Cagnoald had not personally been banned from France, but followed Columban out of love and care. He returned after Columban's death, took up his bishopric, and died himself in the year 633.

Sozon

A young shepherd-boy named Tarasius lived in Cilicia at the beginning of the fourth century. In spite of the dangerous lives led by Christians in that persecuting age, he was baptized and changed his name to Sozon. As he slept out in the fields one day, he had a dream in which Jesus told him to lay aside the weapons which he used to protect his sheep and – taking only his shepherd's crook – to get himself ready to die for his faith.

Sozon seems to have known exactly what to do. The main town of the neighbourhood was called Pompeiopolis. There was a pagan temple with a great golden idol. Sozon marched into the temple and with his crook smashed down the golden idol. He then broke off one of the idol's golden hands and gave pieces of it to the poor of the town. It seemed that he might escape unpunished; but some other Christians were arrested and accused of smashing the idol. Sozon could not allow them to be punished on his behalf, so he confessed his crime. With nails driven through the soles of his shoes Sozon was forced to walk to the amphitheatre. The magistrate wanted to release the courageous prisoner and asked him to play a tune on his pipe to the crowd. Sozon refused. He had, he said, once played to sheep. Now he would play only to God. He was then burned to death.

Adrian and Natalia

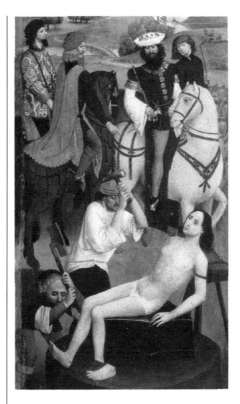

In the year 304 twenty-three Christians were being beaten before the Emperor Maximian. Such was their bravery that one of the imperial officers shouted, 'Let me be counted as one of these, for I too am a Christian' – even though he had not even been baptized.

His name was Adrian. He and his wife Natalia had been married scarcely thirteen months, but when she learned why he had been arrested she was extremely proud of her husband.

In disguise Natalia managed to accompany her husband to the executioner's block where he was to be cut up bit by bit. As the axe dismembered Adrian, Natalia managed to save one of his hands.

A few months later a pagan official began pestering Natalia to marry him. She had no intention of consorting with the heathen who had been responsible for Saint Adrian's martyrdom, so she set sail for Argyropolis, near Constantinople where she died.

Peter Claver

Peter Claver had joined the Jesuits at the age of twenty. He was educated at the University of Barcelona and at Montesione College in Palma, Majorca. There St Alphonsus Rodriguez fired him to go to the New World, to teach the black slaves the faith. In 1610 he had reached New Grenada and was ordained at Cartagena (in what is now Colombia) five years later.

Claver now declared himself to be 'for ever the slave of the Negro'. Each ship that arrived in the New World disgorged men who were scarcely alive, stinking and dying, having been penned up like cattle for the duration of the crossing. Peter Claver said the priority was to 'speak with the hands' and not with the lips. Medicine

and food, tobacco and final unction was what these men craved, and the saint gave it to them. Women had given birth to children in the indescribable filth of the slave holds. Peter Claver baptized them. He found seven interpreters who could speak the language of the slaves, and sought through them to teach the rudiments of the Christian faith.

Nicholas Tolentino

Protus and Hyacinth

In 1845 a priest named Joseph Marchi was excavating part of the Old Salarian Way in Rome when he found a wall tomb, shut up with a slab on which was inscribed in Latin, 'Buried on 11 September the martyr Hyacinth'. Joseph Marchi opened the tomb and found inside a piece of cloth, wrapped around human ashes and fire-blackened bones. Another inscription close by Hyacinth's tomb read: 'The tomb of the martyr Protus'. According to ancient legend, Protus and Hyacinth were the slaves of Eugenia, the Christian daughter of a prefect of Egypt. She and her two faithful servants fled from Egypt to Rome where they were captured by the pagan authorities and put to death by fire. Almost certainly the martydom took place during the reign of the Emperor Valerian.

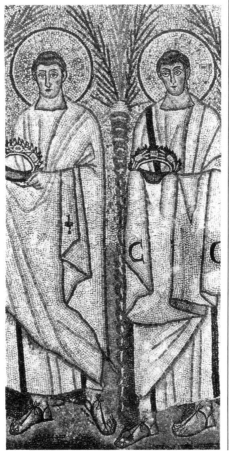

Born at Sant'Angelo, Ancona, in 1245 to middle-aged parents who had almost despaired of being sent a child, Nicholas was brought up as a special gift from God. His mother used to say that God had destined her son to be a saint, and she made sure he came under the influence of their parish priest. When the young Nicholas heard an Augustinian friar preaching on the text, 'Do not love the world, nor those things that are of the world,' he was fired to join the Augustinian order. For a while he thought his vocation lay in a monastic community, but one day as he prayed he heard a voice calling, 'To Tolentino.' Soon he was sent to preach and serve that town, and there he stayed for thirty years until his death in the year 1305.

Victoria Fornari-Strata

John Chrysostom

In 1579 Victoria Fornari of Genoa married Angelo Strata. She was seventeen years old, and the marriage was extremely happy. Then, after nine years of marriage, Angelo died. For some time his widow was distraught. She was also deeply anxious about her children's future. For their sake she was about to marry again, when she was granted a vision of the Virgin Mary. Victoria later wrote down the Virgin's words to her. 'Be brave and courageous. I shall take both you and your children under my wing. Live in peace, without anxiety. Trust yourself to my care and above all devote yourself to the love of God.' The vision was more than fulfilled. Although Victoria still lived charitably, giving away most of her wealth, her children never felt any want.

In 1604 with money provided by one of her wealthy friends, Victoria and ten other women began the practical work of setting up a religious house. All eleven were professed as nuns the following year. So successful was their venture, that a second house of 'Blue Nuns' (as they were called from the colour of their cloaks) was set up in 1612, and soon the order had spread from Italy to France. Victoria remained their superior until 15 December 1617, when she died aged fifty-five.

John Chrysostom, against his own wishes, was made Patriarch of Constantinople in the year 398. But in 403, at the Synod of the Oak, John's enemies conspired to have him deposed and exiled. In exile he wrote many letters which reveal the hardships he endured, and his enemies eventually ensured that he died, as a result of forced marches in frightful weather.

His health had been impaired by the savage austerities he imposed on himself as a hermit. This physical breakdown was what made him return from the mountains to city life and ordination. A trained lawyer, he now used his marvellous oratorical powers to expound the Scriptures in a powerful series of sermons which earned him the title 'golden-mouthed' (or 'Chrysostom'). He was one of the finest preachers of all time and many of his sermons survive. He said, for instance, that for a believer, 'Death is a rest, a deliverance from the exhausting labours and cares of this world. So when you see one of your family departing, do not fall into despair. Think deeply. Examine your conscience. Cherish the thought that soon this end awaits you too.' He added: 'Think to whom the departed has gone – and take comfort.'

Notburga

Nicomedes

Notburga was born shortly after the middle of the thirteenth century to poor peasants in the Tyrol. At the age of eighteen she became a kitchen maid, working for Count Henry of Rattenberg. The rich castle daily squandered more food on pig-swill than Notburga's own parents ate in weeks. Notburga soon started to give this to the poor who swarmed at the castle gates. In case this was not enough for the poor, the saint would add to the pig-swill some of her own food.

Count Henry's mother entirely approved of Notburga's charity, but the count's wife did not, and when her mother-in-law died, she took care to have Notburga dismissed.

Notburga went to work for a farmer near Eben. She worked hard, though she would insist on her right to worship on Sundays even if her employer wanted his servants to go on working.

Meanwhile life was not treating Count Henry of Rattenberg well. His wife died. Next, the Count of Tyrol quarrelled with the Duke of Bavaria, and the quarrel spread to Count Henry's lands. He began to attribute all his misfortunes to the unjust sacking of his peasant kitchen maid. He married again. His second wife needed a good woman to manage her household. Count Henry speedily brought back Saint Notburga, and from then on till her death in 1313 all went well.

She has become one of the patron saints of servants. So revered was this humble woman that her relics were cherished at the nearby church of St Rupert, Eben, and in the year 1718 placed in a position of honour over the high altar.

The Emperor Constantine Copronymus thought that the relics of the saints and martyrs were worthless objects, and that anyone who collected the bones of the holy ones was a fool. He therefore set about finding as many of these sacred remains as he could and throwing them into the sea.

Pope Pascal I, who was elected in 817, thirty-two years after the emperor's death, disagreed. Whereas Constantine Copronymous had got rid of saintly bones, Pascal I conceived it his duty to find as many replacements as possible. The church of Santa Prassede in Rome is filled with all that he collected, their names inscribed on marble tablets close by the sanctuary.

Amongst them are the earthly remains of Saint Nicomedes, brought in the year 817 from their catacomb on the Via Nomentina.

Nicomedes had been a priest, possibly very early in the second century, in the years when Christians had to keep their faith secret or be killed. His own beliefs came to light when he bravely obtained the bones of another martyr, Saint Felicula, to give them Christian burial.

Nicomedes was given the chance of apostatizing by offering sacrifice to heathen gods. 'I sacrifice only to the almighty God who rules over us all from heaven,' was Nicomedes' response. Nicomedes had signed his own death warrant. He was beaten with whips that had been made crueller by means of lead lining, and under this torture, died.

The saint's body was thrown into the River Tiber, so as to deny it the Christian burial Nicomedes had granted Saint Felicula. But another Christian named Justus boldly rescued it and placed the corpse in a tomb on the Via Nomentina, just outside the Porta Pia. And there it remained till the year 817.

St Notburga

Ninian

Hildegard

'Those who desire to do the work of God, should never forget that they are fragile vessels.'

St Hildegard of Bingen

Ninian's father was a Cumbrian chief. When his son embraced Christianity, he decided to visit Rome, where for many years he advanced in holy virtue and self-discipline. But Ninian never forgot the fellow-Britons who still did not know the Gospel. He decided to return home.

In 394 Ninian was consecrated bishop by Pope Siricius. On his way back to Britain Ninian was befriended by Saint Martin of Tours. He founded his see at Whithorn, and there built a stone church which became renowned as the 'White House'. When Ninian heard of Martin's death he dedicated the church to his friend.

Almost certainly this White House was the oldest Christian foundation in Scotland. Ninian founded a monastery close by, and from here he and his monks persuaded the southern Picts inhabiting the Grampians to 'abandon the errors of idolatry' (as the Venerable Bede put it) 'and accept the true Faith'.

Saint Ninian travelled tirelessly. His diocese was huge, stretching from near present-day Glasgow as far as Westmorland. Although later pagan invaders undid much of his work, his memory lingered; and his success in converting the rulers of Wales was considerable.

Throughout the later middle ages the German nation produced a remarkable stream of Christian mystics whose deep union with God was expressed in the most marvellous language and images. One of the first of these was Hildegard of Bingen.

Though she lived to be eighty, Saint Hildegard was always sickly. As a child she was entrusted to the special care of Jutta, the devout sister of Count Meginhard of Spanheim. Even as a very young child, Hildegard's spiritual experiences and visions were overwhelming; but she preferred to keep them to herself, too shy to appear to be boasting about them. 'I saw a light so great that it frightened me,' she later wrote, of a vision experienced when she was three, 'but the shyness of a child stopped me telling anyone about it.'

Later she felt bold enough to tell her confessor of her visions, and he encouraged her to have them written down. Hildegard's writings combine several useful books (of medicine, for instance), with the lives of the saints, with hymns, and visions. She had the gift of extremely vivid imagery. She saw devils transformed from great sparkling lights into black coals. She insisted that she saw everything perfectly awake, not in some trance or dream. And her fame grew.

Eventually Hildegard became a Benedictine nun and then abbess. She moved her convent to Rupertsberg near Bingen, on the Rhine, in 1147, and founded another one at Eibingen around the year 1165. The pope wrote authorizing her to publish whatever parts of her visions she thought would help the faithful. She corresponded as an equal with emperors, bishops and kings.

Just before she died in 1179 she found herself in trouble for allowing the burial in her convent cemetery of a man who had been excommunicated. Hildegard argued that she was right because the man had received the last Sacraments; even though her convent was placed under an interdict, she refused to change her mind.

181

Joseph of Copertino

Januarius

St Joseph of Copertino

Joseph of Copertino was such an extraordinary saint that his fellow-Christians could scarcely cope with him. First of all he was forgetful, even as a child, often not turning up for the scanty meals his impoverished widowed mother prepared. He would wander about the village of Copertino, Italy, where he was born, gazing open-mouthed at everything. He found it hard to learn anything. And he was clumsy.

When he was seventeen he decided he wanted to become a monk or friar. The Franciscans would not take him because, they said, he was too stupid. The Capuchins threw him out after eight months because he broke everything. Eventually a Franciscan house at La Grotella accepted him as a stableboy.

He prayed and fasted and did his best to perform every task to perfection. Eventually the delighted brothers decided to accept him as one of their equals, and in 1628 he was ordained priest. From that time onwards Joseph of Copertino was continually passing into ecstatic trances, sometimes even appearing to float above the ground. No meals could be taken in the monastery without some extraordinary interruption because of Joseph's miraculous behaviour. For thirty-five years the community decided that he should be kept out of the choir and refectory.

Naturally enough his miracles and above all the reports of his supernatural levitations attracted countless curious visitors. In 1653 the church authorities transferred him to a Capuchin friary in the hills of Pietarossa and kept him completely out of sight. Finally Saint Joseph was allowed to join his own order at a place called Osima, but he was still kept out of sight until his death in 1663. All this he bore without the remotest complaint. Fittingly the twentieth century has made the saint patron of pilots and airline passengers.

Januarius was Bishop of Benevento, Italy, the city of his birth, when the Emperor Diocletian turned his fury on Christians. Dracontius, the pagan governor of Campania, took prisoner some deacons and lay Christians, interrogated them until they confessed their faith, and then put them in a dungeon.

Mindful of the Biblical injunction to visit those in prison, Januarius came to comfort them. The jailers informed the authorities, and the saint too was arrested. He was brought to the city of Nola, along with two other Christians, Festus and Desiderius, who had been visiting Januarius when his captors arrived.

The governor decided to torment the three Christians by making them carry heavy chains before his chariot as he rode from Nola into Pozzuoli. Here lay those Christians that Januarius had so charitably visited in the first instance. All were flung into the same dungeon, awaiting execution of the emperor's orders that wild animals should tear them in pieces.

Eustace

The charming legend of Saint Eustace tells how a Roman general named Placidus was once out hunting. He pursued a noble stag, which suddenly turned and approached him. Between the stag's antlers Placidus saw a crucifix. A voice was calling him by name.

The hunter himself had been caught. The vision converted Placidus. He changed his name to Eustace, and gave away much of his money.

The saint still felt able to serve the Roman emperor. Taking up his command again, he led the legions to great victories. By this time his family had become Christian too, and all four of them – Eustace, his wife Theopista, and his sons Agapetus and Theopestus – refused to make sacrifices to pagan gods in the celebrations following his own victories.

All four were accordingly put to death in a bizarre fashion. They were taken to the colosseum in Rome, encased in a brazen bull, and roasted to death.

Although these events are supposed to have taken place around the year 118, no account of Saint Eustace and his family has been found prior to the seventh century. Yet he became one of the most popular saints in the middle ages, celebrated in prose and poetry as well as in art and popular devotion.

Matthew

If the man who wrote the first of the four Gospels in our New Testament was the person called Matthew who became one of Jesus's first apostles, then he had been a collector of taxes for the Romans, working and living at Capernaum, till Jesus changed his life.

Writing first of all for his fellow-Jews, Saint Matthew longed to show them how Jesus had fulfilled all the deepest hopes of the Jewish people. Matthew brought a message of a Saviour who would never desert his followers. The last words of Matthew's Gospel quote Jesus's command that his followers must baptize disciples from all mankind, and then Jesus's promise: 'Lo, I am with you always, to the end of the world.'

Yet although Matthew meant his Gospel in the first place for his fellow Jews, he alone tells us of the first non-Jews to worship the Saviour – the three Magi who followed a star that led them to the stable at Bethlehem, and brought gifts of gold, frankincense and myrrh to the infant Jesus.

Matthew too was the Gospel writer who set down in order the words of Jesus which we know as the Sermon on the Mount. Matthew also was clearly concerned to see developing a strong organization to disseminate and guard the Christian faith. Of all four Gospel-writers, he is most of all concerned with the rules for dealing with a fellow-Christian who is straying, and his Gospel is in fact the only one that uses the word 'church' at all.

Of the parables that Matthew tells us which we know from no-one else, one stands out especially: the story of the sheep and the goats, a parable by Jesus about the Last Judgment. This parable (in the 25th chapter of Matthew's Gospel) ends with Jesus's warning that what we do to the least of his brethren, we do to him.

We do not know when or how Matthew died, though some church traditions say he was martyred in Ethiopia.

Maurice and Companions

In the first half of the fifth century Eucherius, Bishop of Lyons, wrote down a remarkable story of a unit in the Roman army known as the Theban Legion. Serving under the general Maximian Herculius about the year 287, this legion had been recruited entirely from Christians in Upper Egypt.

They were sent to Gaul to put down a revolt by the Bagaudae tribe. Arriving with his army at Martigny on the River Rhone, Maximian ordered every soldier to make a sacrifice to pagan gods, in the hope of ensuring success in battle. The Theban Legion refused to a man. In a form of Christian mutiny, the legion withdrew from the rest of the army and pitched camp at Saint-Maurice-en-Valais.

When Maximian could not persuade them to sacrifice, he commanded that every tenth man be killed. Saints Maurice, Exuperius and Candidus urged their men to stand fast to their beliefs.

Maximian swore that he would kill every single man, unless each one sacrificed to idols. The men declared their readiness to obey any order that was not contrary to the laws of their God. 'We have seen our comrades killed,' they said. 'Rather than sorrow, we rejoice at the honour done to them.' At this Maximian commanded the butchery of these Thebans.

Thecla of Iconium

Three-quarters of the way through the second century a priest in Asia composed an account of the amazing piety and exploits of a woman named Thecla, a follower of St Paul.

The story tells us that Paul – 'a small, bald-headed man, with a long nose, beetling eyebrows, portly girth and bow legs' – was preaching in the house of Onesiphorus at Iconium and there greatly impressed a girl named Thecla who was about to be married. Paul's theme happened to be on the great virtues of celibacy, and Thecla was inspired to reject her fiancé. He and the girl's parents did everything in their power (even enlisting the help of the local magistrates) to make her relent, but Thecla ran away to join Saint Paul.

Her fiancé now had completely turned against her. He accused Paul of breaking up happy couples. He persuaded the magistrates to have Thecla flogged. Since she was no longer his, he determined that no-one should have her, and obtained a sentence putting her to death by fire. The story continues happily, when a tremendous thunderstorm put out the fire and Thecla again escaped.

She was still a beautiful girl, and a leading citizen of Antioch named Alexander tried to carry her off against her will. She fought him off. After several more attempts to torment her and even put her to death, Thecla decided her best hope of a peaceful life was to dress as a young man. In this guise, she rejoined Paul, who judged her well able to preach the Gospel alongside him. As Paul journeyed elsewhere, Thecla retired and spent the remaining seventy-two years of her life in prayer and seclusion in a cave in Seleucia.

The story of Saint Thecla is in fact a long paean of praise for the virtue of chastity, written in an age of great licentiousness.

Pacificus of San Severino

Sergius of Radonezh

St Sergius of Radonezh

Born in 1653 at San Severino in Ancona, Charles Antony Divini was orphaned at the age of three and brought up by a selfish, unkind uncle. At seventeen, he offered himself as a friar and took the name Pacificus on Holy Innocents' Day, 1670. An extremely intelligent student, he was ordained at twenty-five and for the next couple of years taught philosophy. But Pacificus wished for a more active life. He begged his superiors to let him work in the villages surrounding the monastery, preaching, visiting the sick, hearing confessions, missionizing, teaching the young.

Then, at the age of thirty-five, an illness took away both his sight and hearing. And next he suffered a long-term disease which made it almost impossible for him to walk. In 1705 the blind, deaf and crippled saint was transferred to the friary at his home town of San Severino. There he lived for the rest of his life. Instead of rushing hither and thither in the service of his Lord, he now offered a different, equally acceptable work to God: that of prayer and self-discipline.

Born of a high-ranking Russian family at Rostov in the year 1314, Sergius (who was baptized Bartholomew) and his family lost every possession when he was fifteen years old in the civil war between Moscow and Rostov. Forced to flee they settled at Radonezh, living as poor peasants, fifty miles north of Moscow.

Five years later Bartholomew and his elder brother Stephen decided to live as Christian hermits in the savage forests surrounding Radonezh. He and Stephen built a log cabin and a tiny timber church, dedicated to the Holy Trinity. But the elder brother could not bear the Russian winter, the lack of food, the marauding wild beasts, and he returned to Radonezh.

Bartholomew was professed as a monk by a local abbot, took the name Sergius, and yet remained in the forest. His hopes to live quite alone came to nothing. More and more people came to consult this strange, wise, ascetic man. Some begged to join him. Russian monasticism had virtually disappeared in the wake of the Tartar invasions, so that Sergius's community was recreating one of the central elements in the Russian religious tradition, and Sergius never turned anyone away.

In 1380 the prince of Moscow, Dmitri Donskoy, hesitating before the might of the Tartars, consulted Sergius. Sergius declared that if the Russian troops would fight in faith for their country, they would be victorious. Dmitri believed him, the Moslem Tartars were defeated, and Russia remained a Christian land.

The saint now devoted himself to bringing peace to his divided country, reconciling rival princes and nobles. In 1378 he had refused to be consecrated Patriarch of Moscow: 'Since the days of my youth I have never worn gold. Now that I am an old man, more than ever I adhere to my poverty,' he said. He cared for his monastery (and another forty he had founded) for four more years, and then resigned as abbot to die in tranquillity about the year 1382.

Cosmas and Damian

Cosmas and Damian were twins. Born in Arabia, both studied medicine as young men in Syria. They set up practice together at Aegeae in Cilicia. They were extremely proficient. But what marked them off from other doctors at that time was their refusal to charge any fee for their services. They believed that as Christians this was the best form of charity that they could practise. In consequence they are still known throughout Eastern Christendom as Saints Cosmas and Damian the moneyless.

Unfortunately the Diocletian persecutions soon began. Lysias, governor of Cilicia, had no hesitation in arresting such distinguished Christians, in spite of their good works. The two men remained steadfast in the faith. Once they had healed the bodies of others; now their own bodies were broken. They were hanged on crosses and the mob threw stones at them. Archers fired arrows into their helpless torsos. Finally they were cut down, still alive, and beheaded.

All this took place around the year 303. The corpses of the two doctors were taken to Syria, where they had studied, and buried at Cyrrhus. In later ages many notable sick persons, including the Emperor Justinian I himself, would dream of these two saints when ill, learning various medicines from these visions. After such a vision, Justinian rebuilt a church in their honour in the city of Constantinople. In these ways Cosmas and Damian were revered as patron saints of physicians.

Vincent de Paul

Eustochium

As he sailed from Marseilles to Toulouse in 1605, Vincent de Paul's ship was captured by brigands. Vincent and the rest were sold as slaves, and eventually, Vincent found himself in the household of a lapsed Christian. Later the man repented, and released Vincent.

Having suffered so much himself, Vincent de Paul conceived a deep sympathy for the poor and miserable. He had been ordained in 1600 and now Queen Margaret of Valois made him her chaplain. This work brought him to Paris, where he became tutor to the children of Count Philip de Gondi.

Now Saint Vincent de Paul used his contacts with the rich to serve the poor. The Countess de Gondi offered him as much money as he needed to start a mission. Rich women in Paris helped him to fund hospitals for the sick – including one at Marseilles for galley-slaves. He rose to be an intimate adviser of the French royal family and used this position to inaugurate much relief work among the suffering poor. His headstrong nature was restrained by humility, and he died aged eighty-five in the year 1660.

Saint Paula and her daughter Eustochium (*below, centre*) joined Saint Jerome at Antioch. Paula's fortune was added to what money Jerome possessed to found a monastery near Bethlehem. Jerome lived in a cave nearby, 'to make sure (said Paula) that if Mary and Joseph came again to Bethlehem, there would be somewhere for them to stay'.

Three communities of women were founded close by St Jerome's monastery, and Paula took charge of one of them. Eustochium took care of every material need, including the cooking. But Jerome relied on her for much more. He was busy translating the Bible into Latin. When his eyes began to fail, he would have been obliged to abandon the work, had not Eustochium and her mother been there to help him. He reckoned that they were better able to judge the value of his work than most men, and dedicated some of his writings to them.

When Paula died in 404 Eustochium (said Jerome) wished she could have been buried with her. But instead she took over the community abbey. She died in 419.

This day is also the feast day of Wenceslas, the martyr-king of Bohemia who died in 929.

> **'Set before your eyes the blessed Virgin Mary, whose purity was such that she earned the reward of being the mother of the Lord.'**
>
> *St Jerome's counsel to St Eustochium*

Archangels Michael, Gabriel and Raphael

There are two passages in the New Testament where the archangel Michael (*right*) engages in a great cosmic battle against the Devil. In the book of Jude we read of Michael contending with the Devil over the body of Moses, rebuking the evil one in God's name. The imagery reveals that with the triumph of Jesus evil no longer reigns throughout the cosmos, but remains on earth as the enemy of all who seek to follow God's will.

The New Testament here takes over a figure from the Old – for in the Book of Daniel Michael is twice represented as the helper of God's chosen people. Gabriel too is an archangel who assists Daniel, this time in understanding his visions. And Gabriel has a special role in the New Testament. To Zechariah, the father of John the Baptist, he announces the future birth of this prophet. And his is the message to the Virgin Mary that in the power of the Holy Spirit she will bring forth the Saviour Jesus (*left*).

Raphael (*below, left*) appears in the Books of Tobit and of Enoch as one of the seven archangels who stand in God's presence. Tobit represents him as hearing the prayers of godly men and bringing them before the Almighty. Enoch speaks of fallen angels defiling the earth, which is then healed by Raphael.

Raphael in fact means 'God heals'. The meaning of Gabriel is 'man of God'. And Michael means 'the one who resembles God'. All three repeatedly appear in later Christian writings, with Michael usually envisaged as the leader of the heavenly host, and sometimes as the receiver of the souls of the departed to which the Negro spiritual 'Michael, row the boat ashore! Alleluia!' refers.

Michael the Archangel

Jerome

One of the greatest Biblical scholars of Christendom, Saint Jerome was born of Christian parents at Stridon in Dalmatia around the year 345. Educated at the local school, he then studied rhetoric in Rome for eight years, before returning to Aquilea to set up a community of ascetics. When that community broke up after three years Jerome went to the east. He met an old hermit named Malchus, who inspired the saint to live in a bare cell, dressed in sackcloth, studying the Scriptures.

He learned Hebrew from a rabbi. Then he returned to Antioch and was reluctantly ordained priest. With his bishop he visited Constantinople and became friendly with Saints Gregory Nazianzen and Gregory of Nyssa. And then in 382 he went again to Rome, to become the personal secretary of Pope Damasus. Here he met his dearest friends, a wealthy woman called Paula, her daughter Eustochium and another wealthy woman named Marcella.

Here too he began his finest work. Commissioned by the pope, he began to revise the Latin version of the psalms and the New Testament, with immense care and scholarship. Jerome eventually translated the whole of the Bible into the Latin version which is known as the Vulgate. But when Damasus died, his enemies forced the saint to leave Rome.

Accompanied by Paula and Eustochium, Jerome went to Bethlehem. There he lived for thirty-four years till his death in 420, building a monastery over which he presided and a convent headed first by Paula and after her death by Eustochium. The saint set up a hospice for the countless pilgrims to that place. His scholarship, his polemics, his treatises and letters often provoked anger and always stimulated those who read them. 'Plato located the soul of man in the head,' he wrote, 'Christ located it in the heart.'

October

'O Divine Master, grant that I may not so much seek to be consoled as to console; to be understood as to understand; to be loved as to love. For it is in giving that we receive; it is in pardoning that we are pardoned; and it is in dying that we rise to eternal life.'

Francis of Assisi (October 4)

Bavo

Saint Bavo as a wealthy landowner lived a life completely devoted to his own whims. To make more money he would sell his servants as serfs to others. Only when his wife died did the saint realize how selfish his life had been.

His homeland was Brabant, near Liège. Resolved to start a new and better life, Bavo gave all his money away, including a large estate at Ghent. This last was offered to Saint Amand, who built a monastery there. Bavo begged to enter it, and so great was his repentant life that after his death the name of the house was changed from St Peter's monastery to St Bavo's.

By great good fortune he came across one man he had sold as a serf many years before. Bavo begged the man to lead him by a chain in humiliation as far as the city jail. Similar humility marked everything he now did. Saint Amand allowed him to become his companion on missionary expeditions throughout France, during which Bavo's personal mortifications were the wonder of all who saw them.

The austerities even of monastic life soon were not enough to satisfy Saint Bavo's desire to discipline the body that he had once so much indulged. He begged Amand to give him permission to live as a hermit. When permission was given, at first Bavo made his dwelling in a hollow tree. He later built a tiny cell, close by Ghent in the forest of Malmédun. He lived on vegetables and water, seeing no-one save Amand and another friend, the saintly Abbot Floribert, until his death in the year 633. He was buried at a monastery near by which later took the name Saint Bavo in his memory.

So great was the impression left by Saint Bavo that nine hundred years later when the diocese of Ghent was created, he was made its patron saint. In art he is sometimes represented as a hermit; but often the saint is shown in his unreformed days, dressed as a duke out hunting with a falcon on his wrist as he is shown here, far left.

The Guardian Angels

In the year that King Uzziah died the prophet Isaiah was in the Temple and saw the Lord, sitting on a throne. Six-winged seraphim flew above him, crying, 'Holy, holy, holy is the Lord of hosts; the whole earth is full of his glory.' This notion of a multitude of heavenly beings, worshipping God and ready to do his bidding has been taken from Jewish thought and placed at the heart of Christian worship.

The ancient Jews believed that these angels served both individuals and nations. Jesus saw no reason to reject this idea. For him angels were spiritual beings. He said they would support him at his second coming. Once he took a little child and spoke to his followers about becoming like children and caring for them. 'See that you do not despise one of these little ones,' said Jesus, 'for I tell you that their angels always behold the face of my Father in heaven.'

The notion of Guardian angels is thus implicit in our Lord's own teaching. And in his own earthly life they are constantly seen by the Gospel-writers as ready to serve and minister to him. They succour him in the wilderness. They care for him as he agonizes in the garden of Gethsemane. Had he wished, they would have fought against his captors. They are present at his resurrection.

Teresa of Lisieux

Louis Martin, a watchmaker of Alençon in France, and his wife Azélie-Marie, were granted a daughter in 1873 whom they baptized Marie-Françoise-Thérèse. When she was fifteen she told her father that she was so much devoted to Jesus that she wished to become a Carmelite nun. The Carmelites and her bishop thought she was too young, but Teresa persisted and they eventually relented.

Teresa clearly loved her life. She would have gone as a Carmelite missionary to China in 1896; but she began to haemorrhage at the mouth. Suffering from incurable tuberculosis, she was taken to the convent infirmary and died there on 30 September 1897. Her last words were, 'I love him. My God I love you.'

Perhaps she would have been forgotten. But her superiors had ordered her to write an autobiography, called 'The Story of a Soul'. They published it, revised by themselves, along with an account of her death at the age of twenty-four. The appeal of the book was immediate and astonishing.

Teresa's attraction lay in her utter simplicity. No scholar, no great student of the Bible or the fathers, she simply longed to be a saint, as she believed any ordinary person could. 'In my little way,' she wrote, 'are only very ordinary things. Little souls can do everything that I do.'

She was full of fun. She drew a coat of arms for herself and Jesus, surmounted with her initials, M.F.T., and the divine ones I.H.S. She made superbly innocent and happy jokes. She recorded that she would pretend she was at Nazareth in the Holy Family's home. 'If I am offered salad, cold fish, wine or anything with a strong flavour, I give that to good Saint Joseph. I give the warm dishes and the ripest fruits to the holy Virgin. I give the infant Jesus soup, rice and jam. But if I am offered a bad meal, I say gaily to myself, "My little girl, today it is all yours".'

She suffered physical pain. She was scolded (for example, for pulling up garden flowers instead of weeds). Yet she always thanked God for everything. Teresa was canonized in 1925.

'In any great trouble, in any strong temptation, call upon your Guardian angel, who is your guide and your helper, in any difficulty and in any time of need.'

St Bernard

'Ah, How I love the memory
Of my blessed childhood days!
To keep safe the flower of my innocence
The Lord surrounded me always
With love.'

St Teresa of Lisieux

Francis of Assisi

The great founder of the Franciscans was born in 1181 and had been a soldier. His father was a wealthy cloth merchant who lived at Assisi in Umbria. A succession of visions of Christ calling him to poverty moved the saint to make a pilgrimage in rags to Rome. There he met a leper and not only gave him money but went so far as to kiss the man's diseased hand – an unthinkable act at this time.

Then in a ruined chapel near the gates of Assisi he seemed to hear a voice from the crucifix before which he was praying: 'Francis, go and repair my house which you see is now close to ruin.' Francis rushed to his father's warehouse, took as much cloth as a horse could carry, sold the cloth and the horse and gave the money to the priest in charge of the ruined chapel. When his father angrily summoned Francis before the bishop, the saint solemnly took off all his clothes and gave them back. The bishop gave him a cloak. And Francis said he now had only one father, his Father in heaven.

Now he took absolutely literally the rule in Saint Matthew's Gospel that Christ's apostles should have virtually nothing of their own. He soon gathered followers and made out a simple rule of life for them. Poverty was, he said, his 'lady'. Any illness was to Saint Francis 'a sister'. His body he called 'brother donkey'. He loved every created thing, 'brother sun', 'sister moon', even loving 'sister death' as God's gift. His order spread throughout Italy as more and more followers were attracted to this holy man.

He was beginning a forty-day fast in 1224 when he had a vision of a suffering crucified figure that was so intense as to leave permanently imprinted on the saint the prints of the nails and sword that had pierced Jesus at his passion. For the two more years of his life, the saint kept these stigmata a secret. A Franciscan brother announced them after Francis's death. In death, wrote another, it seemed as if Francis had just been taken down from a cross.

In 1979 Francis was declared the patron saint of ecologists.

Placid and Maurus

In the early sixth century so great was the reputation of Saint Benedict throughout Christian Italy that parents longed to entrust their sons to his care. A patrician named Tertullus sent his son Placid to the saint. A rich man named Equitius sent his son Maurus. Placid was no more than seven years old at this time, and Maurus was twelve.

Benedict was reputed to have eyes in the back of his head, like any great school-teacher. One day Placid fell into the lake at Subiaco where they all lived. Benedict, in his monastery, did not stir, calling instead to Maurus: 'Hurry brother! The child is in the water.' Maurus ran to the lakeside and pulled out Placid by grasping him by the hair.

Later Placid was despatched to Sicily to found a monastery at Messina, dedicated to St John the Baptist. Some years passed, and Placid had gathered together a good number of monks there with himself as abbot. Around the year 546 a fleet of pirates landed and slaughtered them all.

Many historians today think this story an invention, but in 1588 when the church of St John the Baptist, Messina, was undergoing extensive alterations, many skeletons were found, buried under the apse.

'Sanctify yourself and you will sanctify society.'

St Francis of Assisi

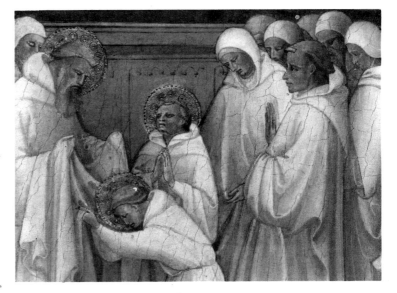

Bruno

Justina

'Only those who have known the silence and solitude of a hermit's cell can understand its blessings and joys.'

St Bruno

Archbishop Manasses of Rheims made Bruno chancellor of the diocese in the year 1075. Already Bruno's career was distinguished. Born in Cologne, he had studied at Rheims University, and was made a professor of theology there. Soon he was appointed head of the whole university, responsible for education throughout the diocese.

Bruno soon perceived that Manasses was unfit to be archbishop. At a Council at Autun, which Manasses refused to attend, Bruno boldly denounced his patron's evil ways. Manasses in a rage expelled the saint from his diocese, but Manasses was later excommunicated by the pope.

For a short time Bruno returned to Rheims when Manasses was deposed; but his aim now was to found a monastery more austere than any before. In 1084 he and six companions obtained from the Bishop of Grenoble a sparse and mountainous stretch of land known as La Grande Chartreuse. Here, living in separate cells, with a common oratory, they founded the Carthusian Order. Poverty, worship, hard manual work and study were the basis of their rule.

Around the middle of the fifth century a church was dedicated in Padua, Italy, to Santa Giustina. Today very little is known about her. Yet in the middle ages she brought more fame to the city of Padua than anyone else.

Venantius Fortunatus, a famous poet, who was also Bishop of Poitiers in the late seventh century, wrote a poem which urges anyone visiting Padua to kneel in the church there and kiss Justina's shrine. She has brought to the Christian world a supreme example of chastity and holiness, he wrote.

The church at Padua also contained the relics of the city's first bishop, Saint Prosdocimus. Later legends recount that this bishop converted Justina, who was later put to death by the sword for her faithfulness. Although many have suggested that this legend embroiders the truth, there is little reason to doubt that during the persecutions of the early church, the saint was in fact martyred, probably in the early fourth century at the time of the Emperor Diocletian.

OCTOBER 8	OCTOBER 9

Demetrius

Denis of Paris

One of the patron saints of France, Saint Denis, was an Italian, sent to Paris in the year 250 or thereabouts along with six other missionaries, including two bold assistants, Eleutherius and Rusticus. The pagan citizens of the Roman city were disturbed by the success of the Christian Gospel, as a result of the labours of the missionaries. The Roman governor, Fescenninus Sisinnus, arrested the three and put them in prison. For a long time they suffered privations, until about the year 275, when the three of them were beheaded and their corpses thrown into the River Seine. Montmartre, 'Martyr's Hill', marks the place of their death.

Demetrius of Thessaloniki is one of the great warrior-saints of history and legend. He inspired many pupils and disciples to face martyrdom, if necessary, for their faith. One of these, named Nestor, was thrown into the arena to face the Emperor Galerian's favourite gladiator.

Unfortunately for Galerian's champion, Nestor killed him. The emperor took revenge not only on Nestor but also on his teacher. Both Nestor and Demetrius were put to death.

All this took place in the fourth century. But Christendom had not heard the last of Saint Demetrius. The martyr was soon reputed to be a great worker of miracles. He was especially famous for defending Thessaloniki in the year 586 against the Slavs. The Slav intruders far outnumbered the warriors defending Thessaloniki. Yet they were repulsed. The Slavs themselves explained that to their surprise a great force opposed them. Its commander was dressed in dazzling armour, seated on a white stallion and wearing a white cloak. Clearly, the citizens reasoned, their supernatural commander was Saint Demetrius himself.

A superbly worked silver-gilt reliquary purporting to contain a bone of Saint Demetrius is kept in the monastery on Mount Athos.

The abbey church of Saint-Denis remains their finest tribute. Saint Geneviève restored it in the year 575 and added a priory in memory of the saints. King Dagobert I enriched this priory and began the rebuilding of the church, in which he himself planned to be entombed. Since that time nearly every French king was laid to rest in this holy spot. Abbot Fulrad of Saint-Denis decided to rebuild the church in 750, and twenty-five years later Charlemagne was present at its consecration. But a greater abbey-church was to arise, when the famous Suger became abbot in the year 1122. Suger's magnificent house of God substantially survives to this day.

Francis Borgia

Bruno the Great of Cologne

St Bruno

After ten years as a counsellor of Charles V, Francis Borgia (*below, right*) became Viceroy of Catalonia. He married Eleanor de Castro, who bore him eight children. And when his father died in 1543, he in turn became Duke of Gandia.

When his wife died three years later the saint conveyed all his fortune and lands to his eldest son and joined the Jesuits. Francis Borgia desired solely to lead a humble, hidden life, a student of theology, a disciple of Saint Ignatius Loyola. But of course no-one could hide forever the talents of such a man. Ignatius Loyola himself made Francis Borgia his emissary in Portugal and Spain. He would sign himself 'Francis the Sinner' till Ignatius ordered him not to. New Jesuit houses were founded under his inspiration. And in 1565 he himself was made general of the Jesuit order. He died in 1572.

Bruno was the youngest son of Saint Matilda and the Emperor Henry the Fowler. At the age of four his parents sent him to Utrecht, where a fine cathedral school was flourishing under the auspices of Bishop Baldericus. Naturally such a privileged childhood presaged a privileged career. Bruno was called to the court of his brother, the Emperor Otto I, when he was only fourteen years old. In 940 Otto made him his personal secretary. Ten years later Bruno had been consecrated Archbishop of Cologne.

His religious duties in no way conflicted in his mind with the call to serve also as a secular prince. Otto I made Bruno Duke of Lorraine. When the emperor went to Rome to be crowned by the pope, Bruno and his half-brother were appointed co-regents of the Holy Roman Empire. Together the two co-regents became guardians of their nephew, the young King of the Romans.

Perhaps the finest memorial to his religious impulse that survives to this day is the abbey church of St Pantaleon in Cologne. Bruno wished to found a Benedictine monastery in his native city. He rebuilt, as the basis of this convent, a small church outside the city gates. The building marked a new age of great architecture in Cologne. Work did not in fact begin until the year 980, fifteen years after Bruno's death. But the inspiration is his. St Pantaleon's church was to represent what a Romanesque age took to be the Holy City.

That was the dream of this great saint and prince-bishop. He saw no contradiction between the call to serve God in the world and the call to serve God in his church. Both callings demanded the attempt to rebuild the heavenly Jerusalem on earth.

Wilfrid

In the year 664 a great synod was held at Whitby, where the Abbess Hilda presided over a monastery containing both monks and nuns. The chief question was how to date Easter. The Celtic church and the Roman church differed over this, and (the Venerable Bede tells us) many humble and noble Christians were deeply troubled over this division in Christian Britain.

King Oswy opened the synod. He said that all who served the one God ought obviously to observe one rule of life. Bishop Colman of Lindisfarne then argued that the Celtic rules for observing Easter were correct. He said they derived their method of calculating Easter from St John. At this Saint Wilfrid spoke. 'Far be it from me to charge St John with foolishness,' he said. But he added that his – the Roman way of calculating Easter – derived from St Peter. When he had finished speaking, King Oswy said, 'I tell you, Peter is the guardian of the gates of heaven. Our Lord gave him the keys of the kingdom. I shall not contradict him. In everything I shall do my best to obey his commands. Otherwise, when I reach the gates of the kingdom of heaven, he who holds the keys may not agree to open up for me.'

Wilfrid was the son of a thegn of Northumbria and had been educated at Lindisfarne. Yet his studies at Rome had convinced him that his own Christian upbringing, though rich in traditional learning and spirituality, was in some respects cut off from important religious wealth. He ended his life peacefully in the year 709, content to serve the north of England as Bishop of Hexham.

Ethelburga of Barking

A contemporary of Saint Wilfrid was Saint Ethelburga of Barking (*right*) – the first abbess of a monastery for men and women there. She was the sister of a bishop and (wrote the Venerable Bede) 'lived an upright life, as the sister of a bishop ought to do.' Ethelburga died in about 676.

SAINT ETHELBURGA ABBESS of BARKING

Edward the Confessor

On 28 December 1065 a superb new abbey church was consecrated at Westminster, London. It had been created by King Edward the Confessor, who had lavishly rebuilt a former Benedictine church on this site. He intended his own shrine to be housed here. One week after its consecration, he was dead.

Nothing remains of Edward the Confessor's church. In the thirteenth century it was pulled down to make way for the superb Gothic church built out of the munificence of King Henry III. But the Confessor's shrine remains virtually the one medieval shrine to survive the English Reformation.

King Edward's youth had been spent in Normandy, till he was acclaimed king of the English in the year 1042. In 1045 Edward married the powerful Earl Godwin's daughter, Edith, though some say they remained celibate.

This monarch was certainly ascetic and devout. He ruled an unfamiliar country. His vassals were plotters and often self-seeking. Edward was generous to the poor, would lay his hands on men and women in the hope of healing them through prayer of any sickness, and clearly loved peace. These characteristics, which after his death greatly contributed towards his reputation as a saint, did not make him a weak man or a king easily swayed by others. In 1051 he even banished his father-in-law. When Godwin returned with an army the following year, Edward managed to negotiate an honourable peace.

Callistus

Teresa of Avila

Callistus began life as a slave whose master gave him a large amount of money to invest. Unfortunately he lost it all, along with other large sums entrusted to him by his master's friends. Callistus ran away. Reaching Portus, he set sail, was followed, flung himself overboard, was rescued, and found himself recaptured by his master.

Callistus's master decided to punish him by confining the slave to a treadmill. Other creditors secured his release; but the unfortunate Christian tried to borrow money off some Jews, was denounced by them for his faith and was now in trouble with the pagan authorities. He was scourged and banished to work in the insalubrious mines of Sardinia. Eventually he persuaded his jailers to release him. His health was so weakened that his fellow-Christians sent him to recuperate at Antium.

Soon he was ordained. Pope Zephyrinus obviously liked him, and Callistus was put in charge of the first ever public cemetery run by Christians. He became the pope's trusted adviser. When Zephyrinus died in the year 217, Callistus was elected to succeed him. As pope this extraordinary Christian was attacked for – of all things – his kindness; many found his teaching that any sin sincerely repented could be forgiven hard to accept.

About the age of twenty, Teresa entered a Carmelite convent at Avila in Castile where she began to experience visions and ecstasies. They included a remarkable experience as if a spear of divine love were piercing her heart.

In 1568 she founded her own reformed Carmelite monastery at Durelo. She founded more with the help of her close friend Saint John of the Cross. In the end seventeen new convents were set up, all of them disciplined, poor and enclosed communities where the priority of the sisters was prayer.

Saint Teresa wrote a treatise, *The Way of Perfection*, for her nuns. She could be warm and affectionate. 'For the love of God get well,' she wrote to a sick prioress, 'eat enough and do not be alone or think too much.' She was humorous. (Being a small person, she described herself as 'half a friar'.) She once wrote to an ally that, 'God treats his friends terribly, though he does them no wrong in this, since he treated his Son in the same way.' Although her discipline was stern, she loved cheerfulness, once crying, 'God deliver me from sullen saints!' She travelled widely, striving against much opposition to reform the whole Carmelite order. She wrote an autobiography, countless letters and a second spiritual masterpiece, *The Interior Castle*.

> *'Though we do not have our Lord with us in bodily presence, we have our neighbour, who, for the ends of love and loving service, is as good as our Lord himself.'*
>
> St Teresa of Avila

Hedwig

Ignatius of Antioch

'Keep your body as a shrine of God. Love unity. Flee divisions. Become followers of Jesus Christ as he was a follower of the Father.'

St Ignatius of Antioch

When she was only twelve, Hedwig was married to the future Duke of Silesia who was eighteen. She had been born in Bavaria to the wife of Duke Berthold of Croatia and Dalmatia. Till her marriage she was brought up in the monastery of Hitzingen. Her husband's name was Henry.

In the year 1202 Hedwig's husband became duke. Hedwig had brought a large dowry to her marriage. She now persuaded her husband to use it to found a monastery for Cistercian nuns at Trebnitz, north of present-day Wroclaw. Henry had the fine idea of using as labourers all the criminals of Silesia. Built between 1203 and 1218, this was the first women's convent in the region, had room for a hundred nuns and space to educate another nine hundred young women.

Henry and Hedwig had six children. The boys grew up to be quarrelsome nobles who caused much anxiety to their parents. Their daughter Gertrude became abbess of the nunnery at Trebnitz. Henry, who was a pious man, eventually agreed that Hedwig should herself retire there. He himself from that time never shaved and never wore rich ornaments or clothing (he was known in consequence as Henry the Bearded). Hedwig too exchanged her regal state for one of poverty and humility. She would always walk to church barefoot, even in winter. She would teach the poor the rudiments of religion – for some of them did not even know the Lord's Prayer. Living such sparse lives did not make Hedwig and her husband less generous to others. He started a hospital at Breslau. At Neumarkt she founded a home for women lepers.

Duke Henry died in 1238 and was succeeded by his son, the one boy who had distressed his parents. Hedwig went into the monastery at Trebnitz. Two years later Duke Henry II was killed in battle against the Tartars. Hedwig dried her tears with the words, 'To see my son alive was what I desired; but I know a greater joy since by his death he is for ever united to God in his glorious kingdom.' She died in the same year, 1240.

'From Syria to Rome I seem to be fighting with wild beasts, night and day, on land and sea, bound to ten leopards. I mean a bunch of soldiers whose treatment of me grows harsher the kinder I am to them.' The writer of those words was a Bishop of Antioch, who had been condemned to death for his faith and was being taken for execution in Rome early in the second century. He was to be thrown into the arena with wild beasts. 'I pray that they will be prompt with me,' Saint Ignatius's letter continued: 'I shall entice them to eat me speedily.'

The saint insisted that in spite of his sufferings, he remained a sinner, saved only because of the love of his Lord, who had been crucified for him. 'My Eros is crucified,' said the saint, looking forward to the end of sensuality as his death approached.

Through his letters we have access to the mind and personality of a man who may well have been a disciple of St John. Saint Ignatius loved vivid images to express his beliefs. The Eucharist he described as 'the medicine of immortality, the antidote against death.' Jesus on the cross lured the devil, like a fish, with the bait of his own body, Saint Ignatius declared. He is shown in the picture above holding his bishop's crosier.

Luke

We know Saint Luke intimately, from reading the third of the Four Gospels and the Acts of the Apostles, which he also wrote. Saint Luke was a non-Jew, and Jesus's attitude to non-Jews fascinated him. Jesus's life was spent almost entirely among Jews; but Luke reminds us that the Saviour once told his apostles and followers that 'people will come from east and west and from north and south, and sit at table in the kingdom of God.'

Whenever Jesus has dealings with, for example, Syrians, or praises a Roman centurion, Luke tells us about it. But he also shows Jesus's especial friendship with the outcasts in society. He shows Jesus caring for the poor, and even pointing to the poor as specially blessed. These elements are found in the other three Gospels too, but Luke above all loves to stress them. He shows us Jesus caring for the black sheep of society.

And in a way that no other Gospel does, Saint Luke's depicts a Jesus who cares for the status and salvation of women quite as much as he does for men. The status of women in those days was usually low. But Luke – who may well have learned much about Jesus from the Virgin Mary herself – brings to the fore those parts of Jesus's life and teaching which raise and enhance women.

We learn from the letters of Saint Paul that Luke was a doctor of medicine, and that he was with Paul in Rome. Luke continued the story of the beginnings of Christianity by writing the Acts of the Apostles as well as his Gospel. He was a fine and careful historian. But he also had been an eyewitness himself of some of the events he describes in the Acts of the Apostles.

Later church tradition adds that Saint Luke was also an artist. He has thus been made patron saint of artists as well as of doctors and surgeons. We have no record of what happened to the saint after the time he was with Paul in Rome; but traditionally he is said to have died well into his eighties, somewhere in Greece.

Frideswide

Acca

St Frideswide

Frideswide was the daughter of Didian, a Mercian prince whose lands included the upper reaches of the River Thames. She took a vow of perpetual virginity. A local prince named Algar refused to accept that she would not marry him. He pursued the saint, only to be struck blind. His sight returned once he had renounced his plan to make her forsake her vow.

Frideswide had hidden herself from Algar in a village near present-day Oxford called Binsey. Eventually she founded a nunnery there and became its first abbess. There she lived until her death around the year 753.

The nunnery flourished and her name was not forgotten. In the twelfth century her nunnery was refounded, this time as a convent for Augustinian canons. In 1180 in the presence of the Archbishop of Canterbury and King Henry II of England her remains were translated to a new shrine in the monastery church. A yet greater shrine was built nine years later. Countless pilgrims visited her relics. Twice a year the University of Oxford held a solemn feast in her honour and came to venerate her bones. In 1440 the Archbishop of Canterbury declared her patroness of the university.

Then in 1525 Cardinal Wolsey suppressed St Frideswide's monastery. Two decades later the monastry church became the new cathedral of Oxford. But the shrine containing Frideswide's relics had been broken up by Protestant reformers. The stone was used for building; but happily some Catholics preserved the saint's bones. Meanwhile the wife of the Protestant professor Peter Martyr had been buried in the Cathedral. In 1561, in an extraordinary burst of fanaticism a canon dug up her bones and mixed them with those of Saint Frideswide, adding the epitaph *Hic jacet religio cum superstitione* ('Here lies religion with superstition'). Today the place where her remains finally rested is marked with four elegant candlesticks in Christ Church.

After serving for several years as chaplain to the redoubtable Saint Wilfrid, Bishop of Hexham in Northumbria, Acca succeeded to the bishopric on Wilfrid's death. Wilfrid had been the first English prelate to appeal to Rome in a dispute. Acca too believed that the English church needed to be brought into line with Roman customs; but his concern was above all for the beauties of the Roman liturgy rather than for the Roman legal system.

'He invited a famous singer named Maban, who had been trained by the followers of Pope Gregory's disciples in Kent, to come and teach him and his clergy,' wrote the Venerable Bede. This man taught church music for twelve years – reviving old forgotten chants as well as bringing new ones. Acca also sang beautifully, says Bede (who knew him), and encouraged this revival by his own example.

From his youth he had been close to the great saints of the time, brought up in the household of Saint Bosa of York, accompanying Wilfrid to Rome (and there, says Bede, 'learning many valuable things about the organization of the church which he could not have found out in his own country'). He loved and studied the Scriptures. He refurnished the churches with sacred vessels and lights. Above all he enlarged and beautified the cathedral of St Andrew at Hexham. He built up a fine library to which scholars and students were drawn, all of whom received the patronage of Bishop Acca.

For some reason Acca was forced out of his diocese in the year 732. He was exiled to Withern, Galloway; but he returned before his death in 742 and was buried at Hexham.

Ursula

Donatus of Fiesole

Ursula is alleged to have been the daughter of a Christian king of Britain. Ursula took eleven companions who set sail in eleven ships, each of her companions taking with her a thousand maidservants. They sailed to Cologne, then along the River Rhine to Basel. At Basel they moored their ships and crossed the Alps, in order to visit Rome.

Ursula decided to lead her companions back to Cologne. There the leader of the Huns fell in love with her, was spurned, and massacred both the British princess and her eleven thousand companions.

The story is difficult to believe as it stands. The earliest reference to the legend of her companions speaks of only ten companions. The present story began to be told only in the eighth century. Yet some truth attaches to the tale. An ancient stone let into the wall of St Ursula's church in Cologne records that a certain Clematius built a church over some graves on that spot in the fourth century.

In the ninth century an Irishman named Donatus decided to go on a pilgrimage to Rome. Returning home he went to Florence and visited nearby Fiesole. Donatus, who was a small and unaggressive person, slipped into the cathedral there just when the people had come together to pray for enlightenment before electing a new bishop.

The moment Donatus entered the cathedral of Fiesole the bells are said to have begun to ring. All the cathedral lamps and candles are supposed to have lit themselves, without any human help. The Christians present could only conclude that this was a divine sign, indicating that the stranger who had just come in was destined to be their next bishop. Unanimously the puzzled Irishman was elected.

Fortunately he was a man of exemplary piety, and also a scholar and a poet. He wrote his own epitaph, which still survives and describes him as a splendid teacher, specializing in grammar and fine writing. The epitaph adds that the bishop loyally advised and served the Frankish king Lothaire and the Emperor Louis. Almost certainly he taught them and members of their household.

He was also a generous supporter of monastic foundations, giving in 850 a church and hospice of St Brigid at Piacenza to St Columban's monastery at Bobbio.

Saint Donatus was not averse to taking up arms himself to defend the property of the church. He took the lead in raising an army to fight the Saracens. At the same time he remained a most cultivated man, ever willing to instruct the young. He ruled as bishop for forty-seven years, dying in the year 876.

St Donatus of Fiesole

Severinus Boëthius

Mark and Senoch

St Severinus Boëthius

'In other living creatures the ignorance of themselves is nature, but in men it is vice.'

St Severinus Boëthius

Boëthius was a member of a noted Christian family, the Anicii. Born in the year 480 or thereabouts, he lost his father as a boy and was brought up a member of a senatorial family of outstanding integrity, marrying the daughter of the house, a woman named Rusticana.

In 510 Boëthius became a Roman consul and then between 520 and 522 served as head of the civil service of the Ostrogothic King Theodoric. Then came his downfall. Boëthius was accused of conspiring against Theodoric in an attempt to put the eastern Emperor Justin I on the throne instead. He was accused of being a magician and of writing letters subversive of good order.

Boëthius was imprisoned in Pavia. During his nine months imprisonment he wrote his most famous work, *The Consolation of Philosophy*. Then Boëthius was tortured and put to death.

As well as *The Consolation of Philosophy* Boëthius wrote on the Trinity; a treatise attacking the heresies of Eutyches and Nestorius; and three other theological works. He wrote on arithmetic and music. He translated books by Aristotle and Porphyry, as well as writing commentaries on Aristotle and Cicero.

But his *Consolation of Philosophy* remains his masterpiece. Its five books are filled with snatches of poetry. He recounts how suffering has brought him to a premature old age. But he takes comfort that God rules the world. He begins to learn the true nature of himself. Evil, philosophy tells him, can have no real existence, since the all-powerful God does not wish it. Vice never goes ultimately unpunished. Virtue in the end is rewarded. And true happiness can be found only in God himself.

Two centuries after Boëthius's death in 524 his body was placed in the huge crypt of the church of San Pietro in Ciel d'Oro, Pavia, and there it lies to this day.

Two sixth-century saints, an Italian named Mark and a Frenchman named Senoch, both commemorated on this day, displayed lives of heroic self-discipline with just a hint of self-satisfaction.

Mark lived as a hermit in a cave in Campania. He had in his early days, he said, suffered many temptations of the devil and came to fear no earthly danger. His cave was not very safe, and one overhanging rock seemed likely to fall at any moment. Some of his followers begged leave to loosen it, so as to let it crash down harmlessly. Mark agreed – provided that he could stay in the cave while they worked. His friends had no choice but to agree, and the saint meditated, unconcerned that at any moment the rock might come crashing down and kill him. Fortunately, it missed.

Then he took to chaining himself to the ground. At this Saint Benedict of Nursia intervened. Mark, he believed, was indulging in public display. Benedict told him that God's servants needed only the spiritual chains of Christ to bind them, not links of iron. Rebuked, Mark humbly threw his chain away.

Senoch, born at Tiffauges in Poitou, founded a small monastery about the year 536, making himself abbot over three disciples. They built their house in some Roman ruins and there fasted or lived on bread and water. Senoch was friendly with Bishop Euphronius of Tours, and when that saint died, went to his funeral and there met Euphronius's successor, Saint Gregory of Tours.

The abbot was fond of spending much time alone in his cell, not speaking and hardly eating. He paid a visit to his home town and there was so much admired that he came back exceedingly conceited. Fortunately Saint Gregory of Tours reproved Senoch and made him spend far more time with his three fellow-monks.

Crispin and Crispinian

Crispin and Crispinian were brothers who lived devout Christian lives in Rome until the persecutions there drove them to Gaul. They turned their exile to good account by becoming missionaries.

Although nobly born, they had left all their possessions behind. They therefore decided to become shoemakers. During the day they would preach the Gospel. In the evenings they plied their trade, taking only what pay men and women could afford or were prepared to give them. They found a new home in the city of Noviodunum, which is now called Soissons.

For several years they lived in peace, delighting many pagans with their charitable lives and converting a good number of them. But when the Emperor Maximian visited Soissons, some pagans complained about their missionary activities. The two saints were delivered over to a man named Rictius Varus, who hated Christians. He tortured them, but failed to make them flinch. Rictius Varus was clearly a man whose own mental state was in disorder, for when he saw that his cruelty had no effect on the composure of Crispin and Crispinian, he went quite mad and drowned himself (though others say he died by leaping into a fire that he intended for the two saints).

The Emperor Maximian commanded that the two saints be beheaded, and so Crispin and Crispinian died. Crispin and Crispinian are the patron saints of leatherworkers of all kinds.

Evaristus

Frumentius

Evaristus was born like his Saviour in Bethlehem. A Hellenic Jew, he was converted to Christianity and eventually reached Rome. There he accepted the dangerous office of pope, after the death of St Clement between the years 97 and 100.

Evaristus contributed to the growing organization of the Christian church in those early years. He divided Rome into various parishes. He appointed seven deacons to serve the city, just as the early apostles had appointed seven deacons to serve the poor of Jerusalem.

Saint Evaristus, who died around the year 107, is deemed a martyr, though we have no direct evidence that he did die a martyr's death. But virtually any prominent Christian in the early centuries of the faith was likely to be brutally put to death because of his beliefs.

Two young Christians named Frumentius and Aedesius were learning philosophy from a teacher named Meropius who decided around the year 330 that he would like to visit Abyssinia (or Ethiopia as it was then called). To the young men's overwhelming delight, he offered to take them with him.

The journey went well, but on their way home the ship docked at Adulis to take on board fresh supplies. There the natives of Adulis took them as slaves to the court of the king of Aksum. The fortunes of the young Christians prospered. Frumentius was made the king's chief secretary. Aedesius became his cup-bearer. They gained permission even to open some churches in Ethiopia and to try to convert the people. And when the king died, he gave the two men their freedom.

Eventually the two princes, named Abreha and Asbeha, came to the throne, and Aedesius returned to Tyre. Frumentius, however, urgently desired the church to send a bishop to Aksum to consolidate all that had been done there for Christ. A synod unanimously chose Frumentius for the work. After his death the Abyssinians dubbed him 'Abuna' (which means 'Our Father') and 'Aba salama' (which means 'Father of peace').

Simon and Jude

Narcissus of Jerusalem

Of these two members of Jesus's first twelve apostles, Simon is said (by the Gospels of Matthew and Mark) to have been a Canaanite. Saint Luke also tells us that he was a 'Zealot', which probably implies that he was a member of a party of Jewish patriots who were later prepared to revolt against the Roman occupation of their country.

Saint Jude is described in the New Testament as a relative of Jesus and also the brother of James. He may also have been the author of the shortest book in the New Testament, the letter of Jude (though verse 17 of that letter half implies that the apostles of Jesus have already died).

The letter of Jude was written by a man passionately concerned both about the purity of the Christian faith and the good reputation of Christian people. The writer had, he tells us, planned to write a different letter, but hearing of the misleading views put out by some false teachers in the Christian community, he is urgently writing to warn the church not to heed them.

Later legends describe the martyrdom of both Simon and Jude in Persia, though other traditions say that Simon died peacefully at Edessa.

Narcissus, who was a Greek, was appointed Bishop of Jerusalem in his old age. The saint's great age did not make him a weak bishop. He was a severe father in God, censuring slackness throughout his see, whether amongst the laity or the clergy. Inevitably he made enemies. Some of them hinted that he was guilty of some dark crime. Most of the Christians in the diocese of Jerusalem simply refused to believe such a lie; but Narcissus himself for many years had wanted to spend some time in seclusion, meditating and praying without the distractions of his office. He took the opportunity of leaving Jerusalem. For several years no-one saw him. Another man was put in office to look after the diocese while Narcissus was absent. He died and a second temporary bishop was appointed. Then Saint Narcissus reappeared. People thought he had risen from the dead, so long had he been away. He was so old that he appointed a second-in-command, a bishop named Alexander, to ease the burden of his episcopate, and he died still at work, venerated and wise around the year 220. If our records are correct, he was about a hundred and twenty-two years old though his long life was not the result of easy living.

'Now to him who is able to keep you from falling and to present you without blemish before the presence of his glory with rejoicing, to the only God, our Saviour through Jesus Christ our Lord, be glory, majesty, dominion and authority, before all time and now and for ever. Amen.'

The Blessing of St Jude

Alphonsus Rodriguez

Wolfgang

'The difference between adversity suffered for God and prosperity is greater than that between gold and a lump of lead.'

St Alphonsus Rodriquez

Alphonsus Rodriguez, born the son of a Spanish wool-merchant in Segovia in the year 1531, inherited his father's business at the age of twenty-three. He married. His daughter died as a child. Then his wife died, shortly after giving birth to their only son. The business too did not prosper, so he sold it and took his son to live with the boy's two aunts. From these devout ladies Alphonsus learned to meditate for at least two hours each day. He was an assiduous communicant. His life was austere and happy, though he still longed to devote himself even more to God.

When the saint's son died, Alphonsus decided finally to try to become a Jesuit, if possible as an ordained priest. He had given away most of his money by now, so he became a hired servant, hoping to pay for his necessary extra education by this and by begging. But the Jesuits of Segovia were not willing to take a man in poor health whose education was incomplete. Happily the provincial of the order spotted the saintliness of Alphonsus Rodriguez's life and overruled those who had refused him permission to join the Jesuits. Alphonsus became a lay brother. As hall porter till his death in 1617 his influence on those who met him proved remarkable. Crowds (including the bishop and the viceroy) attended his funeral.

Wolfgang was born in Swabia in the tenth century. After being taught as a little boy by a friendly priest, he was sent to the abbey of Reichenau on Lake Constance, to continue his schooling. There he became the best friend of a young nobleman named Henry whose elder brother was Bishop of Würzburg. The bishop set up a great school there, employing a brilliant Italian named Stefano of Novara to teach in it, and Henry persuaded Wolfgang to journey with him to study at the Italian's feet.

Wolfgang was incomparably the better pupil, though both young men were devout. In the year 956 when Henry was made Archbishop of Trier, he asked Wolfgang to go there with him to teach in the cathedral school.

Henry died in the year 964. Wolfgang had stayed by his side faithfully, but now left Trier to become a monk at Einsiedeln. The abbot, an English Benedictine named George, soon saw that he had with him a teacher of genius, and he put Wolfgang in charge of the abbey school. It became the best in the land. Later the Emperor Otto II recognized his worth and made Wolfgang Bishop of Regensburg.

November

'In Jesus humility was taken up into majesty, weakness into strength, mortality into eternity; and to pay the debt that we humans had incurred, an inviolable nature was united with a nature capable of suffering. He assumed the form of a servant without the stain of sin, enhancing what was human, not detracting from what was divine.'

Leo the Great (November 10)

Benignus

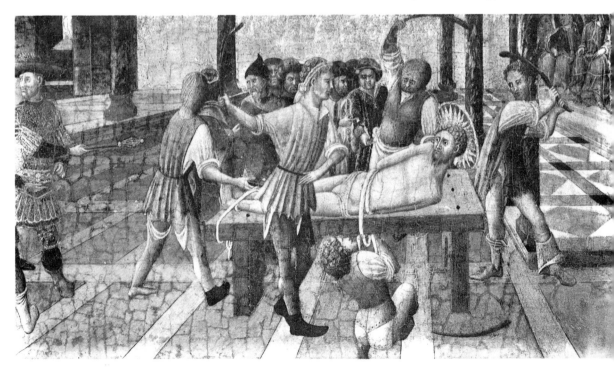

St Benignus

Benignus, along with another priest and a deacon, were sent, according to a sixth-century tradition, to preach the Gospel in Gaul in the second century, by Polycarp, Bishop of Smyrna. Their adventures included being shipwrecked at Corsica, landing at Marseilles and making their way perilously up the rivers Rhône and Saône. They reached Autun, where Benignus converted a nobleman who later was martyred (Saint Symphorianus, celebrated in the calendar on August 22).

He and his companions separated, to missionize different parts of Gaul. He worked openly, despite the danger to Christians from Roman persecutors. Inevitably Benignus was denounced to the authorities and put on trial. He refused to sacrifice to pagan idols, or to Caesar. He refused to deny Christ. Attempts were made to make him change his mind by savage tortures. Eventually he was put to death.

This day is also celebrated as the feast of All Saints.

Victorinus

Victorinus (*below*) became Bishop of Pettau in Pannonia and was martyred about the year 303 in the persecutions of the Emperor Diocletian.

One of his beliefs was that Christ would come a second time to reign on earth for a thousand years. This was later considered an error and a heresy. The result, sadly, is that scarcely any of Victorinus's writings have survived, for – although a saintly man and a martyr – his views were considered tainted. All we possess is a commentary he wrote on the last book in the New Testament and another book, a mixture of speculative science and theology, about the creation of the world.

In fact he was the first Christian ever to write Latin expositions of the Scriptures. Saint Jerome admired him, and tells us he wrote about many Old and New Testament books. Thus a piece of unnecessary censorship has denied us access to the mind and thinking of one of our early Christian forefathers. Even the account of his sufferings and death at the hands of the emperor has disappeared.

Hubert

In medieval times many saints derived both the pleasure of sport and some of their food from hunting. Both Saint Eustace (celebrated in the calendar on September 20) and Saint Hubert came upon a stag with a crucifix between its antlers. The stag's warning to Hubert was sterner than that to Saint Eustace, since Hubert had been hunting on Good Friday. Stopped in his tracks by the sight of the stag and crucifix, Hubert heard a voice warning him that unless he turned to Christ he was destined for hell.

This was in the forest of Ardenne. Hubert had been a courtier whose wife died giving birth to their son in the year 685. He retired from the service of Pepin of Heristal and became a priestly servant of Bishop Lambert of Maestricht. For ten years Saint Lambert taught the future Saint Hubert self-discipline by makng him live alone as a hermit in the forest.

Around the year 705 Lambert publicly criticized King Pepin for his adultery with the sister of his wife. The woman called on her brother and some other men to murder Lambert in the tiny village of Liège. Hubert was elected Lambert's successor.

Hubert courageously cherished the memory of Saint Lambert. Since the saint had been murdered at Liège, Hubert decided that his bones should not lie in the cathedral at Maestricht. He transferred them to Liège and also made that village the seat of his diocese. In consequence Liège grew to be a great city. There today Saint Lambert is regarded as patron of the diocese and Saint Hubert as patron and founder of the city.

In the eighth century, the forest of Ardenne was filled with men and women to whom the Gospel had not ever been preached. They worshipped idols. The saint assiduously worked to convert these people and destroy their pagan gods. He loved to go in procession through the fields, chanting Christian prayers and blessing the crops. He died, murmuring the Lord's Prayer on 30 May 727.

Charles Borromeo

Zechariah and Elizabeth

Saint Luke's Gospel tells us that Elizabeth (*left*, *below*) and Zechariah were both 'righteous before God, walking in all the commandments and ordinances of the Lord blameless.' Their one sorrow was that Elizabeth was barren and both were now old.

While Zechariah was performing his priestly duties, the angel Gabriel appeared to him, announcing that his wife would bear him a son and they were to call the boy John. Zechariah scarcely believed the angel, so that Gabriel decreed he remain dumb until the prophecy was fulfilled.

The time came for the birth of John (who was to be known as the Baptist). Zechariah was still dumb, and Elizabeth's neighbours and relatives wanted to call the baby after his father. But Elizabeth said, 'He shall be called John.' Zechariah too wrote the name 'John' on a tablet. So the boy was circumcised. Speech came back to the old father, who praised God, for (he said) 'he has visited and redeemed his people'. John, he said, would 'be the prophet of the Most High and go before the Lord to prepare his ways'.

A later tradition holds that Zechariah was murdered in the Temple for refusing to tell Herod the whereabouts of his son.

On 26 October 1569 Charles Borromeo, Archbishop of Milan, was at evening prayer. He had been attempting to bring to order a corrupt religious group known as the Humiliati, which had no more than seventy members but which possessed the wealth of ninety monasteries. One of the Humiliati, a priest named Farina, shot at the archbishop as he knelt before the altar. When it turned out that the wound was not mortal, Charles Borromeo rededicated himself to the reform of the church.

At this time the diocese of Milan stretched from Venice to Geneva. It comprised three thousand clergy and six hundred thousand lay men and women. Born an aristocrat, Charles Borromeo decided he ought to identify himself with the poor of this huge diocese. He travelled its length and breadth.

In 1575 when the plague struck Milan Charles Borromeo refused to leave the city. During the famine of 1570 he managed to find food for three thousand people a day. He died in the arms of his Welsh confessor in 1584, aged only forty-six, with the words, 'Behold, I come. Your will be done.'

Leonard of Noblac

Herculanus

Leonard of Noblac, converted by Saint Remi of France who had baptized Clovis, King of the Franks, had no desire for earthly rewards. He renounced the life of a Frankish nobleman; and when the king offered him a bishopric, he turned it down. Instead he built himself a little hut in a forest near Limoges.

One day the king went hunting in this forest, accompanied by his wife, who was pregnant. The moment of birth arrived, and it was clear that the queen was in difficulties. Leonard fell to prayer on her behalf, and her baby was delivered safely.

Bishop Herculanus of Perugia suffered dreadfully when the Goths under King Totila captured the city in the year 549. Before the saint was beheaded, the king said that a thin slice of skin would be pulled off every single part of his body. Happily the pagan soldier detailed to perform this execution took pity on Herculanus, and before all his body had been flayed, executed him.

Engelbert

Engelbert, Archbishop of Cologne, had been excommunicated for threatening the Emperor Otto IV with armed violence, but he redeemed himself in the eyes of the church by crusading against Albigensian heretics. Probably only a fighting bishop could have looked after the diocese of Cologne in those turbulent times. Although Engelbert insisted on discipline for the clergy and religious in his diocese, both groups knew they could always rely on his protection.

This led to the saint's murder. His cousin, Count Frederick of Isenberg, was in theory administrator and protector of the nuns of Essen. In practice he stole their lands and goods. The archbishop vigorously protested against the abuse of his position at Essen. The count and fifty retainers waylaid the archbishop on 7 November 1225, and left him dead with forty-seven wounds in his corpse.

In gratitude the king said that the saint should be given as much land as he could ride round in one day on his donkey.

Leonard rode all day, was granted many acres and there founded the abbey of Noblac which he used as a base to preach the Gospel throughout the whole region. King Clovis promised that any prisoner converted by the saint would be released – so that he is today regarded as a patron not only of women in labour but also of prisoners of war.

Four Crowned Ones

St Theodore the Recruit

On the Caelian Hill at Rome stands the church of Santi Quattro Incoronati. In it is a chapel specially dedicated to the guild of marble-workers. A church has stood in this place since the sixth century and probably before that time too.

Oddly enough, it commemorates not four but five Christian martyrs. They came from Pannonia, and were brilliant stone-carvers. Their names were Simpronian, Claudius, Nicostratus, Castorius and Simplicius.

When they were living at Smirnium an order came for them to carve on behalf of the Emperor Diocletian a statue of Aesculapius, the Greek god of medicine. The commission would have brought renown as well as pay. But the five stone-carvers were Christians and simply refused to co-operate in any fashion with the worship of idols.

The stone-masons were then ordered to make a sacrifice to the Sun god. This was even less acceptable than the notion that they should carve a statue of Aesculapius. They were bound, fastened in leaden boxes, and drowned in the river.

Theodore the Recruit

Theodore (*far left*) was a young man newly enlisted in the Roman army when severe regulations were published continuing under the new rulers of the empire the persecutions that had been started by Diocletian. His legion was wintering at Amasea in Pontus when orders came that everyone should join in pagan worship. The recruit refused to do so. Though his life was seriously at risk, Theodore made no attempt to conceal his faith in Christianity.

The tribune of the legion and the governor of Pontus summoned the soldier before them, asking why he proclaimed belief in Jesus Christ when the Roman authorities threatened anyone who did so with death. 'Jesus Christ is my one God,' replied Theodore. 'Since you dislike my words so much, why not cut out my tongue. There is no limb that I am not ready to sacrifice when God demands it.'

Both the tribune and the governor had no desire to put their new recruit to death. They sent him back to his quarters, resolved to try to convert him to paganism later. Theodore, believing that the time had now come for a public demonstration of his hatred for the pagan idols, went to the centre of Amasea where a temple to Cybele, the mother-goddess, had been erected and set fire to it.

Even now the governor and the tribune were disposed to be lenient. They bribed the young soldier with the promise that he would be made a priest of Cybele, if only he would recant and deny Jesus. Theodore pointed out that the pagan priests were the most reprehensible of all, since they misled the rest.

At this the authorities sentenced Theodore to be whipped. He made no cry of pain as his skin was lashed. He spent a further time in jail, awaiting sentence, which was that he should be burned alive.

On 17 February 306 the young recruit was thrown into a furnace and perished. A good Christian woman named Eusebia buried his ashes.

Leo the Great

In Jesus Christ 'was born true God in the entire and perfect nature of true man'. The words are from the famous 'Tome' of Saint Leo the Great, sent to the Council of Chalcedon in 451 through Patriarch Flavian of Constantinople, to present a proper understanding of the nature of Christ's incarnation. 'The Son of God,' Leo continued, 'came down from his throne in heaven without withdrawing from his Father's glory, and entered this lower world, born after a new order, by a new mode of birth.'

The immediate aim of Saint Leo was to combat the teaching of a monk named Eutyches, who had insisted that Jesus had only one nature, since (Eutyches maintained) his human nature had been absorbed into his divine nature. Flavian had excommunicated Eutyches. The monk had appealed – in vain – to Pope Leo for support. But the 'Tome' also greatly enhanced the papacy, for the Council of Chalcedon recognized Leo's teaching as 'the voice of Saint Peter'.

Leo the Great (*below*) was a Tuscan who succeeded Sixtus III as pope in 440. In 432 surviving letters and ninety-six sermons he defends papal primacy in the jurisdiction of the church, securing the support of Emperor Valentinian III, although he did not manage to persuade the whole eastern church to accept his jurisdiction.

Mennas

Mennas was born in Egypt and may well have been a camel-driver before he enlisted in the Roman army. He was also a Christian. When his legion reached Phrygia the persecution of Christians under Diocletian began. Mennas deserted his post in order to escape death and hid in a mountain cave.

But as more and more Christians were put to death under Diocletian's edicts, Mennas decided he too ought to make a public profession of his faith. He carefully chose his time. During the annual games in the arena at Cotyæum in Phrygia, Mennas suddenly appeared before the spectators and announced that he was a Christian. He was tortured and beaten, but would not recant, and so he was put to death by beheading.

Martin of Tours

Martin of Tours, a Hungarian army officer, was at Amiens in France in the year 337 when a semi-naked beggar approached him in bitterly cold weather. Martin's memory became immortal at that moment, for he sliced his military cloak in two and gave half of it to the starving man. Although the saint longed to be a hermit, the church forced him to lead the life of a loving and energetic Bishop of Tours.

St Mennas

Joseph of Polotsk

Josaphat Kunsevich was born at Vladimir in Poland at a time when the attempts of some Christians to bring about a reunion between Rome and the Russian Orthodox Christians were causing deep dissension. The boy's father adhered in his religion to Rome. The boy was apprenticed to a merchant at Vilna. But his interests were in the church. Instead of learning the trade, he learned church Slavonic, the language of the Byzantine liturgy.

In 1604 Josaphat was admitted to the Holy Trinity Monastery of Vilna. He rose to be abbot.

In 1617 Josaphat (or Joseph as he was known in the west) was elected first Bishop of Vitebsk and then Archbishop of Polotsk. The dispute between East and West was breaking his see asunder. The laity were confused. The secular rulers were causing havoc in church affairs.

The archbishop strove to bring order. He knew that some of his opponents hated him enough to kill him if they could do so. He once addressed an angry mob with the words, 'I, your shepherd, am happy to die for you.'

On 12 November 1623 this is precisely what happened.

Frances Cabrini

Frances Cabrini, the first American citizen to be canonized as a saint, was in fact born in Italy, at Sant' Angelo Lodigiano, Lombardy, on 15 July 1850. At eighteen she was orphaned, and – though qualified as a teacher – felt called to be a nun.

The Bishop of Todi invited her to start an order of missionary sisters who would educate girls. The Sisters of the Sacred

Heart soon spread to Milan, Rome and other cities in northern Italy.

Frances longed to missionize in China, but realized that Italian immigrants in the United States of America needed all the help that her order could give them. Under the patronage of Archbishop Corrigan of New York, she arrived in America in 1889 with six of her sisters. For twenty-eight years she travelled throughout the United States. She established four hospitals, as well as another fifty orphanages, convents and schools. The sisters of the Sacred Heart spread to Britain, France and Spain as well as to South America. Frances became a naturalized American. She died in 1917 and was canonized in 1946. She is regarded as a patroness of immigrants.

Gregory Palamas

The monks of Mount Athos believe that by perfect quieting of a person's body and mind, the Christian may be granted an extraordinary vision of God's uncreated light. It is a gift from God bringing purity and deep spiritual insight.

In late medieval times some members of the Eastern church believed that these mystics (known as 'hesychasts') were wrong. A Greek monk named Barlaam said that this 'uncreated light', the light that surrounded Jesus at his transfiguration, was part of God's essential unity and that no human being could experience it.

Hesychasm would almost certainly have been condemned at the Council of Constantinople in 1341 had it not been vigorously defended by Gregory Palamas.

Gregory Palamas insisted that for true meditation a Christian must take a mentor, never forget the supremacy of the Eucharist and if possible be attached in some way to a monastic community. Nevertheless two synods condemned his views, although the monks of Mount Athos never ceased to support him. Gregory Palamas was appointed Bishop of Thessaloniki in 1347. In 1368, eight years after his death, a synod declared him Father and Doctor of the church'.

Albert the Great

Albert the Great was born at Lauingen in Swabia in 1206, the son and heir of the Count of Böllstadt. Whilst a student at the University of Padua he joined the new order of Dominicans. He continued his studies at Paris, where he began to read the writings of Aristotle.

He then moved to the University of Cologne. Here his pupils included Saint Thomas Aquinas, with whom he struck up a friendship that lasted until Saint Thomas's death.

Albert the Great introduced Aristotle's thought to the Dominican order and had the greater ambition of making it intelligible to the whole western Christian world. He was the first western theologian to make a sharp distinction between faith and reason to both of which he gave its due. He insisted that 'purely from reason no-one can attain to knowledge of the Trinity, the incarnation of Jesus and the resurrection'. His encyclopedic brain perceived the difference between the Greek and Arabian way of looking at human knowledge and the outlook of the early Christian fathers. He spotted with great clarity that theology and philosophy were two distinct methods of reasoning.

BEATVS·ALBERTVS·MANGNVS·

'The prayer of the heart is the source of all good, which refreshes the soul as if it were a garden.'

St Gregory of Sinai (Palamas)

Margaret of Scotland

Elizabeth of Hungary

St Elizabeth of Hungary

In 1057 at the age of twelve, Margaret the daughter of Prince Edward (the exiled son of King Edmund Ironside of England), arrived at the court of the English King Edward the Confessor. Ten years later she and her mother were in exile again, fugitives after William the Conqueror defeated Harold at the Battle of Hastings.

They fled to Scotland. The beautiful princess loved the religious life. But in 1070 in deference to the wishes of her mother, she married King Malcolm III of Scotland, to whom she bore six sons and two daughters. Her unlearned and even boorish husband grew daily more graceful and Christian under the queen's influence. And she brought to the people of Scotland all she had learned of Anglo-Norman Christianity.

Saint Margaret brought to Scotland English monks, who settled in a Benedictine priory at Dunfermline, Fife. Here in 1072 she had built a new and exquisite church. She developed a deep friendship with Prior Turgot who built the superb Norman cathedral at Durham, had been one of William the Conqueror's prisoners, and had escaped to Norway where he taught sacred music at the royal court.

Elizabeth of Hungary found tremendous joy in a marriage that was arranged for her when she was four years old. At that age she came to live in the same household as her future husband, who was destined to become Landgrave Ludwig IV of Thuringia. They married in the year 1221. Elizabeth bore Ludwig two girls and a boy. The couple had fallen in love in their childhood. Ludwig never forgot to bring Elizabeth a present after one of his journeys.

Now they were idyllically happy. She built a hospital at the foot of the steep hill on which perched Schloss Wartburg where they lived. She even vacated her own bed for a leper.

Elizabeth's married happiness lasted for six years. In 1227 her husband decided to join the Emperor Frederick II on the fifth crusade. He reached Otranto and died of the plague. 'The world, and all that was joyful in the world is now dead to me,' Elizabeth cried, but worse was to come. Her brother-in-law simply threw her and her children out. Elizabeth had vowed to Ludwig that if ever anything happened to him she would never marry again. After attending his funeral at Reinhardsbrunn, she became a member of the third order of Franciscans, living in a tiny house outside Marburg. With remarkable humility she submitted to the harsh – and some might say utterly unreasonable – discipline of her confessor. He forced her to part from the two friends she had known and loved since she came to Germany from Hungary at the age of four, replacing them with cruel women. He would slap Elizabeth's face and sometimes beat her with a rod that left its mark for weeks. She refused to return to Hungary, but (as she put it) rose after his chidings like grass that a stream has bent. She died two years later in 1231 aged only twenty-four.

Mawes

The lives of the sixth-century Irish saints frequently contain startling elements, and that of Saint Mawes is no exception. Even his birth is said to have been remarkable. His mother was called Azenor and lived in Brittany. One day she was thrown into the sea near Brest, with only a barrel for a boat. There Mawes was born. Mother and son stayed in the cask for five months, till they were washed up alive on the coast of Ireland.

In the days of King Childbert I Saint Mawes decided to return to the land of his mother. On his way to Brittany he visited Devon and Cornwall, preaching out of doors and founding a town on the River Fal named after him. Then he and his followers sailed for Brittany. Landing on an island just off the coast of France, the saint showed his practical skill by clearing it of vermin, setting fire to the dried vegetation to do this. Many churches in the region are dedicated to him – testimony to his influence and missionary skills.

One reason for Saint Mawes's return to Brittany is said to have been to escape yellow fever in Ireland. Ironically, he subsequently became famed for his ability to cure many kinds of sickness. After his death, the earth under which he was buried was often taken away, mixed with water and used as a medicine.

The saint eventually established a monastic community on St Maudez island. One day, it is recounted, the last fire on the island was accidentally extinguished. Mawes sent a serving boy at low tide to cross to the mainland and bring back a flame. As the boy set off back, the tide came in. The waves rose higher and higher, threatening to engulf the flame; but the boy stood on a rock, prayed to Saint Mawes, and discovered the rock rising miraculously so that it never sank beneath the sea. When the tide went out again, the flame was successfully transported to St Maudez.

Barlaam

Saint Barlaam was an illiterate labourer who worked in a village near Antioch in the fourth century, at a time when Christians were still being persecuted. Because of his boldness in proclaiming his faith, Barlaam was brought before a judge, but refused to weaken in his zeal for Christ. He was whipped, and so savagely stretched on the rack that his bones were dislocated.

None of this caused the saint to renounce his faith. The judge, supposing that he could readily trick an unlettered Christian, ordered his officers to set up an altar to pagan gods and light a fire on it. Then Barlaam was brought out of the dungeon. Incense was placed on his hand, which was then put into the flames over the altar. The judge's plan was to watch Barlaam pull his hand away in pain, thus dropping the incense on the altar and apparently sacrificing to pagan gods.

The saint knew what was happening. At no point did he weaken but foiled his tormentors by holding his hand completely steady until it had totally burned away. He was then led away and killed.

Pontian

Pope Pontian, whose feast also falls on this day, was a Roman who succeeded Pope Urban I in the year 230. His was no easy pontificate. The writings of the theologian Origen were causing much controversy and the pope was among those who wished to condemn some of his teachings. This too was the time of Saint Hippolytus's disputes with the papacy. And five years after Pontian's election as pope, the Emperor Maximinus began to persecute Christians.

Maximinus's persecution brought Pontian and Hippolytus together, for the two saints were both exiled to the quarries of Sardinia. There they were reconciled. There they both died. Pontian was beaten with rods; his flesh was torn apart; and he died on 30 October 236. He remained an inspiration to his successors in the papacy and to the Christians of Rome.

NOVEMBER 20

Edmund the Martyr

On Christmas Day 855 a young man aged fourteen was acclaimed King of Norfolk by the ruling men and clergy of that county. The following year the leaders of Suffolk also made him their king. For fifteen years Edmund ruled over the East Angles with what all acknowledged as Christian dignity and justice. He himself seems to have modelled his piety on that of King David in the Old Testament, becoming especially proficient at reciting the psalms in public worship.

From the year 866 his kingdom was increasingly threatened by Danish invasions. For four years the East Angles managed to keep a shaky, often broken peace with them. Then the invaders burned Thetford. King Edmund's army attacked them there but could not defeat the marauders.

The Anglo-Saxon Chronicle records that the Danes 'killed the king and overcame all the land', adding that 'they destroyed all the churches that they came to, and at the same time reaching Peterborough, killed the abbot and monks and burned and broke everything they found there'. He thus remains the only English sovereign until the time of King Charles I to die for religious beliefs as well as the defence of his throne.

NOVEMBER 21

Gelasius I

Pope Gelasius I, who ruled from 492 to 496, had been secretary to the two previous popes, and we know that as pope he still liked to dash off letters in his own hand. He tried to compile a trustworthy list of saints and martyrs. He drew up a compendium of the important decrees of the synods of the church, not only including western ones but incorporating judgments of eastern synods where he thought them relevant.

Gelasius I was convinced that the supreme power on earth was the church. This

he saw summed up in the power of the papacy. Alongside the papacy, the role of the Byzantine emperor was as nothing.

In his day, as the pope realized, Christianity remained only superficial among many converts. For instance, each February Christians still celebrated the feast of the Lupercalia, in honour of the Roman god Pan. Through it they hoped to influence for good the animal and vegetable world. Gelasius vigorously tried to suppress it, publicly writing a refutation of a senator named Andromachus who supported the rites.

Gelasius made little attempt to heal the split between Rome and the East, started when Acacius was Patriarch of Constantinople (471 to 489) and ended only in 518. His aim was different: to assert the superiority of the bishop of Rome over the patriarch of Constantinople.

Cecilia

A patrician woman of Rome who lived either in the second or third century was betrothed and married against her will, having planned to remain devoted only to God. While everyone sang and danced at her wedding, she sat apart, saying only the psalms. Valerian her husband turned out to be a man of great understanding. They retired to their bedroom, and the saint persuaded him to respect her vow of virginity.

He and his brother Tiburtius were both enormously impressed and attracted by his wife's Christian graces, and eventually both men were baptized. They spent much money obtaining bodies of martyred Christians and giving them decent burials. The prefect Almachius learned of this charitable work, summoned them to trial, and when they refused to sacrifice to the pagan gods, sentenced them to be scourged and beheaded. One of his officers, named Maximus was himself converted by the demeanour of these men, and died with them.

Saint Cecilia obtained their bodies and buried them honourably in the cemetery of Praetextatus. She now decided to turn her home into a place of worship. Her religion was discovered. Almachius was as little able to persuade her to renounce Christianity as he had her husband and brother-in-law. His sentence was unusually cruel: Cecilia was to be suffocated in her own bathroom.

The saint seemed immune to such a martyrdom. The story continues that her executioners stoked the furnace under these Roman baths till the heat was seven times the normal temperature and the steam was scalding; but to no avail. Saint Cecilia sat unharmed. At this a soldier was ordered to strike off her head. He was a clumsy man and three times mutilated her neck without immediately killing Cecilia. For three days she lay in pain before finally dying. Her friends gathered round to hear her last blessings. Even now she sang spiritual songs to God, and comforted herself with sacred music.

Clement I

Chrysogonus

'O God, make us children of quietness, and heirs of peace.'

St Clement

'The strong must make sure that they care for the weak. The rich must be certain to give enough to supply all the needs of the poor. The poor must thank God for supplying their needs. . . . We all need each other: the great need the small, the small need the great. In our body, the head is useless without the feet and the feet without the head. The tiniest limbs of our body are useful and necessary to the whole.'

St Clement

'Through jealousy and envy the greatest and most righteous pillars of the church were persecuted and contended unto death. Look to the heroic apostles: Peter through unrighteous jealousy endured not one or two, but many labours, and having thus borne witness went on to his true place of glory. Paul through jealousy and strife, displayed the prize of endurance: seven times in bonds, driven into exile, stoned, a herald for the faith in east and west. . . . Associated with these men of holy life is a great multitude of believers, suffering many tortures because of jealousy, some of them women who, though weak in body, completed the race of faith.'

The writer is Clement of Rome, third pope after Saint Peter. His constant references to the evils of jealousy are to rebuke the church at Corinth, where hot-heads had overthrown the lawful Christian leaders and unbelievers were mocking the Christian faith.

Saint Clement's letter, written in the year 95, is older even than some parts of our New Testament. He shows with Old Testament stories how evil are the results of jealousy. He begs the Christians in Corinth to show mutual tolerance and love and to respect those set in authority. Peace must be the aim of all who follow Jesus, he said.

Chrysogonus was an official at Rome who was converted to Christianity and in turn converted many others to the same faith. He is said to have been particularly close to Saint Anastasia and become her guide in the Christian faith.

The saint's success as a Christian missionary displeased the authorities who imprisoned him. After festering for many months in squalid conditions, Chrysogonus was beheaded during the persecutions of the Emperor Diocletian. His corpse was thrown into the sea, but rescued by a priest named Zoilus. Pope Sylvester I built a church over his tomb in the first half of the fourth century, and this was excavated in the early twentieth century, twenty feet below the present ground level of the church of San Crisogono in Rome.

San Crisogono contains the head of Saint Chrysogonus and one of his arms, now proudly preserved over the high altar. On the superbly gilded and decorated ceiling of the church, which was created in the seventeenth century, Giovanni Guencino painted 'The Triumph of Saint Chrysogonus'.

Saint Chrysogonus probably died around the year 304.

Catherine of Alexandria

The monastery of St Catherine on Mount Sinai is renowned as being the oldest continuously occupied monastery in Christendom. Yet it was first dedicated not to St Catherine but to the Transfiguration of Jesus. Its architect began building the monastery walls in the year 542. Three centuries later, guided by a dream, the monks of this monastery found on the mountain the body of a woman, whom they took to be Saint Catherine – a body presumably miraculously flown there from Alexandria.

Her story is no less remarkable. In the year 305 the Emperor Maxentius carried off many wives and daughters of the citizens of Alexandria. One of them was a rich Christian named Catherine. She was only eighteen years old, yet had studied much. Maxentius brought fifty pagan philosophers to try to convince her that belief in Christianity was foolish. She converted them, and the emperor, in a rage, put them to death.

Because she refused to marry him, Greek Christians call her 'Aeikatharina', that is 'ever pure'. The emperor put her in a dungeon, after she had been beaten. During his absence his wife Faustina and an officer named Porphyrius visited the saint and were themselves converted. Porphyrius converted two hundred men of the imperial guard. On his return Maxentius had them killed and decided that Catherine too must die.

First a wheel, set with razors, was constructed. The saint was tied to its rim. But instead of cutting her to pieces, the wheel broke, and some of its splinters and razors injured the onlookers. Finally Catherine was beheaded. It is claimed that for many years oil oozed from her bones; this oil was prized as medicine and for lamps in holy sanctuaries.

Peter of Alexandria

James Intercisus

When Peter became Bishop of Alexandria in the year 300, he perceived the need for some rules which would lovingly but sternly welcome back into the Christian fold those who – under persecution and even torture – had lapsed from the faith and then returned. These rules were eventually accepted throughout the Eastern church; but others criticized Peter of Alexandria as being far too lenient.

Some of these critics were hypocrites. One of them, a man named Melitius, envied Peter his position as bishop; and when Peter was obliged to hide to avoid being killed by the pagans, Melitius got himself falsely appointed bishop.

Peter of Alexandria excommunicated the man who had usurped his position. Even now, he displayed the hope of reconciling Melitius. His letter of excommunication reads: 'Now take heed to this and hold no communion with Melitius until I meet him, in company with some wise and discreet men, to find out what he has been plotting.'

Eventually Peter returned to Alexandria. But in the year 311 Caesar Maximinus Daia began persecuting Christians again. The bishop was put to death. The Coptic church calls him 'the complement of the martyrs', since he was the last Christian to die for the faith before Constantine granted religious toleration throughout the empire.

'Intercisus' means 'cut to pieces', which is precisely what happened to James, a courtier of the Persian King Yezdigerd I in the year 421.

King Yezdigerd began to persecute Christians in 420. To his later shame, James decided to apostatize from Christianity rather than lose the favour of the king. When Yezdigerd died, the parents of the faithless courtier wrote to their son: 'We ourselves want nothing more to do with you. If you persist in your apostasy, the justice of God will reward you with the same punishment as your friend the king.'

Ashamed, James quit the court of Yezdigerd's successor, King Bahram. Learning that James had become a Christian again, Bahram debated with his counsellors what to do with James, and they decreed that unless he once again denied his faith, the saint should be hung from a beam and his body slowly cut to pieces. Those commissioned to perform this cruel deed tried to make him give way. 'This supposedly painful death is but little to pay for eternal life,' replied James.

So they began slowly to cut pieces from his body. When they cut off his thumb, he began to pray: 'O Saviour, receive a branch of this tree. Let it die, corrupt in the grave and bud again, before being covered in glory.'

Many Christians and others in the crowd begged James to give way. But the saint continued to pray, offering each hacked off piece of his body to God, until finally an executioner cut off his head. His dead body lay in no fewer than twenty-eight pieces.

Catherine Labouré

When the mother of Zoé Labouré died, Zoé was called on by her father to act as housekeeper, and though she seems to have enjoyed her life, it meant that she had no schooling.

From the age of fourteen she felt the call to follow her elder sister into the religious life and in 1830 she was admitted to the Sisters of Charity and given the name Catherine. The order sent her to Paris and there Catherine Labouré was granted a vision in which the Blessed Virgin Mary told Catherine that within her lifetime the Archbishop of Paris would be brutally put to death. (This indeed happened, in 1871.)

Further remarkable visions followed; in one Our Lady appeared to be dominating the whole world, blessing it with light. Catherine saw on the back of this picture a cross surmounting the first letter of Mary's name. Here too she saw Jesus's heart, crowned with thorns, and Mary's, pierced by a sword.

A voice seemed to be ordering Catherine to strike a medal with these emblems. Catherine's confessor gained permission from the Archbishop of Paris, and a hundred and fifty medals were struck.

Sernin of Toulouse

Sernin was born in Rome and about the the year 245 was sent by Pope Fabian to preach the Gospel at Pampluna in Spain. From Pampluna he travelled on to France, where Bishop Trophimus of Arles needed missionaries.

Sernin was consecrated bishop of Toulouse. His preaching soon gained many converts for Christianity. But it also offended the priests of the pagan temple at Toulouse. To show his contempt for the pagan gods, Sernin took a house on one side of it and built a small church on the other side. This is said to have silenced completely the temple oracles, from which the pagan priests drew their principal profit.

These pagan priests, assuming that Sernin's behaviour had displeased their gods, one day hauled him into their temple where there was a bullock about to be sacrificed. The angry priests tied Sernin to it by the feet, and drove the beast out of the temple down a hill. The saint's head was smashed and his brains spilled out on to the ground.

Today the church of St Sernin, Toulouse is the largest Romanesque church in France, and the saint's body lies in the choir, in a great tomb constructed in 1746 and resting on bulls of bronze.

Andrew the Apostle

Among the followers of John the Baptist was a fisherman named Andrew. After John had been arrested. Jesus came into Galilee. His message was, 'The time is fulfilled, and the kingdom of God is at hand. Repent and believe in the good news.'

As he passed by the sea of Galilee he saw Simon (who became the Apostle Peter) and Andrew, who were fishing. Jesus said, 'Follow me, and I will make you fishers of men.' Saint John's Gospel suggests that Andrew was the first to hear this message. He then went to his brother Simon and said, 'We have found the Messiah.' So Saint Andrew was the very first apostle to be called by Jesus. In bringing his brother to Jesus, Andrew also proved to be the first of all Christian missionaries.

The Gospels show Andrew ready to sit humbly at his Master's feet, asking questions on behalf of the others, alongside Peter, James and John, who were the leading apostles. When Jesus had been followed by about five thousand men, none of whom had anything to eat, the disciples wondered how Jesus would feed them. Andrew had enough faith to realize that however small the amount of food available, Jesus would be able to find food for all those present. He was the one who found the lad with five barley loaves and two fish – though in bringing these to Jesus he did ask 'What are they among so many?' Jesus used them to fill all five thousand men, with twelve basketfuls of fragments left over.

Andrew is mentioned as being in the Upper Room in Jerusalem when the Holy Spirit came on Jesus's disciples after the resurrection and ascension. He is said to have preached the Gospel in Scythia and Greece and even in Byzantium, before being crucified (on an X-shaped cross) at Patras in Achaia in the year 60.

December

'Beloved, let us love one another,
for love is of God; and everyone
that loves is born of God and
knows God. See what love the
Father has given us, that we
should be called children of God;
and so we are.'

John the Divine (December 27)

Eligius

Eligius's father was a goldsmith and metalworker who lived near Limoges, and when his son showed similar talent, he apprenticed Eligius to the master of the mint at Limoges. Eligius acquired great skill at working in precious metals, and decided to seek his fortune in Paris. There he came to the notice of Bobbo, treasurer to King Chlotar II. The king needed a treasurer at Marseilles, and the post was given to Eligius. He held on to this post during the reigns of Chlotar's successors, Kings Dagobert I and Clovis II.

Soon he was rich. His wealth was devoted to the poor. Once a stranger asked the way to his home in Paris and was told he would recognize it by the great concourse of poor persons outside. Eligius developed into a deeply religious man. When King Chlotar gave him land at Solignac, he founded a monastery there, as well as setting up the first ever workshop for producing Limoges enamels.

Soon after Clovis II came to the throne, Eligius was elected Bishop of Noyon and Tournai. He spread the Gospel through his vast diocese and into Flanders. His most loyal assistants included several men and women who had been slaves, until Eligius bought and freed them. He founded nunneries, and ruled as bishop for nineteen fruitful years. As death approached in the year 659, Eligius said to his flock, 'Do not weep. Congratulate me instead. I have waited a long time for this release.' His body lies in Noyon cathedral.

Viviana

Apronianus, governor of Rome in the year 363, lost an eye in an accident and decided to blame the Christians for this. A former prefect of the city named Flavian and his wife Dafrosa were amongst those unjustly punished for this. Flavian's face was horribly burned with a red-hot piece of metal. When he succumbed, his wife was taken outside the city and beheaded.

These two Christian martyrs had two daughters, Viviana and Demetria. All their goods were now confiscated by Apronianus. For five months the two girls lived in terrible poverty, but their faith did not waver. Apronianus came to visit them, supposing that they would have by this time renounced Christ. Angered at their constancy, he summoned them to trial. In court Demetria spoke first. She boldly professed Christianity. Then she fell down dead.

A pagan woman named Rufina took the other girl into her home, instructed by the governor to make her forsake her Christian beliefs. But nothing could disturb Viviana's composure. Apronianus sentenced her to be executed cruelly, ordering that the soldiers tie the saint to a pillar and scourge her with lead-loaded whips.

Francis Xavier

In 1534 the first seven Jesuits came together to form the Society at Montmartre in Paris. One of them was a Basque, Francis Xavier. Three years later he was ordained. And in 1540 Ignatius of Loyola commissioned Francis to go to preach in India. The saint set sail from Lisbon on 7 April 1541 and after a journey lasting over a year arrived at Goa.

Churches and clergyman were to be found in Goa itself, but what 'bruised' the saint's soul, as he put it, was the scandalous behaviour of the so-called European Christians. They were greedy and loose-living. They treated the natives despicably.

For seven years Francis laboured in that region, converting many thousands to a proper understanding of Christianity. In 1549 he sailed for Japan. He gained permission to teach there, but the life was harsh, there was much opposition from the Buddhist priests, and he converted fewer than he had hoped for – though his converts still numbered thousands by the time he returned to Goa.

In April 1552 Saint Francis Xavier decided to sail for China. At that time no foreigner was allowed into that country, but he arranged to be landed secretly from a Chinese junk. While waiting there the saint fell ill and died on the island of Shangchwan. He was forty-six years old.

Barbara

A fanatical pagan named Dioscorus lived at Heliopolis in Syria at the time of the Emperor Maximinus Daia. He grew fearful that his daughter Barbara was growing friendly with Christians and may even have taken up their faith. To prevent this, if he could, he shut her up in a high tower. All this was in vain. Barbara's faith was only strengthened.

Eventually her father reported her to the pagan authorities. They tortured the saint, but she refused to recant. At this the judge ordered Dioscorus himself to slay his own daughter. He took Barbara up into a mountain and killed her with his sword.

As Dioscorus was coming down the mountain he was struck by lightning and killed. As a result Barbara is regarded as one who protects men and women both from lightning and from sudden death.

Sabas

In the sixth century, many monks lived lives of virtually complete solitude. Sabas learned of a famous saint named Euthymius, who lived in a cave in the wilderness between Jericho and Jerusalem. At the age of eighteen Sabas went to Euthymius, asking if he could join the handful of disciples Euthymius allowed to live around him. Euthymius told him to come back when he was thirty years old. He sent Sabas to a nearby monastery run by another saint named Theoctistus.

So Sabas trained himself for the life of a desert father. And at the age of thirty Euthymius gave him permission to live for five days a week in a cave. Each weekend he had to return to the monastery. Euthymius would not let him simply devote himself to prayer. Sabas had to make ten wicker baskets a day, taking all fifty back to the monastery each Saturday.

When Euthymius died Sabas spent four years completely alone in the desert, before founding a monastery of his own, where solitaries could occasionally worship together. Soon he was made superior of all the desert monks of Palestine. The Patriarch of Jerusalem often sent him on missions, for Sabas's reputation for great wisdom was widespread; but always the saint returned to the desert, founding other monasteries, and building hospitals. His greatest monastery, Mar Saba, is still inhabited by Orthodox monks. The saint died in the year 532 aged ninety-four.

Nicholas

The governor of Myra in south west Asia Minor in the fourth century took a bribe to condemn to death three innocent men. The executioner was about to kill them when the bishop of the city, Nicholas, appeared and prevented this. Turning to the governor, the saint upbraided him till he confessed his sin and begged to be forgiven.

Nicholas was born in a well-to-do family at Patara in Asia Minor and was probably imprisoned as a Christian during the terrible persecutions of the Emperor Diocletian.

The Emperor Justinian built a church in his honour in sixth-century Constantinople. His shrine at Myra was a centre of pilgrimage until 1087, when Italian sailors stole the saint's earthly remains and brought them to Bari, where the Normans built for them a superb new church. Saint Nicholas became the patron saint of Greece and Russia and of great cities, such as Moscow and Fribourg. Since he is said to have rescued sailors in his lifetime, seafarers too have made him their patron. Throughout Europe in the middle ages his feast on 6 December was the occasion for electing a Boy Bishop, who reigned until the feast of the Holy Innocents on 28 December.

Saint Nicholas's final transformation into 'Father Christmas' and 'Santa Claus' occurred among Protestants. Dutch Protestant settlers in New Amsterdam – now New York – took with them traditions of 'Sinter Claes', which spread throughout the USA and then back into European children's lore. He is the patron saint of children and sailors.

Ambrose

Ambrose was a much-loved Bishop of Milan. He had been elected by popular acclaim when still being instructed as a Christian and not yet baptized. Born at Trier in the year 340, he had returned to Rome with his widowed mother and trained as a lawyer. The emperor appointed him governor of Liguria and Aemilia, whose capital was Milan. When the bishop died in the year 374, the city was so much divided over the new appointment that it needed a man of great strength and charity to step into his shoes. Ambrose was baptized and made bishop on 7 December 374.

Ambrose was strong enough to call the greatest in Christendom to public penance. A mob at Thessaloniki killed the Roman governor in the year 390. In reprisal the Emperor Theodosius I commanded a savage massacre of citizens. Ambrose forced him to submit to public penance. 'The emperor belongs to the church,' said Ambrose, 'but is not its superior.'

He was adamant that the Christian religion should be supported by the empire. Pagan senators wanted the heathen goddess of Victory honoured by a new statue in Rome. Ambrose persuaded the Emperor Valentinian II to forbid it. He refused to give one of his churches to the Arian heretics, in spite of an order from the regent Justina telling him that he must do so.

Quite consciously Saint Ambrose set out to be an exemplary bishop. On his election he began to study the fathers of the church and the Scriptures in great depth. Thenceforth his life was one of poverty and humility. His personal possessions were given away. Whenever he baptized new Christians, Ambrose always washed their feet, even though he knew this was not the usual Roman custom. A superb preacher, Ambrose was the close friend of Saint Augustine's mother Monica, and it was he who finally showed the still doubting Augustine that a person of intelligence could find the Christian faith totally satisfying. In 386 Saint Ambrose baptized Saint Augustine.

Romaric

Romaric belonged to the royal house of the Merovingians, but this did not prevent Queen Brunehild ordering the death of his father. The young Romaric was forced to quit the life of a nobeman's house in the Vosges and for several years wandered with nowhere of his own to lay his head. But he was a person of courage and resourcefulness and climbed his way back until he became a courtier of King Chlotar II. He amassed a fortune and became owner of a large number of serfs.

Then he met a holy saint named Amatus, who converted him to such a belief in and commitment to Jesus that in the year 620 Romaric founded a monastery for men and women on his estates at Habendum on the River Moselle. Saint Amatus became the first abbot of this house, which afterwards became extremely famous as the abbey of Remiremont.

On entering the monastery, Romaric freed all his serfs, but such was their love for him that many followed him into the religious life. After three years Saint Amatus died and Saint Romaric became abbot, ruling the monastery for thirty years.

Leocadia

Saint Leocadia was martyred in the year 304. Leocadia was the daughter of a noble family who lived in Toledo, but rather than give up her Christianity during the persecutions of the Emperor Diocletian, she submitted to torture and died in prison.

Peter Fourier

In 1595 Peter went to the Jesuit University at Pont à Mousson, and by the time he was twenty had become a member of the Regular Canons of St Augustine at Chamousey.

But his real work did not begin until he became parish priest of the village of Mattaincourt in the Vosges. Spiritual life at Mattaincourt was at a low ebb. It did not seem an attractive place for an ambitious man but Peter Fourier worked there for the next thirty years.

He opened a school for poor children that was to be entirely free. An innovation was to persuade the authorities that nuns were ideally suited for this work. His school for boys failed. For girls he found an ideal teacher, Alix Le Clerq, who became superior of the Regular Canonesses of the Congregation of Our Lady.

Eulalia

Daniel the Stylite

Eulalia who died in the year 304 became the most famous martyr of Spain in part because even as a child she knew that the only true response of a Christian to the savage persecutions of the Roman emperors was to embrace death at their hands rather than the shame of denying her Lord. Even in far away Northumberland the Venerable Bede rejoiced at her example, 'Eulalia, who submitted to the scorching heat of the flames.'

The saint planned to meet Dacian the local judge and attack him for trying to threaten or bribe Christians to give up their beliefs.

Eulalia was twelve years old and had not the slightest fear of what the judge might do to her.

The executioners were brought in. With metal hooks they began to rip apart the saint's young body. Then they set fire to her with torches. Fortunately Eulalia's hair caught alight, so instead of burning to death, she was smothered by the smoke.

The most famous pillar saint (or 'Stylite') Saint Simeon was sitting on his pillar when a young man was taken to see him by the abbot of the monastery where he was

being educated. Saint Simeon allowed this young man, whose name was Daniel, to climb up the pillar, and gave him a blessing.

Daniel stayed in the monastery till he was forty-two years old. But he never forgot the impression made on him by Simeon. When the abbot died, the monks asked Daniel to take his place. He refused. Eventually, after many adventures and pilgrimages, Daniel decided to live alone in an old temple near Constantinople.

In the year 459 Saint Simeon died. Daniel now decided that the time had come to imitate his saintly hero and he lived on pillars for the next thirty-three years. He refused to come down even to be ordained, so that the Patriarch of Constantinople who ordained the saint said the first part of the service at the bottom of the pillar and then climbed up to lay his hands on Daniel's head. Countless people came to trust the saint's wisdom, including two emperors. The only time Daniel descended his pillar was to chastise one of these emperors. He was eighty before he died in the year 493, leaving for his followers his last testament – a summary of Christian virtues, emphasizing above all the virtue of charity.

Frances de Chantal

In the year 1604, Frances de Chantal met Saint Francis de Sales and confided in him her desire to enter a Carmelite nunnery. Francis de Sales had, he said, a better idea. For many years he had meditated about forming a community of nuns, dedicated to the Visitation of the Blessed Virgin Mary. His idea was to create a community where girls and widows who were not equal to the rigours of other convents, might learn to lead the religious life.

Many times she must have wondered why she had taken on such a task. Some of the young girls who offered themselves for the Order of Visitation felt that their high birth gave them the right to reject any irksome discipline. Many of the widows were irritatingly self-centred. But with the support of Saint Francis de Sales she persevered, coping not only with the problems of guiding these difficult women to sanctity but also with her own years of arid torments when God seemed far away. Among her sorrows was the death of one of her beloved sons, fighting against the English in 1627. But Saint Frances de Chantal lived to be almost seventy, and by the time she died more than eighty convents of the Visitation had been successfully established.

Lucy

Lucy hoped to remain single, consecrated to Christ alone but her suitor, an unbeliever, wanted revenge. The persecutions of Diocletian had begun and the suitor accused Lucy of being a Christian before the pagan governor of Syracuse.

The judge ordered her to be thrown into a brothel. Somehow Lucy managed to preserve her honour. Then the guards were told to set fire to the young woman. This failed to kill Lucy. Later legends say that to make herself ugly she tore out her own eyes, which were miraculously restored. Thus Lucy became specially renowned for healing diseases of the eyes.

Finally Lucy was killed by a sword-thrust through her throat. Her story has seemed legendary to many historians. Yet an early authority for the genuineness of her life is an inscription to her discovered in the cemetery of St John in Syracuse.

John of the Cross

Mary di Rosa

'"Now woe is me,"
cried the shepherd
lad,
"A loved one's absence
is my torment
here. . ."
He waited long; then to
a Tree above
Mounted. His feet and
yearning arms he
spread
And from his
outstretched arms he
now hangs dead,
His sad heart wounded
mortally with love.'

Poem on the crucifixion by
St John of the Cross

So powerfully did Saint John of the Cross support the attempts made by Saint Teresa of Avila to reform the Carmelite monasteries of Spain that the general of the Carmelites had him imprisoned in 1577 and again in 1578.

In intense poems and his other mystical writings, John of the Cross set out the schema of a Christian's mystical ascent to God. In his greatest work, *The Dark Night of the Soul*, the saint describes how a mystic loses every earthly attachment, passing through a personal experience of Jesus's crucifixion to a rhapsodic union with God's glory. To pass through this darkness is, he says, 'a fortunate adventure to union with the Beloved'.

For a time Saint John of the Cross was reconciled to the general of his order. He became vicar provincial of Andalusia and a prior at Segovia. But when disputes broke out once again among the Spanish Carmelites, Saint John of the Cross withdrew to complete solitude.

Spiridon of Corfu

A Cypriot shepherd, Spiridon (*below*) was so admired by his fellow-Christians that he became Bishop of Tremithus while still continuing to tend his sheep. He was martyred during Diocletian persecutions.

Mary di Rosa quite simply wore out her frail body serving those in need in her native Brescia from the age of seventeen until she died in 1855 aged only forty-two.

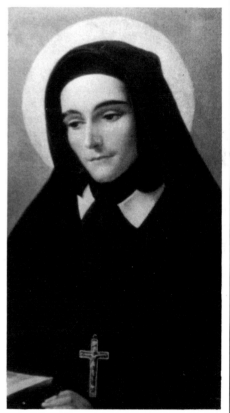

She longed to take seriously Jesus's words that whoever helped the least of his brethren did it for him. Mary began to help in any way she could the downtrodden factory workers of Brescia, especially women and girls whose working conditions were atrocious. She was daily visiting hospitals, taking especial care for the deaf and dumb. And at the age of twenty-seven she set herself to put all this work on a properly organized basis, by founding the society of the Handmaids of Charity. Her order flourished. And first of all the war with Austria of 1849, followed by the disastrous cholera epidemic of 1852, gave the members as much work as anyone could bear.

Adelaide

Begga

The Empress Adelaide, who lived in the tenth century, maintained her piety and goodness in spite of many cruel shifts of fate. Her first husband was poisoned by his

Saint Gertrude of Nivelles and Saint Begga were both daughters of a man named Pepin, who was mayor to the palace of three Frankish kings. Gertrude never married, chosing instead the life of a nun; but Saint Begga married a son of Saint Arnulf of Metz and bore him Pepin of Heristal, who started the dynasty of French kings known as the Carolingians.

In 692 Saint Begga's husband Ansegis was killed while hunting. The widow decided to make a pilgrimage to Rome. She returned home, and at Andenne on the River Meuse founded seven churches to match the seven famous churches of Rome. Nuns from her sister's convent joined her in an abbey she set up at the same place, and there Saint Begga died in the year 693.

successor. When Adelaide refused to marry the murderer's son, she was imprisoned. King Otto the Great freed her and married her. He died, and her daughter-in-law forced Adelaide to quit the royal presence. Later her son begged forgiveness for this unjust exile; but after his death Adelaide was once more forced to leave the court, returning only in her old age. Yet throughout these troubles she remained gracious and loving, and was canonized about a hundred years after her death which occurred on 16 December 999 in the convent at Seltz in Alsace that she herself had founded.

Winebald

St Winebald

Saint Richard the Saxon, an important landowner in eighth-century Britain, took his two sons, Willibald and Winebald, on a pilgrimage to Rome.

From Rome Willibald went on to the Holy Land (the first Englishman in recorded history to go there). Winebald did not have his brother's stamina. He was ill by the time they reached Rome. He decided to stay there as a student for seven years. There he became a monk, returning to England, but twice coming back with friends on further pilgrimages to Rome. He was there in 739 when Saint Boniface arrived.

Boniface's supreme achievement was to bring the Gospel to much of Germany. Although Winebald was still a sick man, Boniface persuaded his fellow-countryman to join his mission to the Germans. It was dangerous work, but Winebald soon arrived in Thuringia and was ordained priest. In spite of his ill-health, he took over the care of seven churches. The German Saxons continually tried to hamper his work, but he pressed on into Bavaria, working there for several years until the call of the cloister proved too strong for him and he joined his brother Willibald at Eichstätt.

Willibald was by now Bishop of Eichstätt, and he longed to found a monastery for both men and women in his diocese. Winebald he perceived to be the perfect abbot of the men. The two brothers decided that their sister Walburga, who was still in England, should rule the nuns. So Winebald went to a remote spot near Heidenheim, and built the double monastery. Walburga came to join him. All this the saint accomplished in spite of continual illness. His last three years were spent as an invalid in great pain. Sometimes he could not even leave his cell to worship with the other monks. Yet he bore the sickness patiently. And when he died, in December 761, Willibald and Walburga were by his side.

Urban V

William de Grimoard, later Pope Urban V, had a most distinguished academic career, both studying and teaching at four universities: Montpellier, Toulouse, Avignon and Paris. He became abbot of St Germain, Auxerre, in 1352 and abbot of St Victor, Marseilles, nine years later. He was on a papal mission to Naples when he learned that Innocent VI had died and that he himself had been elected pope.

For fifty years the papacy had been based at Avignon but in 1366 Urban decided to bring back the papacy to Rome. The Emperor Charles IV was won over to a new treaty with the papacy. Even the Greek emperor, John V Palaeologus, was reconciled to Rome, in an attempt to heal the deep rift between the Eastern and Western church. But many princes remained hostile. The *condottieri*, led by Barnabo Visconti, remained his implacable enemies. The Perugians rose against him. The leaders of France threatened the stability of the church. Sadly Urban left Rome on 5 September 1370, and returned to Avignon; within four months he died.

Dominic of Silos

The child of Spanish peasants, Dominic was destined to become one of the most famous monks of his century.

Dominic was born at Canas, Navarre. The monastery of his choice accepted him, and he became a Benedictine of San Millan de Cogolla. He was a model pupil and a devoted member of the community, and eventually his fellow monks elected him as their prior.

At this point in his placid and yet busy life the greed of King Garcia III of Navarre interrupted Dominic's career. Garcia claimed that some of the monastic estates really belonged to him. So savagely did the king persecute Dominic for strenuously defending the monastery's rights that eventually the prior and two other monks fled for protection to King Ferdinand I of Castile. Fortunately Ferdinand recognized the saint's worth.

King Ferdinand had suzerainty over the monastery of San Sebastian, Silos, in the diocese of Burgos – a house that had been for some time in spiritual torpor. He asked Dominic to take over as abbot. When the saint arrived at Silos he found that the monastery's finances were also totally awry. But he and his two companions from San Millan de Cogolla accepted the challenge.

The former shepherd boy loved the great illuminated manuscripts of the church – books of liturgy, the psalms, the Scriptures, and books of prayer. He set up a scriptorium at Silos which was soon producing some of the finest Christian books that Spain has ever seen. The decayed buildings of San Sebastian's monastery were restored. The whole monastery soon had to be enlarged as more and more monks arrived, attracted by Dominic's piety and renown. Rich men and women began to endow the monastery. And by the time Saint Dominic died in 1073 the monastery of San Sebastian, Silos, was one of the greatest in the land.

Peter Canisius

In the disorders of the sixteenth-century Catholic church which helped to create the Protestant Reformation, one man stood out from all the rest as a scholar and theologian whose courtesy and learning commanded the respect even of his opponents. Peter Canisius was born in 1521 in Holland and went to the University of Cologne with the intention of becoming a lawyer. But he grew more and more entranced by the study of theology, and under the inspiration of a Jesuit named Peter Fabre, joined the Society of Jesus in 1543.

A stream of works in defence of the Catholic faith poured from his pen. Whereas many felt that the Protestant Reformers were by far the most learned and intelligent of the controversialists, in Peter Canisius they met their equal. He used some of their weapons. The Bible, he believed, could be used in support of the ancient faith as well as enlisted on the side of Protestantism. Where Canisius thought his opponents were right, he courteously said so. But he believed that his own statement of the Catholic faith could hold its own in any Christian debate. His finest work was a *Catechism* of two hundred and eleven questions and answers. Published in 1555 it went through 130 editions.

St Dominic of Silos

Chaeremon and Ischyrion

In the year 250 Christians in Egypt were suffering grievously from the persecutions of the Emperor Decius. In their attempt to escape this persecution many Christians fled, only to perish in exile. Such appears to have been the fate of the aged Bishop Chaeremon of Nilopolis. He and a number of companions escaped to the mountains of Arabia. This was the last anyone saw of them. Even when their fellow-Christians went searching for them, they found no trace.

Those who stayed behind fared little better. Ischyrion was the procurator of an Alexandrian magistrate. The saint's employer insisted that he renounce his Christian faith and make a sacrifice to pagan gods. When Ischyrion refused to obey, the magistrate turned against him and ordered that Ischyrion be first beaten and then cruelly put to death by impaling.

Jutta of Diessenberg

Jutta of Diesenberg was born in Germany in the late eleventh century, the sister of Meginhard, Count of Spanheim. She gathered together a group of dedicated Christian women and was their abbess for twenty years.

Entrusted to the care of Jutta was a weak girl who was to become one of Germany's greatest mystics, Saint Hildegard of Bingen. Jutta taught the young girl to read Latin, cared for her physical needs, and taught her hymns and psalms.

When Jutta died in 1136 Hildegard became prioress in her place. Hildegard added her own testimony to Jutta's goodness. 'Jutta was like a river with many tributaries,' she wrote, 'overflowing with the grace of God. Until the very moment that a joyful death freed her from this mortal life, she never ceased to fast, pray and wait on God, keeping her body under control by many acts of penance.' Countless men and women of the region continued to venerate Jutta's memory and visit her tomb.

John of Kanty

Kanty is near Oswiecim in Poland, and John was born there on 23 June 1390. His parents spotted that he was a bookish boy and they had enough money to send him to university at Cracow. There he seemed destined to stay all his life. He graduated and was given the post of lecturer in the study of the Bible. But his success bred envy in others. They managed to get him transferred to the humble post of parish priest at Olkusz. Here John was not happy. He loved the academic life. He felt himself unequal to the duties of a curate of souls. But he worked hard. When he was recalled to the university as a professor eight years later, his parishioners wept to see him go.

He returned to the life of a teacher with relish. So great was his fame that long after his death candidates for higher degrees at Cracow University were dressed in his old gown. What also astonished his contemporaries was his complete devotion to poverty and charity. The second created the first. John of Kanty gave away virtually everything he possessed. He needed little. He never ate meat. He used the floor for a bed. He walked everywhere – even as far as Rome for his four pilgrimages to that city.

John of Kanty died aged seventy-seven on Christmas Eve, 1473.

Charbel Makhlouf

Anastasia

In December 1898 the Lebanese monk Charbel Makhlouf had lived as a hermit for twenty-three years. His home consisted of four tiny rooms and a chapel. For all these years Charbel had not tasted meat. He had spoken to another monk only when it was absolutely necessary. He had drunk no wine, save a drop at the Eucharist. He had eaten no fruit.

Instead of a bed Charbel Makhlouf had used a duvet filled with dead leaves, on top of which he used a goatskin for cover. His pillow was a piece of wood. His one companion Charbel also regarded as his superior.

Thus in the nineteenth century Fr. Charbel Makhlouf – along with a few other saintly men – had tried to live again

the austere life of the desert fathers of the early church. He belonged to the Christian body known as Maronites, a group which traces its name back to Saint Maro, a friend of Saint John Chrysostom. This group of Christians, most of whom still live in the Lebanon, have been united to the Western church since the twelfth century, thus bringing into Western Christendom traditions of great value that might readily have been forgotten. These traditions are ones of enormous self-discipline, and few have exemplified them better than Charbel Makhlouf. After twenty-three years he fell ill celebrating the Eucharist in his chapel, dying on Christmas Eve, 1898.

Anastasia is said to have been the daughter of a high-born Roman named Praetextatus. She learned her Christian faith from Saint Chrysogonus, though she was married to a pagan named Publius. When the Emperor Diocletian started persecuting Christians, Anastasia visited them in prison, to give them comfort. Anastasia moved to Aquilea where Chrysogonus was living, and once more began to visit those in jail.

Soon she was discovered at this work and summoned to the tribunal of the prefect of Illyricum at Sirmium – now Mitrowitz in Yugoslavia. Anastasia resolutely refused to abandon Christianity, and she was sentenced to be drowned. She and some pagan criminals were put on board an unseaworthy vessel and abandoned to the waves. But a saint who had visited her in prison managed to get on board and steered them to safety. At this many of the pagan criminals joyfully embraced Christianity.

This did not mean that Saint Anastasia escaped martyrdom. First she was tortured by being staked to the ground and set alight. Then she was taken to the island of Palmaria near Terracina, and there buried alive.

Stephen

Stephen, the first Christian martyr, was a Greek-speaking Jew, chosen by the apostles to be one of seven men who would look after the needs of widows, who tended to be neglected in the daily distribution of charity.

Stephen, 'full of grace and power' as the Acts of the Apostles describes him, did many great wonders, so that his enemies amongst his former associates plotted to bring about his death. They accused him of planning to destroy the Jewish Temple.

When Stephen was called before the Jewish Council to defend himself, his speech was one of great provocation. He tried to show how always in the past the people had turned against those sent by God, just as finally they killed Jesus. 'Which of the prophets did your fathers not persecute?' asked Stephen. 'They killed those who announced the coming of the Righteous One. Now you have betrayed and murdered him.'

He accused his hearers of always resisting the Holy Spirit. They grew so angry against him that they threw him out of the city, especially when they heard him cry that he saw the heavens opened 'and the Son of Man standing at the right hand of God.'

Then they stoned Stephen to death. Holding the coats of those who threw the stones was a man from Tarsus named Saul. This was the future Saint Paul, still at this time one of the most dangerous enemies of the Christians.

As they were stoning Stephen he prayed, 'Lord Jesus, receive my spirit.' He knelt down and said, just as he died, 'Lord, do not hold this sin against them.'

Devout men buried Stephen and wept over him. Nearly four centuries later, in the year 415, his relics are said to have been found again at Paphargamala.

John the Divine

The last book of the Bible, the Revelation or Apocalypse, was written by John, who describes himself there as our brother, sharing tribulation with patient endurance, exiled on the island of Patmos 'because of preaching the word of God and the evidence about Jesus'. His book is a superb conclusion to Holy Scripture. The book of Genesis begins the account of man's spiritual odyssey by describing our expulsion from the Garden of Eden. The book of Revelation is a vision of our restoration to Paradise. 'Let him who is thirsty come and take the waters of life.'

It is in the Book of Revelation that we find the compassionate invitation of Jesus to the world: 'Behold, I stand at the door and knock. If anyone hears my voice and opens the door, I will come in to him and eat with him, and he with me. He who conquers, I will grant to sit with me on my throne, as I myself conquered and sat down with my Father on his throne.'

'I looked and behold a great multitude which no man could number, from every nation, from all tribes and peoples and tongues, standing before the throne and before the Lamb, clothed in white robes, with palm branches in their hands, crying out with a loud voice, "Salvation belongs to our God who sits on the throne and unto the Lamb."'

From the Revelation of
John the Divine

The Holy Innocents

*'O martyrs, young and
  fresh as flowers,
Your day was in its
  morning hours
When Christ was
  sought and you were
  found
Like rain-strewn petals
  on the ground.'*

From 'Salvete, flores martyrum'
by Prudentius

Herod the son of Antipater was designated procurator of Judea by Julius Caesar and king under Augustus Caesar. He ruled from 47 BC to 2 AD, and was therefore king when Jesus was born.

Herod assumed the title 'the Great'. Yet he was fanatically determined to stamp out any messianic threat to his throne. When he learned from the three Magi who had come to worship the infant Jesus that 'a ruler shall come from Bethlehem who will govern my people Israel', he decided to kill the child. The Magi, warned in a dream not to tell Herod where to find Jesus, returned to the East by a way which avoided Jerusalem. In his rage King Herod decreed that every male child under two years old in Bethlehem and that region should be killed.

Only because Mary's husband Joseph had been warned in a dream by God that this would happen and accordingly fled with his wife and Jesus to Egypt was the Saviour spared. The other innocent children were put to the sword.

The number killed under Herod's order has often been exaggerated. Perhaps two dozen male children under the age of two would have been found around Bethlehem at that time. Yet Herod's savagery has become a deep historical memory. He later had his own son murdered, so that Augustus Caesar allegedly said, 'Better to be Herod's pig than Herod's son.'

Thomas Becket of Canterbury

On 29 December 1170 four knights arrived at Canterbury cathedral determined to murder Archbishop Thomas Becket and believing that they had the blessing of King Henry II in doing so. As he was killed by successive blows, Thomas Becket repeated the names of those archbishops that had been martyred before him: Saint Denis and Saint Alphege of Canterbury. Then he said, 'Into your hand, O Lord, I commend my spirit.'

Before he was consecrated Archbishop of Canterbury, few would have chosen Thomas Becket as a likely martyr. As the king's chancellor he usually supported Henry II's policies. He loved good living, fine clothes, hunting, even war. He had not wished to be made archbishop. But when the office fell to him, his style of life changed radically. He lived austerely, and he preferred exile to any compromise with Henry II over the rights of the church.

King Louis VII of France brought the king and the archbishop together in 1170. But Thomas had scarcely returned to England before they began to quarrel again. King Henry is reported to have said before Becket's death, 'Who will rid me of this turbulent priest?' He was forced to do public penance, and in 1173 Pope Alexander III declared Thomas Becket a saint.

Anysia

Anysia was born at Thessaloniki. Her parents were both rich and pious. She herself led a life of unobtrusive prayer, using the money and estates her parents had left her to relieve the poor.

One day a Roman soldier accosted her as she was on her way to a meeting of Christians. When he discovered her faith, he became even more abusive, deciding to make sport with her by dragging her to a temple to make a pagan sacrifice. Anysia resisted. The retiring saint habitually covered her face with a veil, but the soldier ripped it away to peer at her. She struggled all the more, and in his rage he drew his sword and thrust it through her, killing the saint immediately.

Silvester I

This pope, who reigned from 314 to 335, rejoiced at his good fortune in becoming Bishop of Rome after the Emperor Constantine granted toleration to the Christian church. In consequence an extraordinary fable arose about his pontificate. It was said that Constantine had been told by his doctor that the best way to cure leprosy was to bathe in the blood of children. A vision in which Saints Peter and Paul appeared to the emperor charging him instead to seek baptism at the hands of Silvester changed Constantine's mind. Silvester baptized him; the emperor was healed; and in gratitude granted the pope the islands of Sicily, Sardinia and Corsica. For centuries this 'Donation of Constantine' passed as history – even though the emperor was not baptized till after Silvester's death.

Silvester's own virtues must have been considerable, if only because he is one of the first Christians who did not die a martyr and yet was honoured as a saint. He sent legates to the Council of Arles, and at the famous Council of Nicea in the year 325 his two representatives assisted the presiding bishop.

Saint Silvester also set himself the task of creating churches worthy of the faith in the city of Rome. He made the basilica of St John in the Lateran his cathedral. He either restored or founded the churches of Saint Peter, Saint Lawrence Without the Walls, and Santa Croce. His ancient episcopal chair and his mitre – the oldest one still to survive – can today be seen in the church of San Martino ai Monti, which he built over a house used for worship during the years of persecution.

THE ILLUSTRATIONS

Please note that the contraction 'Men. Bas.' stands for the Menology of Basil II, Biblioteca Apostolica Vaticana, Rome, and *Les Images* for *Les Images de Tous Les Saincts Et Saintes De L'Année* by J. Callot, 1636.

PICTURE ACKNOWLEDGMENTS

The illustrations on the pages listed were kindly provided by the following sources:

A.C.L., Brussels: 38 right, 129 bottom left; Alinari, Florence: 8 bottom right, 12, 17 left, 18 right, 26 right, 33 right, 35, 37 left, 38 left, 40, 104, 111 bottom, 113 top, 114, 166 right, 177 right, 221 right, 226 right; Antikvarisk-Topografiska Arkivet, Stockholm: 58, 139 left; Archivio IGDA: 8 top, 8 bottom, 11, 15 right, 16, 17 right, 19, 20 top, 21, 22 left, 23 right, 25, 30 left, 32, 34, 39 right, 44, 45 right, 49 top left, 54, 55, 59, 64, 65, 67, 71 right, 74 top left, 78, 79, 84, 86, 87, 93, 96, 100 left, 105, 110 top right, 112, 118, 119, 122, 123 top, 127, 128 bottom left, 131 bottom right, 132, 137, 138 right, 139 right, 140, 149, 150, 151, 152, 153, 156, 157, 158, 159, 160 right, 163 right, 164, 165, 166 left, 167, 168, 173, 178 right, 183, 184, 185, 186, 188, 189 right, 190, 191 left, 192, 194, 195, 196, 198, 199 right, 200 bottom, 202, 205, 207, 211 left, 212 right, 215, 216, 223, 225, 227, 230, 234, 235, 236, 238, 239 right, 243 right, 245 right, 247, 248, 250; Bavaria-Verlag, Munich: 243 left; Bayer. Landesamt Für Denkmalpflege, Munich: 41 right; BBC Hulton Picture Library: 66 right, 107 top right; Bildarchiv Foto Marburg: 52 right; Bridgeman Art Library: 111 top, 191 right, 206, 219 left; Bulloz, Paris: 101, 217 left; Jean-Loup Charmet: 73; Corvina Archives, Budapest: 18 left; Arnold Desser/Orbis: 102 bottom; Documentation Des Réunion Des Musées Nationaux, Paris: 61 right; Mary Evans Picture Library: 9 top right, 51 right, 53 left, 130, 133, 200 top, 239 top left; Werner Forman Archive: 10 left; Giraudon, Paris: 14, 15 left, 20 bottom, 24 right, 47, 75 right, 82 right, 99, 107 bottom, 120, 141, 162, 209, 214 top left, 219 right, 232, 241 left, 246; Jenny Gray, Hastings: 89 left; Sonia Halliday: 10 right, 23 left, 110 bottom left, 123 bottom, 224 left, 249 left; Hirmer Fotoarchiv, Munich: 124; Kunstbildarchiv, Hamburg: 187 right; Mansell Collection: 33 left, 66 left, 75 left, 76, 80 right, 97 right, 113 bottom, 135, 161, 170, 174 left, 214 bottom, 233; Mas, Barcelona: 45 left, 95 left, 134 left, 143 right, 148 left, 229 right; Dr Philip Mavroskoufis: 62 left; National Council of Tourism in Lebanon: 245 left; National Monuments Record: 108; Pictorial Archive, Jerusalem: 31 right; Betty Rawlings: 201; St Frances Xavier Cabrini Chapel, New York: 220 right; Scala, Florence: 22 right, 24 left, 29 right, 82 left, 85, 91, 92, 116, 126 bottom right, 142 left, 143 left, 144, 147 left, 163 left, 169, 174 right, 181, 189 left, 203, 208, 226 left; Seton Shrine Center, Maryland: 9 bottom; Ronald Sheridan's Photo-Library: 9 top left; Dr G. Sutton: 48 left, 81, 136, 146; Ullstein Bilderdienst, Berlin: 155; VAAP, Moscow: 221 left.

INDEX

Numbers in italics refer to illustrations.